THE SPANISH STRUGGLE
FOR JUSTICE
IN THE
CONQUEST OF AMERICA

BARTOLOMÉ DE LAS CASAS, BISHOP OF CHIAPA
AND APOSTLE TO THE INDIANS

THE SPANISH STRUGGLE
FOR JUSTICE
IN THE CONQUEST OF AMERICA

LEWIS HANKE

1/04

New Introduction by Susan Scafidi and Peter Bakewell

•

Previously Unpublished Personal and
Professional Reminiscence by the Author

•

Published in cooperation with the
William P. Clements Center for Southwest Studies

SOUTHERN METHODIST UNIVERSITY PRESS
Dallas

Requests for permission to reproduce material from this work should be sent to:
Rights and Permissions
Southern Methodist University Press
PO Box 750415
Dallas, Texas 75275-0415

Cover Photograph: Peter Bakewell
Cover Design: Tom Dawson

LIBRARY OF CONGRESS CATALOGING-IN-PUBLICATION DATA
Hanke, Lewis.
    The Spanish struggle for justice in the conquest of America / by Lewis
    Hanke ; new introduction by Susan Scafidi and Peter Bakewell ; personal and
    professional reminiscence by the author.— 1st Southern Methodist University
    Press ed.
        p. cm.
Originally published: Philadelphia : University of Pennsylvania Press, 1949.
"Published in cooperation with the William P. Clements Center for Southwest Studies."
    Includes bibliographical references and index.
    ISBN 0-87074-466-6
    1. Spain—Colonies—America. 2. Indians, Treatment of—Latin America.
3. Indians—Legal status, laws, etc.—Latin America. 4. Latin
America—History—To 1830. 5. Spain—Foreign relations—Latin America.
I. Title.
F1411.H37 H37 2002
980—dc21

                                                    2002034516

Printed in the United States of America on acid-free paper

10   9   8   7   6   5   4   3   2   1

Dedicatoria

A la

Querida Compañera de Mi Vida

CONTENTS

LEWIS HANKE AND *THE SPANISH STRUGGLE*   xi
FOR JUSTICE IN THE CONQUEST OF AMERICA:
RECENT HISTORIOGRAPHY AND FUTURE JURISPRUDENCE
New Introduction by Susan Scafidi and Peter Bakewell
      Lewis Hanke: Latin Americanist and Historian—Lewis Hanke
      and the Influence of Spanish Law in the United States

FOREWORD   xix
INTRODUCTION   1
      The Aim of This Book—Spirit of This Study—The Climate of
      Opinion in Sixteenth-Century Spain—Free Speech in Spain and
      America—The Nature of the Indians

PART I
The First Cry for Justice in America

I THE SERMONS OF FRIAR ANTONIO DE MONTESINOS   17

II THE BASIS OF SPAIN'S RIGHT TO RULE THE INDIES   23
      The Laws of Burgos—The Dispute up to 1512—The Treatise by
      Matías de Paz—Juan López de Palacios Rubios and His Treatise

III THE REQUIREMENT—A MOST REMARKABLE DOCUMENT   31

PART II
Spanish Experiments in America

INTRODUCTION   39
      Why Did Spain Experiment?

IV COULD THE INDIANS LEARN TO LIVE LIKE
CHRISTIAN SPANIARDS?   42
      The Jeronymite Interrogatory—The Experiments of Rodrigo de
      Figueroa—The Experiencia in Cuba

V COULD THE NEW WORLD BE COLONIZED PEACEFULLY
WITH FARMERS?   54

The Meaning of Las Casas' Attempt to Establish a Colony as an Alternative to the Encomienda System—"The Indians Are Free Men and Must be Treated as Such": The Utopian Memorial of 1517—The First Colonization Plan for America, 1518–19—The First Attempt of 1518–19—The Battle for the Tierra Firme Agreement, 1519–20—The Reality in America—The Aftermath

VI   COULD THE FAITH BE PREACHED BY PEACEFUL
MEANS ALONE?   72
     The Only Method of Attracting All People To The True Faith—The Doctrine—The Vera Paz Experiment in Guatemala, 1537–50—Later Attempts at Peaceful Conversion

VII COULD THE ENCOMIENDA SYSTEM BE ABOLISHED?   83
     The Meeting of the New Laws—Lack of Adequate Materials for a Study of the Encomienda System—The Development of the Encomienda System to 1542—The "Eighth Remedy" of Las Casas and His *Very Brief Account of the Destruction of the Indies*—The New Laws—Why Were the New Laws Decreed?—The Encomienda Is Not Abolished After All—Concluding Reflections on the New Laws

PART III

The Development of the Struggle for Justice, 1550–1600

INTRODUCTION   109

VIII "ALL THE PEOPLES OF THE WORLD ARE MEN"   111
     Development of Regulations for Conquistadores to 1550—Prelude to Combat—Conquests in the Indies Must Stop!—The Two Sessions of the Judges, 1550–51—The Argument—Aristotle and the American Indians—Conclusion

IX   THE WAGING OF JUST WAR IN THE INDIES   133
     Just War in Mexico and in Nicaragua—Just War Against the Chiriguanaes in Peru—Just War in Chile—Just War in the Philippines

X   THE JUST TITLES OF SPAIN TO THE INDIES   147
     Why the Dispute Arose—After Burgos—The Contribution and Influence of Francisco de Vitoria—Las Casas: Political Theorist

XI   JUST TITLE DISCUSSIONS IN MEXICO AND THE PHILIPPINES   156
     The Town Fathers of Mexico City—Trouble in Manila

XII   FRANCISCO DE TOLEDO AND THE JUST TITLES TO
      THE INCA EMPIRE   162
         Defense of the Spanish Title to Peru—The *Informaciones* of
         Viceroy Francisco de Toledo—The *Indian History* of Pedro
         Sarmiento de Gamboa—Epilogue

CONCLUSION   173

NOTES   181

BIBLIOGRAPHICAL APPENDICES   197
         1 Bibliographical Works
         2 Collections of Printed Material
         3 Previous Studies
         4 Manuscript Sources
         5 List of Works Cited
         6 List of Abbreviations Used

INDEX   213

THE DEVELOPMENT OF LATIN AMERICAN HISTORY
IN THE UNITED STATES, 1923–1988: REMINISCENCES,
REFLECTIONS, AND RECOMMENDATIONS   219
Previously Unpublished Personal and Professional Reminiscence by the Author

COVER PHOTOGRAPH

A STATUE OF FRANCISCO DE VITORIA, O.P., GREATEST OF SPANISH
SIXTEENTH-CENTURY LEGAL THEORISTS ON THE RIGHTS OF AMER-
ICAN NATIVES, STANDS BEFORE THE DOMINICAN MONASTERY OF
ST. STEPHEN IN SALAMANCA (SPAIN)—HOME TO THE REMARKABLE
SCHOOL OF SALAMANCA

ILLUSTRATIONS

BARTOLOMÉ DE LAS CASAS   *frontispiece*
ITEM 24 OF THE LAWS OF BURGOS (1512)   *facing page*   24
DR. JUAN GINÉS DE SEPÚLVEDA   *facing page*   114
DOMINGO DE SALAZAR   *facing page*   158

LEWIS HANKE AND *THE SPANISH STRUGGLE FOR JUSTICE IN THE CONQUEST OF AMERICA*:
RECENT HISTORIOGRAPHY AND FUTURE JURISPRUDENCE

Lewis Hanke: Latin Americanist and Historian

Lewis Hanke was the best known historian of Latin America in the United States from the late 1930s until the 1970s. In addition to his scholarly activities of research and writing, he occupied a series of prominent positions in the academic community of Latin Americanists. In "Reminiscences, Reflections, and Recommendations"—the autobiographical sketch published in this volume—Hanke describes his appointment as the first head of the Hispanic Division of the Library of Congress, the section of the Library created in 1939 to gather materials about Spain, Portugal, and their colonies in a systematic way. The Division took over from Harvard the preparation of the annual *Handbook of Latin American Studies*, which became and still is, the most comprehensive bibliography of writings on Latin America in the humanities and the social sciences.

Dr. Hanke headed the Hispanic Division of the Library of Congress for twelve years before moving to a teaching position at the University of Texas at Austin. From 1954 to 1960 he served as editor of the *Hispanic American Historical Review*, which was the senior trade journal at that time for those writing in English about Latin American history. He left Texas to take up a teaching post at Columbia University in New York.

The early 1960s was a time of increased interest, both public and private, in Latin America, largely as a result of the Cuban Revolution of 1959. Fidel Castro's administration soon proclaimed the aim of exporting Marxism and revolution to the rest of Latin America. Public policy in the United States supported the academic study of Latin America as an effective way of dealing with the Marxist threat there. In New York, Hanke was geographically at the center of discussions and action, and he pressed for greater governmental funding of research. Undergraduate enrollment in courses on Latin America grew rapidly, and new teaching materials were needed. [The publisher] Alfred A. Knopf conceived the idea of offering a series of affordable books for classroom use consisting of edited documents on specific topics, along with essays interpreting the topics. Hanke was chosen to compile and edit these volumes, called "Borzoi Books." Eventually there were thirty volumes dealing with a broad range of topics in Latin American history from the earliest times to the twentieth century.

By the mid 1960s, Hanke was a senior member of the Latin Americanist community in the United States. His scholarly work and efforts to promote the study of Latin America had brought him wide recognition abroad as well. In 1969, after a brief interval at the University of California at Irvine, he began an appointment at the University of Massachusetts at Amherst, where he taught until his retirement in 1975 at the age of seventy. In 1974 he was elected President of the American Historical Association—the first Latin Americanist to occupy that office. For most of the remaining eighteen years of his life he continued, as keen as ever, his scholarly enterprises, some of them departures for him.

As Hanke relates in his "Reminiscences," his scholarly work on the history of colonial Spanish America had three distinct phases, each concentrating on a particular topic. His major concern, after his retirement, was with the history of the viceroys of the Spanish Empire. These men, for almost three hundred years the monarchy's representatives in America and the colonies' chief executives, had been strangely neglected by historians. Hanke decided to remedy that situation by producing a series of volumes containing the letters and other documents of the viceroys in the sixteenth and seventeenth centuries. A set of twelve such books was published in the renowned Biblioteca de Autores Españoles series (Atlas Editorial, Madrid) between 1976 and 1980. Perhaps more useful to historians wanting to study viceroys and what they governed was, however, the three-volume guide to manuscripts in the great Archive of the Indies, in Seville, on viceregal administration that Hanke and his collaborator Celso Rodriguez compiled *(Guía de las fuentes en el Archivo General de Indias para el estudio de la adminstración virreinal . . .*, Bohlau Verlag, Cologne, 1977); and the companion volume, prepared with the help of Gunnar Mendoza, on similar sources in archives in Spanish America *(Guía de las fuentes en Hispanoamérica para el estudio de la administración virreinal...*, Organization of American States, Washington, D.C., 1980).

Hanke's second large research topic was the history of Potosí, the famous silver mining center of the central Andes (in what is now Bolivia), a place so productive of wealth, so large in population, and set on so high and remote a site that it acquired an almost mythic quality. His main contribution to knowledge of Potosí's past was his discovery, transcription, and publication (with commentary) of two central chronicles of the town and its mining activities. The first, fundamental for students of the silver industry, was the late sixteenth-century description by Luis Capoche: *Relación general de la Villa Imperial de Potosí* (Biblioteca de Autores Españoles, Atlas, Madrid, 1959); and the second, prepared in collaboration with Gunnar Mendoza, was the splendidly edited and annotated *Historia de la Villa Imperial de Potosí*, written by Bartolomé Arzáns de Orsúa y Vela in the early eighteenth century (Brown University Press, Providence, 1965).

But the book which first brought Hanke recognition as a major scholar of colonial Spanish America, the work with which his name has been most associated and which will long remain the foundation of his reputation as a historian, is the one that is reprinted here: *The Spanish Struggle for Justice in the Conquest of America* (American Historical Association, University of Pennsylvania Press, 1949; Little, Brown and Co., 1965).

In the "Reminiscences" Hanke lays out fully and clearly the genesis of this book. As Benjamin Keen (another student of early Spanish policies in America but one with often very different views) noted in his obituary tribute to Hanke (*Hispanic American Historical Review*, November 1993), Hanke was one of a small group of historians in the United States who in the mid-twentieth century tried to correct what they saw as a distorted, but prevailing, view of Spain's colonizing activities. That view is summed up in the so-called "Black Legend": the opinion that, in comparison with other European colonial powers of recent centuries, Spain acted with unusual and extreme cruelty towards the native people of the regions it occupied and governed. One of the sources of the Legend had been the famous Spanish Dominican friar, Bartolomé de Las Casas, who for much of the first half of the sixteenth century had sought to defend American native people in the young Spanish colonies against the demands and the maltreatment of the colonists. Las Casas had written violent denunciations of the settlers and had come to criticize the whole Spanish enterprise in America, going so far as to propose that colonization should consist only of missionary activities.

Hanke had found during his doctoral research, however, that Las Casas was far more than the fanatical propagandist he had sometimes been taken for. His polemical writing was outweighed by voluminous other writings and by his political arguments and maneuverings in support of the Indians. Las Casas had developed what could properly be called an anthropological interest in the American peoples, trying to understand them in their own terms.

And from this revisionist, more nuanced view of Las Casas, Hanke came, as he says in the "Reminiscences," to a broader realization that "Spain had been the only European power that carried on its conquests amidst public doubts and disagreements of her people concerning the justice of the conquest." Though Las Casas is the figure who receives most attention in *The Spanish Struggle for Justice,* the subject of the book is that wider story of "doubts and disagreements"—debates in which numerous lawyers, theologians, priests, government officials, and even monarchs took vigorous part for most of the sixteenth century.

After Hanke's book was published, there could be no doubt that influential and educated Spaniards of the age of conquest had engaged honestly and sincerely in those debates. The book therefore helped to move historians' discussions to a new stage, asking whether the debates had served any useful outcome—whether, for example, the laws issued under pressure from Las Casas and others, in favor of Indians, had really benefited the native peoples in any measurable way. Many such questions are still open. Beyond that, *The Spanish Struggle for Justice* helped raise the broader issue of the relationship and interaction between Spaniards and Indians in the colonies, not only in the conquest period but throughout the span of the empire. Hanke's book was not the only influence that opened up these topics.

The rising wave of decolonization in the 1950s added to the growing concern with the rights of minorities, and a general questioning of social order in the Western world during the 1960s aroused historians' interest in what happened when Spanish estate owners in the colonies employed Indians to raise their crops and herd their animals; what happened when officials tried to move Indians into new towns and villages; what happened when priests attempted to convert Indians to Christianity; and what happened when those priests discovered that the Indians, while accepting Catholic beliefs, continued to practice their own ancient cults. These and similar questions have been the topic of many doctoral dissertations and many of the best books produced by historians of Spanish America in the English-speaking world (and elsewhere) in recent decades. Through such work we have come to know the economic, social, religious, and cultural realities of life in the Spanish colonies with a density of detail that could hardly have been imagined when *The Spanish Struggle for Justice* was published in 1949. Much of that work can properly be seen as an outgrowth of Hanke's most noted book. The book remains notable precisely because of its generative effect.

Lewis Hanke and the Influence of Spanish Law in the United States

The epicenter of the legal history of the United States is the East Coast. The majority of our scholarship focuses on the legacy of British colonization and the creation of the Constitution, on the activities of Congress and the Supreme Court, on theories of jurisprudence developed at the great New England law schools. Our legal heritage is dubbed the Anglo-American common law, and its diffusion across the several states is largely taken for granted.

Only occasionally does the gaze of American legal historians turn westward, following pioneers, railroads, and land, water, or mineral disputes. Distinguished scholars such as John Phillip Reid have unveiled the dispersal of American legal culture across the Great Plains, and the elaboration of customary law on the frontier and on the West Coast receives periodic attention. Legal historians who remind us of North America's heterogeneous colonial past, thus raising the possibility of other European legal systems infusing American justice, are nevertheless quick to note the triumph of Anglo-American law over weaker strains. Florida, California, and Texas all voted swiftly and deliberately to replace continental civil law with common law, though traces of the original Spanish system persist in areas related to property rights. The endurance of civil law in Louisiana is the exception that proves the rule, appearing in general legal histories more often as testimony to the flexibility of a federal system than as a subject of study in its own right. In the landmark U.S. legal histories of Laurence Friedman and Morton Horwitz, the unique juridical development of the American West casts only a faint shadow on the intellectual trajectory of American law.

In recent years, however, a few legal scholars have turned their attention to early Spanish and French attempts to transplant European law to what would become the United States borderlands. Morris S. Arnold, Charles Cutter, and Joseph W. McKnight have independently unearthed portions of the legal record of Texas and New Mexico, Arkansas and Louisiana, and have begun to reconstruct a juridical past characterized by the pragmatic adaptation of learned law to local conditions. The experience of civil law in the pre-republican Southwest thus stands in contrast not only to Anglo-American colonial law, but also to the legal regime in the centers of Spanish colonial power, as described by Lesley Byrd Simpson, Woodrow Borah, and James Muldoon. As interest in the Borderlands continues to grow, so too will the associated body of legal history.

At the same time, the rise of Native American legal studies as well

as Latino critical theory has prompted new interest in the jurispru-
dential contribution of what is now the American West. Led by scholars such as Rennard Strickland and Robert A. Williams, Jr., recent
scholarship has explored the legal implications of the various Indian-
European encounters and the theories of justice and conquest developed in that context. While the European approach to relations with
Native Americans seems in retrospect a vast miscarriage of natural
justice, it was heavily debated and structured around a series of
formal legal principles. It may be tempting simply to dismiss legal
theories developed in the era of Spanish exploration and conquest as
self-serving political tools or mere weapons in a campaign of cultural
genocide. However, the persistence of certain themes well into the
modern era, including the legal construction of native peoples as a
dependent class under the ostensible protection of the state,
demands our attention to the origins of these legal theories. The
modern study of ethnic or racial identity and law, particularly as
applied to Native American and Latino history, leads directly to the
pre-history of the American West.

In this context, the work of Lewis Hanke provides a critical starting point for legal historians attempting to explore the competing
sources of law that ultimately provide a more accurate and complex
picture of America's European legal heritage. Hanke's vivid description of competing Spanish factions, and in particular the famous
disputation between Bartolomé de Las Casas and Juan Giné de
Sepúlveda over the legal status of the Indians, underscores the seri-
ousness of the lengthy Spanish national debate. Despite the persistence of the Black Legend, Hanke succeeds in convincing the reader
that at least some Europeans were committed to a vision of justice
and to the use of legal rules to establish political, social, and religious
norms in accordance with that vision. This moral debate drew upon
centuries of theology, philosophy, and jurisprudence, and forced all
subsequent European colonial powers to reflect, at least briefly, upon
the legal justification for their exercise of power. Even U.S. Supreme
Court Chief Justice John Marshall, writing in the early nineteenth
century, echoes the questions of legal justification in the assertion of
sovereignty over native peoples that were first raised three centuries
earlier. Hanke's illumination of the "Spanish struggle for justice" is
the first chapter in a much longer legal drama.

While Hanke has provided a valuable service to American historical jurisprudence, dramatically expanding the scope of the field, he
was not himself primarily a legal scholar. As a result, his exploration
of the competing versions of sixteenth-century Spanish justice—or
rather justice and injustice, as he would probably characterize

them—is somewhat limited. Even the perspective championed by Las Casas, which ultimately prevailed in theory if not in practice, would be hard pressed to meet the standards of individual rights championed by the modern liberal state. The reality of changing standards of justice does not detract from Hanke's excellent description of the Spanish colonial struggle, but it does present a challenge for the modern jurist attempting to understand the past on its own terms. Similarly, the lack of a definition of sovereign authority requires modern legal scholarship to supply the missing context. Still, the cross-disciplinary challenge Hanke provides to American legal historians who have too long accepted a homogenous, anglicized version of the past outweighs any technical limitations of his work.

At the end of the day, the Anglo-American common law system prevails, and the faint echoes of civil law or even indigenous law seldom affect the machinery of justice. It is nevertheless the project of legal history, aided by the foundations laid down by Lewis Hanke over fifty years ago, to broaden our understanding of what constitutes American jurisprudence and to reconstruct the elements of a usable past.

We would like to thank the Hanke family and the William P. Clements Center for Southwest Studies for making this edition possible.

Peter Bakewell
Edmund and Louise Kahn
Professor of History

Susan Scafidi
Assistant Professor of Law

Southern Methodist University
Dallas, Texas
2002

FOREWORD

THIS book has been a long time growing. It started in 1930 when, as a graduate student at Harvard University, I had to find a topic to use for a term paper in a course on the history of political thought. By chance a brief but suggestive study by Fernando de los Ríos came to my attention and brought out the fact, new at that time to me, that many theories of government were involved in the Spanish conquest of America. I followed this clue, discovered that the writings of Bartolomé de Las Casas were full of theories, and worked out a monograph on this subject which satisfied the academic requirements for the course and was published in Buenos Aires shortly afterward.

The figure of Bartolomé de Las Casas came to fascinate me, and an Amherst Memorial Fellowship enabled me to go to Spain in the fall of 1932 to search for his papers. I have never ceased to wonder at and be grateful for the action of Amherst College in appointing a non-Amherst man to this fellowship. A second year was made possible by an Archibald Cary Coolidge Fellowship from Harvard, supplemented by judicious borrowing from relatives. I have often thought that few students of history have tried to live abroad with their families on the stipend of a graduate student fellowship. This we did for two years, and they were happy and fruitful years.

But the papers of Las Casas, which during the last few years of his life were so voluminous that they made it difficult for visitors to get in and out of his cell in San Gregorio monastery in Valladolid, simply could not be found. After some months of desperation, I came to realize that the story I wanted to tell did not depend upon finding more Las Casas papers. His essential doctrines and ideas, for the most part, had been published. My real discovery was that he was only one, the most aggressive and articulate one, to be sure, of those Spaniards who sought to have the conquest follow Christian and just principles. With this as my basic conception, I ransacked the Archivo General de Indias, the Archivo de Simancas, and various deposits of manuscript material in Madrid, Paris, and London. The printed material was also of considerable importance, for many documents have been published on this period. Part of my findings were presented in 1936 as a doctoral dissertation at Harvard. Since then many parts of this book have appeared, mostly in Latin-American historical reviews, and I have thus been able to take advantage in this final presentation of various criticisms and suggestions made by reviewers of these printed portions.

Many persons and various institutions have assisted me. During the long periods of research and writing required to complete this volume, my wife has not only kept the home fires burning but has been intimately connected with almost every phase of the work. The dedication to her is no perfunctory gesture but a recognition of the vital role she has played in the prolonged struggle to finish this book.

The Carnegie Institution of Washington has substantially aided me in various ways over a period of years, and the Committee on Research in International Relations of Harvard University and Radcliffe College, the Milton Fund of Harvard University, and the Carnegie Endowment for International Peace have also provided support. Professor C. H. Haring of Harvard University and Dean France V. Scholes of the University of New Mexico have borne with me and my problems since the very beginning of the work. Other friends who have generously given of their time and knowledge are: Professor James F. King (University of California at Berkeley); Professor Ramón Iglesia (University of Wisconsin); and Dr. Silvio Zavala (Colegio de México).

I feel a special and unusual gratitude for the aid of my friend Sr. Edmundo O'Gorman of the Archivo General de la Nación in Mexico. We do not see eye to eye on some of the most fundamental problems of the Spanish conquest, but conversations with him and his publications have forced me to reëxamine critically my previous positions. His firm and skillful opposition has not convinced me, as yet, on all points at issue, but I value greatly his criticism and no doubt will continue to receive it.

The original manuscript was also read by all the members of the Committee on the Albert J. Beveridge Memorial Fund of the American Historical Association which awarded it the Albert J. Beveridge Memorial Fellowship for 1947. The manuscript was then revised with the assistance of Professor C. H. Haring, who served as special consultant to the Committee for this purpose.

Hard as all these readers have worked to comb out the errors and misinterpretations from this text, it is certain that some mistakes will soon be found. For these, of course, I am wholly responsible.

L. H.

Washington, D. C.
1948

INTRODUCTION

The Aim of This Book

THE purpose of this work is to demonstrate that the Spanish conquest of America was far more than a remarkable military and political exploit; that it was also one of the greatest attempts the world has seen to make Christian precepts prevail in the relations between peoples. This attempt became basically a spirited defense of the rights of the Indians, which rested on two of the most fundamental assumptions a Christian can make: namely, that all men are equal before God, and that a Christian has a responsibility for the welfare of his brothers no matter how alien or lowly they may be.

In the written history of America the undeniable courage and spectacular daring of the *conquistadores* have hitherto been emphasized, as well as the impressive stability of the far-flung empire which Spain brought within the orbit of European civilization and ruled for over three hundred years. There is more, however, to Spain's contribution to the New World, noteworthy as these aspects of her work will always be. Other nations sent out bold explorers and established empires. But no other European people, before or since the conquest of America, plunged into such a struggle for justice as developed among Spaniards shortly after the discovery of America and persisted throughout the sixteenth century. This study attempts to examine this unique quality of Spanish effort and to show how it influenced Spanish action in America.

The struggle occurred because of the widespread concern felt by soldiers, ecclesiastics, and the crown that all Spain's laws and actions in America be just. What constituted justice and how it could be achieved were questions raised with every important step Spaniards took in the discovery, colonization, and administration of their new dominions. This concern for justice, which can only be understood in relation to the political and spiritual climate of opinion in sixteenth-century Spain, to be described later, led to sharp and basic controversies on a variety of particular issues.

What political and economic rights should Spain enjoy from her overlordship there? Were the Indians rational beings, and, if so, what were their rights? How should the faith be preached to them; under what circumstances could they be made to work for Spaniards; and when could war be justly waged against them? All these and other questions were asked and heatedly debated throughout the

1

sixteenth century in both Spain and America and by all classes and manner of men.

The papal bulls of Alexander VI and Julius II conferred upon the crown of Spain even greater power to direct the administration of church affairs in America than that enjoyed by the crown in Spain. The acceptance by the crown of the obligation to provide for the Christianization of the Indians led to a theory of empire and colonial policy in which ecclesiastics, who had always been important in royal councils, became trusted advisers to the crown and to the Council of the Indies, the principal administrative body for ruling America. Although the ecclesiastics never agreed on a united policy and were frequently in direct conflict with the conquistadores and royal officials, their influence was felt in all quarters and ensured that every basic decision made during the conquest be scrutinized from the point of view of Christian justice. The kings of Spain, one after another, were confused and troubled by the multitude of differing voices raised at home and half a world away to advise them on the proper way to discharge their temporal and spiritual responsibilities.

The crown, faced with enormous administrative problems and surrounded by strident champions of widely varying solutions, decided to experiment. This volume describes four extraordinary attempts, made during the critical first half-century with the full approval of the crown, to test certain daring theories put forward by ecclesiastics as solutions for the pressing problems of the New World. Could the Indians learn to live like Spaniards? Was it possible to colonize the new lands peacefully with Spanish farmers? Could the Indians be won over to Christianity by peaceful means alone? Could the *encomienda* system, by which some Spaniards were supported by Indians, be abolished?

Some influential Spaniards believed strongly that the answers would all be "yes," but the experiments or quasi experiments failed to convince the crown and resulted in no fundamental change in royal policy. Hotly debated at the time, they never really had a chance to succeed in the hostile environment of the New World. The experiments appear to us today, from the vantage point of four hundred years, as tragic comedies enacted on doomed little islands around which the ocean of the conquest boiled and thundered until it overwhelmed them. But it is an important fact that the experiments were conducted at all and that many loyal Spaniards gave years of their lives trying to prove the validity of their conviction that the conquest of a new world, conducted by the nation whose military force was probably the greatest in Europe, could be achieved without trampling on the rights of the relatively defenseless natives.

The struggle for justice continued during the second half of the sixteenth century and spread from the islands of the Caribbean to Mexico, Peru, and even to the distant Philippines. Wherever Spaniards carried their banners in the New World opened up by their energy and daring, there also they carried the ideas and concern for justice which led inevitably to those bitter controversies which endow the Spanish experience in America with original characteristics. The eighteenth-century Scottish historian William Robertson realized this truth when he wrote: "The Spanish monarchs, having acquired a species of dominion formerly unknown, formed a plan for exercising it to which nothing similar occurs in the history of human affairs." [1]

Although historians have long recognized the fact that there was a struggle for justice during the Spanish conquest, and have become steadily more interested in the subject, this volume is the first attempt to set forth the story as a whole, to describe historically the conflict of men and ideas as an integral part of the conquest, and to base the account on a foundation of copious printed and manuscript material in the archives and libraries of Europe and America. [2]

Previous studies have been used wherever possible. [2] Philosophers, jurists, and theologians in many countries have made penetrating and in some respects path-breaking investigations, limited largely to the theoretical and legal aspects of the struggle. Other juridical works have been devoted to the treatment of a single theorist such as Francisco de Vitoria, Juan Ginés de Sepúlveda, or Bartolomé de Las Casas. Historians, including the writer, have been busy on monographs dealing with one topic, with an individual incident in the struggle, with the work of a special group such as the Dominicans, or have located and published fundamental documents.

An exception to this rule is the Mexican scholar Silvio A. Zavala, who has produced two brief but important general treatments entitled *New Viewpoints on the Spanish Colonization of America* and *Filosofía de la Conquista.* [3] Valuable as these two contributions are, they are essentially collections of essays and their intention is radically different from that of this volume, which tries to tell the story of the interaction throughout the first century of the conquest between the theories and theorists on the one hand and the laws and events in the New World on the other, and is thus essentially a study in the history and influence of ideas. Although the publications of other scholars have been freely cited, the writer has located and utilized some of the great store of manuscripts available on these topics in an effort to provide greater depth and breadth to the story. Thus this volume aims to be both an original contribution to the subject and an interpretative synthesis of what is known today concerning the struggle for justice in the Spanish conquest of America. An enlarged version in Spanish now in press in Buenos Aires, entitled *La lucha por justicia en la conquista de América,* will be available for any reader desiring greater detail than the present volume provides.

Spirit of This Study

A historian writing today cannot be certain that he has presented the facts of this mighty sixteenth-century struggle accurately. Even now some of the essential facts are not known and the clarification of some problems must await further archival investigation. Interpretation of the available facts is even more difficult. Learned controversies have long raged, and their fires are not yet quenched, over many of the men and events discussed in this book.

Besides the usual doubts and disagreements that spring up among historians, no matter what the subject, those who write the history of Spain in America have often been subject to the special hazard of strong religious or political bias. On this account the struggle for justice has been one of the topics in Spanish history most vulnerable to partisan treatment.

Historians, especially those writing in English, even when they have recognized the existence of Spanish theories dealing with Spain's American problems, have usually confined themselves to pointing the finger of scorn to show how far Spanish practice in America departed from the theory elaborated by the crown in Spain. The Spaniards' concern to work out a policy which they could justify to their own consciences has been dismissed as hypocritical religiosity akin to the spirit of the walrus in *Alice's Adventures in Wonderland,* who shed such bitter tears while busily assisting the carpenter to consume so many oysters. Thorstein Veblen faithfully represented a large body of opinion—outside Spain at least—when he asserted: "The Spanish enterprise in colonization was an enterprise in pillage, inflamed and inflated by religious fanaticism and martial vanity." [4]

Spanish "revisionists," eager to justify their ancestors' ways and to combat the "black legend" of Spanish cruelty and oppression in America, have replied to these critics by quoting long extracts from the humanitarian laws of the Indies with intent to prove the just and enlightened nature of the Spanish conquest and colonial system. Or they point out that other European nations were at least as cruel as the Spaniards, a characteristic defense which appeared most recently in the volume entitled *The Rise of the Spanish American Empire,* [5] by the brilliant Spanish controversialist Salvador de Madariaga.

A completely objective attitude toward the historical controversies centering around a people as vital and as complex as the Spaniards is, of course, impossible to attain. But, allowing for my long-standing and incurable predilection for all things Spanish, my effort has been to be both accurate and honest and to exemplify the spirit so well described by Samuel Purchas over three hundred years ago as he presented an English translation of the writings of the Dominican friar Bartolomé de Las Casas to his countrymen. Las Casas, a loud champion of the Indians, had bitterly accused his fellow Spaniards of horrible cruelty in America. Purchas, explaining his publication of the writings of this partisan figure, prefaced his translation with these words:

And if any thinke that I publish this in disgrace of that Nation (Spain); I answere, Every Nation (We see it at home) hath many evill men, many Devill-men. Againe, I ask whether the Authour (himself a Spaniard and Divine) intended not the honour and good of his Country thereby. . . . For my part I honour vertue in a Spaniard, in a Frier, in a Jesuite. . . . And so farre am I from delighting to thrust my fingers in sores (which yet I doe on necessitie even with the English also) that I have left out many invectives and bitter Epithetes of this Authour, abridging him after my wont, and lopping off such superfluities which rather were the fruit of his zeale, than the flowre of his History.[6]

My ideal has been to follow the counsel of Fernando de los Ríos, whose writings first led me to enquire into this subject. He urged: "Let us judge the Spanish colonial activities, not as Catholics or Protestants, but as observers with the objectivity necessary to one who proposes to study a problem of great significance in history." [7]

The Climate of Opinion in Sixteenth-Century Spain

The almost incredible story of the amusing, curious, and tragic episodes which took place when the theories decided upon in Spain were put into practice in America cannot be understood except in relation to the climate of opinion prevailing in sixteenth-century Spain.[8]

It was an age of theologians who believed that their "duties and functions extended over a field so vast that no argument and no discussion seemed alien to the practice and purpose of theology." [9] Their importance was so widely recognized in that century that even frontier officials in Florida felt the need of a theologian in their midst and requested the crown to send them one.[10]

Religiosity was an integral and vital part of Spanish life. Captains of slaving ships promulgated and enforced strict laws against blasphemy and card playing.[11] Even while Sir Francis Drake was raiding the Spanish coast, Philip II took time to consider how the sailors on the Armada could be kept from swearing.[12] Another example of the

strength of religious formalism has been well described by Alonso
de Ercilla in his great epic poem *La Araucana* (1569) on the conquest
of Chile. The Araucanian chief Caupolicán had been captured and
was about to be put to death when he expressed a desire to be baptized and become a Christian. "This caused pity and great comment
among the Castilians who stood around," according to Ercilla, and
Caupolicán was baptized "with great solemnity, and instructed in
the true faith as well as possible in the short time available." After
this, the Spaniards made him sit on a sharp stake and shot him
through and through with arrows.[13]

Sixteenth-century Spaniards were thoroughly saturated also with
the spirit of legal formalism, and the New World offered many opportunities for the exercise of juridical formalities. The Requirement or proclamation to be read to the Indians before warring
against them, which will be discussed later, was probably the best
single example, but many others could be cited. Spaniards were so
accustomed to certifying every action they took that notaries were as
indispensable to their expeditions as friars and gunpowder. The
extraordinary concern for legality of even the Spanish soldier of the
period reveals itself in the account given by the foot soldier Bernal
Díaz of the encounter between his captain Hernán Cortés and the
Indians at Cholula. Cortés explained that "he had been sent to these
countries to give them warning and to command them not to worship
idols, nor sacrifice human beings or eat their flesh, or practice sodomy
or other uncleanness" and urged the Indians to render obedience
to the king of Spain. The Indians refused to give up their idols but
"as to rendering obedience to our king, they were content to do so.
And thus they pledged their word, but it was not done before a
notary." [14]

But it was not done before a notary! Would a pikeman of any
other European nation have noticed, let alone recorded, such a fact?
And one cutthroat conquistador, Lope de Aguirre, even took the
trouble to rebel against his king in a legal way, drawing up while
deep in the Amazonian jungle a manifesto which announced to the
crown that he no longer considered himself subject to Spanish
law.[15]

The element of Spanish character which most deeply affected the
struggle for justice in America is what Spanish and foreign interpreters alike have termed its "tendency toward polarization, a native
passion for extremes." [16] All the great figures of the conquest were
moved by one or the other of two dominant and diametrically opposed motives.

The conquistador Francisco Pizarro once replied to an ecclesiastic
in his company who was protesting the despoilment of Indians in

Peru and urging upon him that God and the faith ought rather to be made known to them: "I have not come for any such reasons. I have come to take away from them their gold." [17]

There it is in its stark simplicity, the oldest and most familiar motive, the lust for material wealth. But it is deeply significant that the incident showing this motive cannot even be recounted without involving the second one, best set forth in a statement made by Friar Bartolomé de Las Casas, who cried:

The aim which Christ and the Pope seek and ought to seek in the Indies— and which the Christian Kings of Castile should likewise strive for—is that the natives of those regions shall hear the faith preached in order that they may be saved. And the means to effect this end are not to rob, to scandalize, to capture or destroy them, or to lay waste their lands, for this would cause the infidels to abominate our faith.[18]

Here the other face of sixteenth-century Spanish character looks boldly at us, and the second motive compelling Spaniards during the conquest reveals itself: the missionary urge to carry to far places and hitherto unknown men the great message from Christendom— the faith.

Between the two poles—the thirst for gold and the winning of souls, not for Spain but for the glory of God—a variety of mixed motives appeared. Some conquistadores were at times as missionary-minded as the most devoted friars. A few ecclesiastics were as worldly as Pizarro in their search for wealth and a life of ease in America. Many Spaniards, however, exemplified both motives. As the classic statement by Bernal Díaz put it: "We came here to serve God, and also to get rich." [19]

The motives of men are usually complicated and we must avoid undue simplification. But as the conquest proceeded there developed two conflicting interpretations of justice and how to achieve it. One group regarded Indian conversion as important, but secondary, and its members devoted themselves to justifying to the royal conscience the virtual enslavement of the Indians as a means to develop the resources of the New World for the benefit of the crown and for the glory of Spaniards and of Spain. The other group placed primary emphasis on Indian conversion and on the welfare of the Indians, relegating to an inferior place the material development of the continent. Both groups sought political power as the indispensable force required to make their views prevail, the ecclesiastics just as energetically as the conquistadores. Indeed, one writer today suggests that "behind all the discussion of the rights of the crown to the conquered lands lies the plan, very natural in Spain, to erect a spiritual power, over against that of the state. The self-assurance and anti-imperialistic aggressiveness of Las Casas . . . hide a desire for ecclesiastical and utopian imperialism." [20]

However the various motives may be interpreted, the fundamental divergence represented by the quotations from Las Casas and Pizarro remains, nevertheless, one of the abiding truths.

Free Speech in Spain and America

The historian today would know much less about the struggle for justice if the Spaniards had not discussed their American problems so freely and so frankly.[21] In the Archive of the Indies in Seville lie thousands of letters and reports advising, admonishing, exhorting, and even threatening the mightiest monarchs of the time in Europe. Ferdinand and Isabella, Charles V, and Philip II were powerful rulers who usually brooked little opposition. From the very beginning of the conquest and throughout the sixteenth century, however, ecclesiastics, conquistadores, colonists, Indians, and a multitude of royal officials from all the far corners of Spain's New World empire sent personal messages to their kings, explaining what and who was wrong and describing the measures required to remedy the situation. The great distances lying between the various regions of the Indies and the court, the royal policy of playing off one group against another, and the responsibility of the crown for both the spiritual and temporal welfare of Indians as well as Spaniards all tended to stimulate the vast flow of correspondence between America and Spain.

The king's loyal subjects did not sugar-coat the pill of their criticism. Nor did ideas and complaints remain hidden in correspondence, for they often achieved the permanence of print. No one from the king downward was exempt from criticism and no subject seems to have been too small or correspondent too humble for the highest authorities in Spain to lend an ear. Nor was any part of the empire too far away to command the attention of the king. When the Bishop of Manila, the vigorous Dominican Domingo de Salazar, insisted on making the Chinese converts to Christianity in the Philippines cut off their pigtails as a visible symbol of their emancipation from heathenish customs, the opponents of this extreme measure carried their protest to Philip II and won.[22] No problem was too important to touch upon, for the kings allowed and even encouraged at times the discussion of such a tender issue as the justice of their own right to rule the New World.

Always the basic conflict of approaches to American problems impelled Spaniards to speak out and to communicate by letter and messenger with the directing power in Spain. Men of action, men of thought, men eager to consolidate the expanding empire or to govern it, men burning to advance the spiritual conquest by their various plans and devices—all carried their claims and grievances to the crown or Council. Each correspondent or messenger was intent on moving the great machinery at home to the uses he or his faction considered paramount and felt that the success of the whole Spanish enterprise hung in the balance while he struggled to convince the lawmakers at the seat of power.

What makes the freedom of speech enjoyed in sixteenth-century America so notable is that the Spanish rulers not only permitted but encouraged it. As early as August 14, 1509, King Ferdinand ordered that "no official should prevent anyone from sending to the king or anyone else letters and other information which concern the welfare of the Indies," [23] and in 1521 a standard instruction was issued which read:

We order and emphatically maintain that now and henceforth at all times when each and every Royal Official and all other persons who are citizens and residents and inhabitants of the Indies, Islands and Tierra Firme of the Ocean Sea wish to write and give an account of everything that appears to them to be convenient to our service or if they wish to send messengers or come themselves, they shall be allowed to do these things and no one (including Captains, pilots and sailors) is to be permitted to place any restriction or hindrance or obstacle, whether directly or indirectly, under penalty of losing all favors, privileges, and positions granted by Us and loss of all property and under pain of Our displeasure.[24]

Freedom of speech was, of course, subject to restrictions in certain fields such as religion. Nor was the press wholly free as the prohibition against some books, particularly after 1550, indicates. Some of the writings of the opponents of Las Casas, for example, were never allowed to be printed in the sixteenth century although he was able to distribute—all too freely in the opinion of some of his contemporaries such as the venerable Franciscan Toribio de Motolinía [25]— his published and unpublished tracts throughout Spain and the New World. On the other hand, those who challenged Las Casas wrote steadily and extensively to the crown against what they considered his exaggerations and falsehoods. Never during the sixteenth century did the crown attempt to stop the flow of news—good and bad— from the New World to Spain. The historian who digs away today in Spanish archives becomes painfully aware of the results of this policy, for literally tons of reports and letters of the most controversial and divergent nature have been preserved there on every topic of colonial administration.

The crown did not merely provide that mail should be free to move to Spain without censorship. It also encouraged discussion of practically every American problem before the regular and special tribunals that were set up in Spain and America to carry on the vast imperial enterprise. Established institutions, such as universities, were also drawn into these disputes although the royal patience was strained at least once, for the records show that Charles V rebuked the professors and friars of Salamanca on one occasion when he considered they had presumed too far in their consideration of Spain's title to the New World.[26]

What was the real meaning of this freedom of speech? Was it merely a device by which Spaniards of all degrees were encouraged to bear tales simply to keep the crown informed, a sort of Hapsburg intelligence service? Certainly the crown deliberately utilized the material resulting from this freedom of speech in the administration of the Indies toward the end that it might retain its dominance in all things.

In common with every other fundamental aspect of Spanish thought and character, the degree of freedom of speech which flourished in the sixteenth century can be and has been interpreted variously. My own interpretation is that it was not merely a carefully calculated administrative device and not merely a lack of postal censorship. The fostering of discussion on American problems also reveals, it seems to me, both the highly developed individualism of the Spaniards and a deliberate, imaginative, and courageous attempt by the crown and the Spanish people to shoulder the heavy burdens placed on Spain by her political and ecclesiastical dominion in America.

The period in which Spaniards expressed their views most freely coincided with the greatest age Spain has ever known, and some Spaniards well understood that this was no accidental relationship. The plain speaking of sixteenth-century Spaniards must be considered—along with their legal formalism, religiosity, devotion to theology, and passion for extremes—as an important element in the climate of opinion which prevailed during the momentous epoch which Spaniards considered the eighth wonder of the world—the discovery and conquest of America.

The Nature of the Indians

Spaniards not only spoke freely on American problems, they also wrote extensively and heatedly on American history as they were making it. One great topic touched upon by every historian or free-speaking Spaniard was the true nature of the Indians. No other controversy so universally embroiled Spaniards during the sixteenth century or so well illustrates the climate of opinion.[27]

From the very beginning of the conquest, opinion was sharply divided concerning the nature of the Indians—particularly their capacity to live according to the ways of Spaniards and their ability to receive the Christian faith. As the discovery and colonization proceeded, the treatment of the Indians became an issue of prime importance, for the proper treatment to be accorded the Indians, the proper laws to be devised to govern them, depended to a large degree on their nature or at least upon the Spaniards' concept of their nature.

Though more subtle, more moderate, and more realistic theories were eventually developed, the majority of the Spaniards in the Indies during the first half-century of the conquest tended to look upon the natives either as "noble Indians" or as "dirty dogs."

Bartolomé de Las Casas may be taken as an extreme example of the "noble Indian" group when he cried:

God created these simple people without evil and without guile. They are most obedient and faithful to their natural lords and to the Christians whom they serve. They are most submissive, patient, peaceful and virtuous. Nor are they quarrelsome, rancorous, querulous or vengeful. Moreover, they are more delicate than princes and die easily from work or illness. They neither possess nor desire to possess worldly wealth. Surely these people would be the most blessed in the world if only they worshipped the true God.[28]

Gonzalo Fernández de Oviedo, official historian and sworn foe of Las Casas, was one of the most prominent among the rival school. He considered the Indians

naturally lazy and vicious, melancholic, cowardly, and in general a lying, shiftless people. Their marriages are not a sacrament but a sacrilege. They are idolatrous, libidinous and commit sodomy. Their chief desire is to eat, drink, worship heathen idols, and commit bestial obscenities. What could one expect from a people whose skulls are so thick and hard that the Spaniards had to take care in fighting not to strike on the head lest their swords be blunted?[29]

Thus began the inevitable conflict, which continued throughout the sixteenth century. Practically every important figure in the New World and many in Spain delivered a judgment on the capacity of the Indians. Humble friars and renowned theologians, such as Francisco de Vitoria at the ancient University of Salamanca, arose to defend the Indians from the charge of irrationality. One of the greatest battles on the nature of the Indians, which will be described later in the book, took place in Valladolid in 1550 and 1551 when Juan Ginés de Sepúlveda and Las Casas fought bitterly over the question whether the Aristotelian theory that some men are by nature slaves was applicable to the Indians.

As indicative of the bitter and open conflict that raged on the subject, a conflict which still divides historians and influences their history, may be cited the deathbed retraction by Friar Domingo de Betanzos of his previous opinion that the Indians were beasts. This Dominican had been instrumental in persuading Las Casas to become a friar, had later reproved Las Casas for his "indiscreet zeal," had labored in the Indies for thirty-five years, and now in 1549 returned to Spain on his way to die in the Holy Land. After going on foot from Seville to Valladolid, he stopped at the San Pablo monastery where death overtook him. But before this occurred, a solemn and impressive drama was enacted.

Surrounded by his Dominican brothers, Betanzos repudiated the idea that the Indians were beasts. In the words of the notary who was called to witness this event and whose formal record of it was discovered not long ago in a Bolivian monastery:

In the very noble city of Valladolid on September 13, in the year of Our Lord 1549, before me Antonio Canseco, notary public of Your Majesties, being in the monastery of San Pablo of the Order of Preachers, in a room in that monastery there was an old man with head and beard shaven, lying in bed apparently ill but in his right mind, called Friar Domingo de Betanzos. And he handed over to me, the aforesaid notary public, a sheet of paper on which he told me he had written and declared certain matters, which concerned his conscience, and which related especially to the affairs of the Indies, which manuscript and declaration he delivered to me.[30]

This declaration referred to a written memorial Betanzos had presented to the Council of the Indies some years before in which he had declared that the Indians were beasts (*bestias*), that they had sinned, that God had condemned them, and that all of them would perish. Now on his deathbed he believed that he had erred "through not knowing their language or because of some other ignorance" and formally retracted the statements in the memorial.

A few days after signing this declaration, Betanzos died. For him the struggle was resolved. His Dominican brothers, who doubtless were largely responsible for the whole episode, hastened to make sure that his final statement was made public and that the Council of the Indies received a duly certified copy.

But the issue was not resolved for the King, the Council of the Indies, and all those concerned with the administration of the New World. One of the ablest administrators Spain sent to America, Antonio de Mendoza, the first viceroy of New Spain, arrived at what seems to us today a common sense conclusion on the question. Writing a formal memorial of advice to his successor, about the time that the friar Betanzos made his retraction in Valladolid, Mendoza recommended that neither those Spaniards who considered the Indians simple, industrious, humble, without malice or evil, or those who held the contrary view should be believed. "Treat the Indians like any other people," he urged, "and do not make special rules and regulations for them. There are few persons in these parts who are not motivated, in their opinion of the Indians, by some interest, whether temporal or spiritual, or by some passion or ambition, good or bad." [31]

Some Spaniards in America followed this counsel of moderation, but most did not and all continued to grapple with the problem which was directly or indirectly related to practically every event in the history of the struggle for justice, to which we now turn.

Part I

The First Cry for Justice in America

Chapter I

THE SERMONS OF FRIAR ANTONIO DE MONTESINOS

ON THE Sunday before Christmas in 1511 a Dominican friar named Antonio de Montesinos preached a revolutionary sermon in a straw-thatched church on the island of Hispaniola. Speaking on the text "I am a voice crying in the wilderness," Montesinos delivered the first important and deliberate public protest against the kind of treatment being accorded the Indians by his Spanish countrymen. This first cry on behalf of human liberty in the New World was a turning point in the history of America and, as Pedro Henríquez Ureña termed it, one of the great events in the spiritual history of mankind.[1]

The sermon, preached before the "best people" of the first Spanish town established in the New World, was designed to shock and terrify its hearers. Montesinos thundered, according to Las Casas:

In order to make your sins against the Indians known to you I have come up on this pulpit, I who am a voice of Christ crying in the wilderness of this island, and therefore it behooves you to listen, not with careless attention, but will all your heart and senses, so that you may hear it; for this is going to be the strangest voice that ever you heard, the harshest and hardest and most awful and most dangerous that ever you expected to hear. . . . This voice says that you are in mortal sin, that you live and die in it, for the cruelty and tyranny you use in dealing with these innocent people. Tell me, by what right or justice do you keep these Indians in such a cruel and horrible servitude? On what authority have you waged a detestable war against these people, who dwelt quietly and peacefully on their own land? . . . Why do you keep them so oppressed and weary, not giving them enough to eat nor taking care of them in their illness? For with the excessive work you demand of them they fall ill and die, or rather you kill them with your desire to extract and acquire gold every day. And what care do you take that they should be instructed in religion? . . . Are these not men? Have they not rational souls? Are you not bound to love them as you love yourselves? . . . Be certain that, in such a state as this, you can no more be saved than the Moors or Turks.[2]

Montesinos thereupon strode out of the church with head high, leaving a muttering crowd of colonists and officials behind him, who were astounded, but not one was converted. He had come as near

17

to convincing his hearers of their wrongdoing as would a theological student in our day who delivered a soapbox philippic in Wall Street on the biblical text "Sell that which thou hast and give to the poor, and thou shalt have treasure in heaven."

The colonists gathered at the house of the Governor, Diego Columbus, protested against the sermon as a scandalous denial of the lordship of the king in the Indies, and delegated a group which went indignantly to the monastery to exact an apology and disavowal. The vicar, Pedro de Córdoba, unimpressed by the delegation's threat to expel the offensive friar, assured them that Montesinos had spoken for the Dominican group. He promised, however, that Montesinos would preach the next Sunday on the same topic. The colonists thereupon retired, believing they had won their point.

Word of the expected retreat spread quickly, and the following Sunday most of the leading Spaniards crowded into the church. Montesinos mounted the pulpit and announced the disquieting text "Suffer me a little, and I will show thee that I have yet to speak on God's behalf." [3] Rather than explaining away his previous sermon with dialectic subtleties, he proceeded to belabor the colonists anew, with even more passion than before, warning them that the friars would no more receive them for confession and absolution than if they were so many highway robbers. And they might write home what they pleased, to whom they pleased.

These words were soon heard in Spain, even by the King. On March 20, 1512, Ferdinand ordered Governor Diego Columbus to reason with Montesinos. If the Dominican and his brothers persisted in their error, previously condemned by the canonists, theologians, and learned men gathered to deliberate on the problem ten years before, the Governor was instructed to send them to Spain by the first ship so that their Superior might punish them "because every hour that they remain in the islands holding such wrong ideas they will do much harm." [4]

Three days later on March 23, 1512, the Dominican Superior in Spain, Alonso de Loaysa, reproved Montesinos in an official communication to the Dominican Provincial in Hispaniola and ordered him to prevail upon the friars to stop preaching such scandalous doctrine. The Provincial was warned that no more friars would be sent if such preaching were permitted to continue. [5]

Thus began the first great struggle for justice in the New World. But the Spanish conscience had been twinged by American events even earlier in the conquest, for searching questions had been raised concerning the first Indians to reach Spain. Columbus paraded these natives through the streets of Seville and Barcelona on his first triumphal return, to whet the popular interest in his enterprise and to win royal support for further adventuring in the New World. He also sent back to Spain, after his second voyage, a consignment of natives to be sold as slaves, a clear hint concerning the financial possibilities of the land. The crown ordered Bishop Fonseca on April 12, 1495, to sell these Indians, but on the following day another despatch instructed him to hold the money received from the sale until theologians could satisfy the royal conscience concerning the morality of the act.[6]

When Montesinos declared in 1511 that the Spaniards had been so cruel to the Indians that they could "no more be saved than the Moors or Turks," much in the history of the early conquest justified his attack. The men who went to the New World during those early years were usually footloose ex-soldiers, broken noblemen, adventurers, or even convicts. One eyewitness reported that one could see riffraff who had been scourged or clipped of their ears in Castile lording it over the native chiefs in the New World.[7] Many of the Spaniards had taken Indian women to serve them as concubines, and this fact naturally helped to embitter relations between Spaniards and native men. Food also ran short, one crisis after another quickly developed, and Indian labor was increasingly drafted to hunt for gold or to grow crops for Spaniards. After the Spaniards had reached the early and easily taken decision that the proper relationship between colonists and Indians was that of master to servant, they set out to create a legal institution which would both regularize this relationship and reflect the desire of the crown to convert the natives. This institution came to be known as the *encomienda*.

The theory of the encomienda was simple. The Spanish crown gave or "commended" Indians to Spaniards, who became encomenderos, and this grant gave the Spaniards the right to exact labor or tribute from the Indians. In return, the encomenderos were obliged to provide religious instruction for their Indians and to protect them. The encomenderos also, as the system developed, came to owe an obligation to the king, that of defending the land.[8] The early encomiendas were sometimes called *repartimientos* though this term later had different meanings.

In practice, the encomienda system was established by Columbus in 1499 after the failure of his attempt to impose a definite tribute on the Indians of Hispaniola. The pattern evolved that in the islands, where there were relatively few Indians, many of whom died promptly under Spanish rule, service rather than tribute was rendered, whereas on the mainland the encomenderos enjoyed both tribute and service from Indians and were thus enabled to lead a relatively dignified and comfortable life under semifeudal conditions.[9] The encomienda, then, started with Columbus, when he assigned three hundred Indians to Spaniards. When Queen Isabella learned this, she asked her famous question: "By what authority does the Admiral give my vassals away?"

The encomienda was put on an institutional basis by the first royal governor, Nicolás de Ovando, who arrived in April 1502 at Hispaniola, principle seat of Spanish government during the first quarter-century after 1492. A great company of men was with him, some twenty-five hundred in all, but none of them had come to labor with their hands. Ovando carried instructions to take away the Indians from Spaniards, put them under the crown, and require them to pay tribute out of the daily wages they would earn. This attempt failed, and by royal order of December 20, 1503, Ovando was permitted to grant Indians.[10]

Because of the excessive liberty the Indians have been permitted, they flee from Christians and do not work. Therefore they are to be compelled to work, so that the kingdom and the Spaniards may be enriched, and the Indians Christianized. They are to be paid a daily wage, and well treated as free persons for such they are, and not as slaves.

So runs the royal order.

Inevitably questions arose among ecclesiastics concerning the justice of the system, and by a royal letter of August 14, 1509, it was determined that Indians were to serve for a period of one or two years only, and not for life.[11] This order was not strictly enforced, and pressure was exerted to allow encomiendas to be passed on to encomenderos' descendants as inheritances.[12] Thereafter the question was continuously under discussion in Spain and America. The fact remains, however, that the first two decades of Spanish rule was a period of almost unchecked exploitation of the Indians.

The coming of four Dominican friars to Hispaniola in 1510 under the leadership of Pedro de Córdoba changed all this. They found a frontier community callous to the cruelties, deaths, and enslavements being inflicted on the helpless natives. Perhaps the general indifference, at this period, to the sufferings of the Indians and unconcern with their rights are best illustrated by the attitude of Bartolomé de Las Casas, later one of the most remarkable and controversial figures of the conquest. From his boyhood in Seville he had had some familiarity with American problems and with Indians. He was present in Seville in 1493 when Columbus, on his return from his first voyage, triumphantly exhibited through the streets natives and parrots from the New World. His father accompanied Columbus on the second voyage and is supposed to have given Las Casas an Indian slave to serve as page during his student days at the University of Salamanca. Las Casas himself went to America, probably with Ovando in 1502, and was not much better than the rest of the gentlemen—adventurers who rushed to the New World, bent on speedily acquiring fortunes. He obtained Indian slaves, worked them in mines, and attended to the cultivation of his estates. The affairs of the young university graduate prospered. While he did not mistreat his Indians, no doubts concerning the justice of his actions bothered him. In 1512 he participated in the conquest of Cuba and received as a reward both land and the service of some Indians, even though he had taken holy orders.

It was against such men as the Las Casas of those early days of the conquest that Montesinos raised his voice. And Las Casas shared the resistance of the other colonists to the message of Montesinos, for he, like them, took no steps to change his way of life and for more than two years after the sermons continued to play the role of comfortable gentleman—ecclesiastic, although once during this time he was refused the sacraments by a Dominican because he held slaves. The hot dispute that ensued left him disturbed but unconvinced.

But the seed of a great decision must have been growing within this obstinate man, as yet unaware that his destiny was to become the greatest Indian champion of them all. It was while he was on his estate in Cuba near the Arimao River preparing a sermon he was to deliver on Whitsunday of 1514 at the newly established settlement of Sancti Expiritus that his eye fell upon this verse in chapter thirty-four of Ecclesiasticus: "He that sacrificeth of a thing wrongfully gotten, his offering is ridiculous, and the gifts of unjust men are not accepted."

Pondering on this text for several days and turning over in his mind the doctrines preached by the Dominicans, Las Casas became increasingly convinced "that everything done to the Indians thus far was unjust and tyrannical." The scales fell from his eyes, he saw at last what was to be forever after the truth for him, and experienced as complete a change of life as did Saul of Tarsus on the road to Damascus.

Characteristically he did not shrink from entering upon the new life immediately. He gave up his Indians and preached a sermon at Sancti Espiritus against his fellow Spaniards which shocked them as much as the words of Montesinos had surprised and alarmed his congregation. Henceforth he devoted his life to the Indians, and in every book he read "whether in Latin or in Spanish, he found additional reasons and authorities to prove and corroborate the justice of those Indian peoples, and to condemn the robbery, evil, and injustice committed against them." [13]

He was to follow this path, chosen in his fortieth year, for the remaining more than fifty years of his life, and the energy and skill hitherto employed for his own comfort and enrichment were to lead him to far places and very many times across the Ocean Sea to enrage and astonish generations of his countrymen. It is not too much to say that the struggle for justice which this book recounts would have been much less stoutly and less persistently fought without him, that indeed the story of the struggle becomes to a considerable extent the story of his life.

And yet the struggle was larger than any one man. It is symbolic that it was touched off by an almost unknown friar. No writings of Montesinos have come down to us, nor any picture of him, and of his life after the famous sermons we know little, except that he spoke once at the court in Spain on behalf of the Indians and met his death while protecting them in Venezuela.[14] Millions of Americans today have never heard his name. Our only records of his great moment in history appear in the royal instructions ordering him to be silent and in the *History of the Indies* by Las Casas whose description, written four hundred years ago, conveys to us vividly the passion and the force of this first blow struck for human freedom in America.

Chapter II

THE BASIS OF SPAIN'S RIGHT TO RULE THE INDIES

The Laws of Burgos

THE dispute that had arisen in America was carried back to Spain for settlement. The Dominicans were in no way awed by the summary orders from their Superior and their King, and fought back. The issue was too grave to be resolved by an exchange of correspondence, and both sides despatched special emissaries to present their views at court.

The colonists sent a Franciscan, Alonso del Espinal, to represent them, while Montesinos himself was entrusted by the Dominicans to speak for the Indians. When he at length entered the royal presence he so astonished and bewildered Ferdinand with his list of Indian grievances that the King ordered a group of theologians and officials to deliberate at once and draw up proper laws. This group met more than twenty times.[1] Friar Bernardo de Mesa, one of the King's preachers, presented a thesis in which he proved dialectically that although the Indians were free, yet idleness was one of the greatest evils from which they suffered, and hence it was the King's duty to help them overcome it. This tendency to idle away time made absolute liberty injurious to them. Moreover, they were naturally inconstant, and De Mesa therefore concluded that some kind of servitude was necessary "to curb their vicious inclinations and compel them to industry."

Another royal preacher, the Licentiate Gregorio, reached the same result with learned quotations from Aristotle, Thomas Aquinas, Duns Scotus, and Augustinus of Anchona. Gregorio's citation of Aristotle was the opening gun in the campaign to establish that the Indians were slaves by nature. Montesinos replied to these two arguments, speaking from the text "Answer a fool according to his folly, lest he be wise in his own conceit." [2]

The group finally agreed to seven propositions which, while recognizing the freedom of the Indians and their right to humane treatment, concluded that they must be subject to coercion and be kept close to the Spaniards in order that their conversion be effected. It

23

was formally determined that the encomienda system was essentially sound, "in view of the Apostolic Grace and Donation and in agreement with divine and human law." On the basis thus laid down, a council was assembled which proceeded to frame the first comprehensive code of Indian legislation known as the Laws of Burgos, which were promulgated December 27, 1512.[3]

These laws furnish the most complete statement we have of the crown's conception at that time of the ideal relationship between the Indians and their Spanish masters, and covered an extensive range of subjects, from the diet of the Indians to the Holy Sacraments. The encomenderos' many responsibilities were spelled out in great detail. They were to bring together the Indians in villages near the Spaniards, in new houses specially built for them. The old dwellings of the Indians were to be burned, "so that they might lose the longing to return to them, although in the removal violence should not be used but much gentleness."

The laws also provided that the encomenderos were to pay particular attention to the religious instruction of their charges, churches were to be constructed and properly equipped with images and ornaments. Indians were to be taught the creed, prayer, and how to confess. Whenever an Indian died the other members of his village were to be obliged to attend the funeral, bearing a cross. It was ordained that the encomenderos should have Indian children baptized eight days after birth, and that all the sons of chieftains thirteen years and under should be entrusted to the Franciscan friars for four years, to be taught the faith, reading, and writing, and then returned to their own villages. And in order that Latin grammar might be taught to the sons of the chieftains, the King ordered the Bachelor Hernán Juárez to go to the Indies, and his salary to be paid from the royal revenues.

Although one third of all the Indians were to work in the gold mines, as before, meticulous regulations were laid down to prevent ill-treatment and overwork of the Indians, and pregnant women were not to be employed in any kind of labor. The food, clothes, and beds to be supplied them were minutely described. They were to be "persuaded to marry," were forbidden to dance, and were to be prevented from bleeding and painting themselves and from getting drunk. In each town two inspectors were to be stationed to see that the many provisions of the laws were obeyed. The last item contained the significant provision that if at any time the Indians gave proof of being able to live under their own government, they were to be allowed to do so and pay only the ordinary feudal dues of Spain.

These laws had scarcely received royal approval on December 27, 1512, when the Dominican Provincial of Hispaniola, Pedro de Cór-

ITEM 24 OF THE LAWS OF BURGOS (1512), WHICH PROHIBITS
SPANIARDS FROM BEATING INDIANS WITH WHIPS OR CLUBS
AND FROM CALLING "AN INDIAN 'DOG' OR ANY OTHER
NAME UNLESS IT IS HIS REAL NAME." FROM THE
ARCHIVO DE INDIAS, SPAIN; JUSTICIA 299

doba, reached Spain, studied the laws, considered them incomplete, and insisted that they be amended. King Ferdinand agreed, more discussion ensued, and on July 28, 1513, several changes were incorporated into the list and were known as the Clarification of the Laws of Burgos. These amendments were principally concerned with further protection for Indian women and children, but also provided that the Indians were to be compelled to wear clothes, and their children were to be allowed to learn trades if they wished. Finally, Indians were to be compelled to give nine months of each year in service for Spaniards and—"to prevent their living in idleness and to assure their learning to live and govern themselves like Christians, they were also to be compelled to spend the remaining three months working on their own farms or working for Spaniards for wages."

The Laws of Burgos in 1512, and their clarification in 1513, were the first fruits of the 1511 sermons of Montesinos. But they were only a beginning. Other Spanish thinkers, now that the problem had been brought to their attention, began to wonder whether Spain, after all, held a just title to the Indies. These thinkers wrote treatises in which they went far beyond the dispute at Burgos on the proper laws to be drawn up for the benefit of the Indians. They concerned themselves with basic political issues precipitated by the discovery of America, and thereby helped to work out fundamental laws governing the relationships between nations, over a century before Grotius published his study *On the Freedom of the Seas.*

The Dispute up to 1512

Columbus wrote to the Catholic Kings from the coast of Veragua that he was so persuaded of the legitimacy of Spain's title to the Indies that he considered Their Majesties "just as much political lords of this land as of Jerez or Toledo." [4] Columbus based the claim on the papal grant, as may be seen from his letter to the rebellious Roldán which pointed out the danger of giving the Indians a bad example, thereby hindering their conversion, and stated that

the very ample bull granted by the most holy pontiff Alexander VI to the Catholic Kings to conquer new countries was not given with the intention that the new people should be ill-treated but that they should be well rewarded so as to attract them to the holy faith of Christ the Saviour and our Redeemer.[5]

The first serious discussion of the basis for Spanish rule in America and the right of Spaniards to profit from Indian labor seems to have taken place in Spain in 1503. All members of the royal council took part, as well as other learned men, theologians, and canonists. After due consideration of the donation of Alexander VI and other legal documents, they agreed in the presence of and with the advice of the Archbishop of Seville that the Indians should serve the Spaniards and that this was in accordance with law, human and divine. The records for this first consultation are not complete, but it appears that the just title of Spain was the basic issue, for King Ferdinand later expressed great surprise when he heard that Montesinos and other Dominicans were raising questions, and ordered that the friars be shown the donation and the letters "in case they had not been informed of the right by which we hold these islands or the justifications by which these Indians not only should serve as they do but also might be held in more slavery." [6]

Queen Isabella considered the Spanish title secure, as the well-known codicil to her will, dictated as she lay dying in November 1504, indicates.[7] King Ferdinand also was satisfied, for he referred to himself, in an order to Governor Ovando of February 10, 1505, as "perpetual administrator by apostolic authority." [8] Again in an order to Diego Columbus of June 6, 1511, he charged that the Indians be baptized and instructed in "our holy Catholic faith, for this is the principal foundation upon which we base our conquest of these regions." [9]

Learned lawyers and ecclesiastical experts in succeeding centuries have enquired closely into the real meaning of those famous pronouncements in 1493 by which Alexander VI issued his famous donation.[10] Did the Pope intend to entrust the Spanish monarchs with only a missionary task, and grant such power and privilege as would enable them to achieve this limited objective? Or did he really have in mind something different and far greater in scope when he stated that he constituted Ferdinand, Isabella, and their successors the lords of the islands and mainland discovered, "with full, free, ample, and absolute authority and jurisdiction"? Excellent modern studies have been made on this subject, but it is not necessary to plunge now into the intricacies of the argument. Up to the time when Montesinos lifted his voice in Hispaniola, every Spaniard high and low believed that the Pope had granted the newly discovered lands to their kings, and had charged them to convert the Indians. None seems to have enquired any more precisely than that into the true significance of the donation.

The sermons were stopped in Hispaniola by royal order, as we have seen, but the doubts raised by Montesinos were not satisfied and the struggle was continued at Burgos in 1512 before a special council called to decide the matter.[11] The King came to realize, from the heated and frequent meetings of this group, that both the framing of Indian legislation and the justice of his title were most complicated problems, not lightly to be resolved. The Laws of Burgos were, however, agreed upon and duly promulgated.

There was no such agreement on the just title question, and at the Burgos meetings various theologians and jurists were ordered by the crown to present their views in writing.[12] Two of these works have fortunately been preserved. Four hundred years after Las Casas besought the government to publish and circulate them widely throughout Spain and America,[13] one, now to be considered, was published!

The Treatise by Matías de Paz
"Concerning the Rule of the King of Spain over the Indies"
(1512)

Friar Vicente Beltrán de Heredia of Salamanca has both made available the text and provided a learned commentary on this important source for the history of liberty in America.[14] According to Las Casas, Matías de Paz composed the treatise in fifteen days, "opposing the method of using Indian services despotically, and proving that Indians must be governed as free persons and free people." [15]

Matías de Paz was serving as professor of theology in the University of Salamanca when King Ferdinand requested his presence at the 1512 Burgos meeting. He was one of the most able and devoted members of the Dominican Order and enjoyed the friendship and confidence of Friar Juan Hurtado de Mendoza and Cardinal Cayetano.[16] His treatise was written in Valladolid, probably in the summer of 1512, and appears to have been composed somewhat hurriedly. He considers, in scholastic manner, those "doubts which some ecclesiastics have raised concerning the dominion of Our Catholic and Invincible King over the Indians," and gives his opinion on each, stating each proposition, in this fashion:

1. Whether Our Most Christian King may govern these Indians despotically or tyrannically.

Answer: It is not just for Christian Princes to make war on infidels because of a desire to dominate or for their wealth, but only to spread the faith. Therefore, if the inhabitants of those lands never before Christianized wish to listen to and receive the faith, Christian Princes may not invade their territory. Likewise, it is very convenient that these infidels be requested to embrace the faith.

2. Whether the King may exercise over them political dominion.

Answer: If an invitation to accept Christianity has not been made, the infidels may justly defend themselves even though the King, moved by Christian zeal and supported by papal authority, has waged just war. Such infidels may not be held as slaves unless they pertinaciously deny obedience to the prince or refuse to accept Christianity.

3. Whether those who have required heavy personal services of these Indians, treating them like slaves, are obliged to make restitution.

Answer: Only by authorization of the Pope will it be lawful for the King to govern these Indians politically and annex them forever to his crown. Therefore those who have oppressed them despotically after they were converted must make appropriate restitution. Once they are converted, it will be lawful, as is the case in all political rule, to require some services from them—even greater services than are exacted from Christians in Spain, so long as they are reasonable—to cover the travel costs and other expenses connected with the maintenance of peace and good administration of those distant provinces.[17]

As Beltrán de Heredia has pointed out, these conclusions are much the same as those reached by the famous Francisco de Vitoria twenty-seven years later in his magisterial treatises. Important differences existed between them, however, for Paz held that the pope, as Vicar of Christ on earth, enjoyed direct temporal jurisdiction over all the world, a view which was certainly not general and which his fellow Dominican Cardinal Torquemada had expressly denied half a century earlier. Another significant difference was that Paz cited and approved the opinion of thirteenth-century Henry of Susa, the Cardinal-Bishop of Ostia, better known among students of canonical law as Ostiensis, that when heathens were brought to a knowledge of Christ, all the powers and rights of dominion held by these heathens passed to Christ, who became the Lord over the earth in both the spiritual and temporal sense. Christ delegated that supreme dominion to his successors, first St. Peter and then the popes. Applying this doctrine to the situation of his time, Paz found that the justice of Spain's title was unquestionably established upon the grant of Pope Alexander VI.

Despite these two divergences by Paz from the doctrine later to be worked out by Vitoria, it is noteworthy that in this early writing on the justice of Spanish rule Paz clearly asserts that the Indians are not slaves in the sense that Aristotle uses the term in the *Politics* nor are they infidels, who like the Jews, Saracens, and Turks have had an opportunity to learn about God and have rejected Him. Paz here follows the distinction between infidels laid down by Saint Thomas, and places the Indians in the second class of infidels, those who have either not heard the preaching of the faith or have forgotten it. Here Paz quotes persons recently come from the New World on the character of the natives.

Among these people there exist dominions, although in a different form from that to which we are accustomed. I am informed that there also exist in those lands gentle people, not ambitious, avaricious, or malicious, but docile and submissive to our faith, if they be treated with charity. Some observe the natural law, and others pay tribute to the Devil, with whom they maintain speech. Perhaps it was this that led God to inspire our King to send persons to point out to these people the way of salvation.[18]

Here we note at the very threshold of this great debate on human liberty a recognition of a status for the New World natives different from that of other non-Christians, a most important point as will be seen.

Juan López de Palacios Rubios and His Treatise "Of the Ocean Isles" (1512)

Unfortunately this treatise has not yet been published, nor has there appeared an adequate study of the doctrine it contains. The Mexican scholar Silvio A. Zavala is at work and will bring out soon both text and analysis of what was probably the first substantial study of Spain's title to the Indies. Palacios Rubios was one of the foremost jurists of his time and enjoyed the confidence of his monarchs, so it is not surprising that he held strongly royalist views. He had already drawn up, at King Ferdinand's behest, an official apologia for the conquest of Navarre. After condemning the Navarrese ruler as an enemy of the church and a rebel against pontifical authority, Palacios Rubios based Ferdinand's right to Navarre on two papal bulls, which declared that all goods acquired in the "very holy, very just war" against Navarre became the property of the conquerors. Perhaps his best-known work was the commentaries on the laws of Toro, in which he reveals himself so saturated with the absolutist doctrines of Roman law that he deemed it sacrilege to doubt the will of the prince.

Palacios Rubios produced a much more carefully prepared treatise on Indian problems than Friar Matías de Paz but both agreed on all essential points. The title of Spain rests exclusively upon the papal donation, the Indians must be required to come to the faith, and those who use them as slaves or otherwise mistreat them must make due restitution. Palacios Rubios of course accepts the theory of Ostiensis that the pope has direct political power over the world as well as spiritual authority, which caused Las Casas to write on the margin of the manuscript, which has come down to us partly in his own hand, *falsa doctrina*. Las Casas, however, praised Palacios Rubios warmly for his sympathy for the Indians. Palacios Rubios was indeed one of the few secular Spaniards ever to win his approval on such matters. And this praise is justified, for the treatise contains frequent recommendations that the native peoples be treated like tender new plants, worthy of exquisite care and loving protection. In subsequent conversations with Las Casas, the royal councilor always manifested a deep sympathy and keen interest in the welfare of the Indians. It is not strange, therefore, to find Las Casas recommending a few years later to Cardinal Cisneros that he read the works written by Paz and Palacios Rubios and "order them printed and published and carried to the Indies, because this matter of the Indians should not be ignored . . . and it should be known that those Indians are men and free and must be treated as such, and the Devil must be given no more opportunity to blind those who do not wish to see." [19]

The Franciscan Espinal, who had been sent from Hispaniola by the colonists to oppose Montesinos, and Martín Fernández de Enciso, well-known lawyer and cosmographer, also composed "certain chapters" on the right of Spain to the Indies, which ended the controversy at Burgos, according to Enciso.[20]

We do not know what doctrine these chapters contained, for they have not come down to us. We know that they did not produce a decisive victory, but a lull between engagements, for the controversy broke out again. By this time friends of the Indians had become vociferously unwilling to allow a single expedition to sail for the Indies until proper instructions had been drawn up for the prospective colonists to make certain that no unjust wars would be waged against the natives. To this end they raised such a dust and clamor that in 1513 King Ferdinand ordered a committee of theologians to study the problem, and held up the departure of the armada of conquistador Pedro Arias de Ávila (better known as Pedrarias), who was preparing to sail for Tierra Firme, until a decision was reached. It was the theological deliberations of this committee which brought forth the Requirement, perhaps the most arresting single document produced during the century-long struggle for justice in America.[21]

Chapter III

THE REQUIREMENT—A MOST REMARKABLE DOCUMENT

PEDRARIAS, whose expedition was so rudely interrupted, was no mean antagonist. One of the great courtiers of the age and known as "The Gallant" and "The Jouster," he had been appointed by Ferdinand in July 1513 to be governor of Tierra Firme. Despite his advanced age, Pedrarias showed great energy in preparing the expedition which was to carry him to the New World. Keen interest was aroused in Spain, and no less than two thousand young men came to Seville in the hope of joining the fleet, to say nothing of "not a small number of avaricious old men." The King invested fifty thousand ducats in the enterprise, and fifteen ships were secured to transport the "most brilliant company that ever left Spain." [1] Some of these men were Hernando de Soto, Diego de Almagro, Sebastián de Benalcázar, Bernal Díaz del Castillo, Gonzalo Fernández de Oviedo, Francisco de Montejo, and other conquistadores who were to make their mark in the New World. What the aged, though still vitriolic, Governor said when his expedition was forced to idle about in Spain while theologians sought justificatory texts for his future wars in the New World has not been recorded.

A member of his expedition, however, Martín Fernández de Enciso, who later wrote the first book on America to be published in Spanish,[2] becoming thoroughly agitated over the delay in sailing, composed a memorial on the subject and spoke learnedly before the meeting which was held in San Pablo, the Dominican monastery in Valladolid. Enciso considered himself a defender of the royal rights over the Indies, later requested compensation from the crown for service rendered and received it.[3]

Before the friars of San Pablo, the King's confessor, and Lope Conchillos, the Secretary of the Royal Council, Enciso set forth his line of reasoning, reinforcing the argument with copious extracts from the Bible. He endeavored to show that the Spaniards in conquering the New World could literally adopt a biblical solution for their problem of just war in America. God had assigned the Indies to Spain, asserted Enciso, just as the Jews had been given their Promised Land. Elaborating this thesis, Enciso declared:

31

Moses sent Joshua to require the inhabitants of Jericho, the first city in the promised land of Canaan, to abandon their city because it belonged to the people of Israel inasmuch as God had given it to them; and when the people of Jericho did not give up their land Joshua surrounded them and killed them all except one woman who had protected his spies. And afterwards Joshua conquered all the land of Canaan by force of arms, and many were killed and those who were captured were given as slaves and served the people of Israel. And all this was done by the will of God because they were idolaters.[4]

Enciso reckoned shrewdly when he sought to arouse support for his theory by appealing to the strong feeling against idolatry which then prevailed in Spain. Spaniards abhorred idolatry with all the vigor of early Christians, who considered it their first duty to preserve themselves pure and undefiled against the heathen worship of idols.

Las Casas was later to point out, at the Valladolid disputation of 1550, that Christians had no need to follow the harsh law of Moses when Jesus had taught otherwise.[5] Apparently no one in 1513, however, questioned Enciso's dubious interpretation of the early history of the people of Israel, and he proceeded to apply the supposed Old Testament standards to the problem of the Spaniards in America.[6] Intent on forging an unbreakable legal chain of reasoning, Enciso explained to the assembly that the Pope, who now stood in God's stead, had given Spain the Indies and its idolatrous inhabitants in order that the Catholic King might introduce Christianity there. Therefore,

the king might very justly send men to require those idolatrous Indians to hand over their land to him, for it was given him by the pope. If the Indians would not do this, he might justly wage war against them, kill them and enslave those captured in war, precisely as Joshua treated the inhabitants of the land of Canaan.[7]

After some discussion, the "master theologians" of San Pablo accepted Enciso's theory with the proviso that those Indians who gave over their land peaceably to the King's representative should be allowed to continue to live thereon as his vassals. When these decisions were communicated to the King, he commanded that a formal proclamation be drawn up.

It is fairly certain that Palacios Rubios worked out the sonorous periods of the resulting proclamation, which has amazed so many historians and, before them, so many Indians. It was formally signed by appropriate royal officials, copied for the conquistadores before they sailed for America, and filed away among the records in Seville, where it lies today.

This manifesto, or Requirement, which was to be announced to the Indians by interpreters before hostilities could legally be launched, makes curious reading. It begins with a brief history of the world since its creation and an account of the establishment of the papacy, which leads naturally to a description of the donation by Alexander VI of "these isles and Tierra Firme" to the kings of Spain. The middle portion, which gives the document its name, requires the acceptance by the Indians who hear it of two obligations. The first is to acknowledge "the Church as the Ruler and Superior of the whole world and the high priest called the Pope, and in his name the King and Queen Juana in his stead as superiors, lords, and kings of these islands and this Tierra Firme by virtue of said donation." The second is to allow the faith to be preached to them.

If the Indians immediately acknowledge these obligations, well and good. But if they do not, the Requirement lists, in conclusion, the punitive steps the Spaniards will take forthwith. They will enter the land with fire and sword, they will subjugate the inhabitants by force to the church and the crown, and lastly, in the words of the document, the Spaniards warn the Indians:

We shall take you and your wives and your children, and shall make slaves of them, and as such shall sell and dispose of them as their Highnesses may command; and we shall take away your goods, and shall do all the harm and damage that we can, as to vassals who do not obey, and refuse to receive their lord, and resist and contradict him; and we protest that the deaths and losses which shall accrue from this are your fault, and not that of their Highnesses, or ours, nor of these cavaliers who come with us. And that we have said this to you and made this Requirement, we request the notary here present to give us his testimony in writing, and we ask the rest who are present that they should be witnesses of this Requirement.[8]

For the time being the Requirement stilled the clamor against Pedrarias who now set forth for the New World on April 12, 1514, accompanied by his imposing expedition and a copy of the document. The first recorded instance we have of an attempt to read the formidable theological proclamation to Indians occurred on June 14, 1514, shortly after the arrival of the fleet. The Governor ordered notary Gonzalo Fernández de Oviedo (later appointed royal chronicler) to accompany a reconnoitering expedition of some three hundred men about to set out from Santa Marta and to read the Requirement as provided by law. After marching for over two leagues without seeing a single Indian, the expedition entered a deserted village, where Oviedo, in the presence of all, declared:

My Lords, it appears to me that these Indians will not listen to the theology of this Requirement, and that you have no one who can make them understand it; would Your Honor be pleased to keep it until we have some one of these Indians in a cage, in order that he may learn it at his leisure and my Lord Bishop may explain it to him.[9]

Oviedo then handed over the document to the captain who "took it with much laughter, in which all those who heard the speech, joined."

A complete list of the events that occurred when the Requirement formalities ordered by King Ferdinand were carried out in America, more or less according to the law, might tax the reader's patience and credulity,[10] for the Requirement was read to trees and empty huts when no Indians were to be found. Captains muttered its theological phrases into their beards on the edge of sleeping Indian settlements, or even a league away before starting the formal attack, and at times some leather-lunged Spanish notary hurled its sonorous phrases after the Indians as they fled into the mountains. Once it was read in camp before the soldiers to the beat of the drum. Ship captains would sometimes have the document read from the deck as they approached an island, and at night would send out enslaving expeditions, whose leaders would shout the traditional Castilian war cry "Santiago!" rather than read the Requirement before they attacked the near-by villages. Sometimes Indian messengers were sent to "require" other Indians.

On one occasion the proclamation was made according to the King's instructions, but at the same time the Spaniards judiciously plied the Indians with food, drink, bonnets, cloth, shirts, hoods, and "other little trifles from Castile." This combination of theology and gifts seems to have been effective. The outcome was far different when Captain Juan de Ayora captured a number of Indians, linked them together with ropes fastened to their necks, and then read them the Requirement. According to Oviedo:

It appears that they had been suddenly pounced upon and bound before they had learnt or understood anything about Pope or Church, or any one of the many things said in the Requirement; and that after they had been put in chains someone read the Requirement without knowing their language and without any interpreters, and without either the reader or the Indians understanding what was read. And even after it had been explained to them by someone understanding their language, they had no chance to reply, being immediately carried away prisoners, the Spaniards not failing to use the stick on those who did not go fast enough.[11]

The sight of Spanish swords and dogs and of their own dwellings in flames was often the first knowledge the Indians had of the presence of Christians in their midst. And as Oviedo concludes, "If all were written in detail as it was done, there would be neither time nor paper to enumerate all that the captains did to destroy the Indians and to rob and ravish the land."

Ever since this Requirement was made part of the baggage that every conquistador was expected to carry with him to America, various and divergent interpretations have been placed upon it. Foreign critics naturally seized upon it to illustrate what they considered the hypocrisy of sixteenth-century Spaniards. The eighteenth-century rationalist philosophers saw in the Requirement another piece of evidence of the all-pervading folly of human nature.

Modern historians have usually treated it in a derisive or ironical spirit, have condemned it for one reason or another, and have substantially agreed with Louis Bertrand and Sir Charles Petrie, who state that "the invaders brandished bulls and theological texts, a whole rubbish heap of documents, by way of justifying their invasions." [12]

Spaniards themselves, when describing this document, have often shared the dilemma of Las Casas, who confessed on reading it he could not decide whether to laugh or to weep.[13] He roundly denounced it on practical as well as theoretical grounds, pointing out the manifest injustice of the whole business. Others found it infinitely ridiculous and even its author, Palacios Rubios, "laughed often" when Oviedo recounted his own experiences and instances of how some captains had put the Requirement into practice, though the learned doctor still believed that it satisfied the demands of the Christian conscience when executed in the manner originally intended.[14] Apologists or semiapologists, however, are to be found even today. Constantino Bayle, the Spanish Jesuit who has been vigorously combatting the black legend, declares: "What was wrong with the Requirement was that it was intended for men, but read to half-beasts (medio bestias)." [15]

Whatever else may be said of the Requirement, it is clear that no one stepped forward to oppose it at the time it was being formulated. No one was present to speak on behalf of the Indians of the New World while their fate was being decided in Spain. The document did embody theories held valid at that time by some highly placed Spaniards, including the Dominicans of the court, and the ease with which the royalist theorists lulled the King's conscience with the Requirement leads one to speculate on how different the conquest might have been if no aggressive Indian champions had arisen to challenge the ideas of those who would ignore the rights of the Indians. Certainly the Requirement would never have been approved so easily, if at all, had Las Casas been converted immediately by the sermons of Montesinos. At the time it was determined upon, he was far away in Cuba living a pleasant and profitable life—all at the expense of the Indians. If Las Casas and others like him had not appeared on the scene later and had not thrown their great power and energy into the fray, the struggle for justice might have been a perfunctory, puny thing, and the King's conscience easily and permanently satisfied. There might have been no struggle at all.

The formulation and proclamation of the Requirement demonstrate that the sermons preached by Friar Montesinos had at least disturbed the court. Many Spaniards of the time would have brushed aside the inconvenient questions asked concerning the justice of the encomienda system, the basis for the title of Spain to the Indies, and the just means of waging war against the Indians. But the King heard Montesinos, even such a worldly and "practical" king as Ferdinand, and convoked some of the best minds in Spain to consider these problems and advise him on the action he should take.

And take action he did, by promulgating the first comprehensive code for the administration of the Indians, the Laws of Burgos, though twenty years before Spain had not known that such beings as Indians existed. He stimulated the composition of the first serious juridical treatment in Spain on his title to the New World, and he officially approved the Requirement.

The narrow span of years which separated Montesinos' first cry for justice in America from the official decisions in Spain on the questions he raised was a decisive period in the history of America. During the years 1511–13 the most searching questions any colonial nation can ask of itself were raised and answered.

They were not answered, however, to the satisfaction of everyone and, though the conquest rolled on, determined protests against the way it was moving never died out during the sixteenth century. The spiritual successors of Montesinos and those other bold friars did more than issue protests. They had a program for action, which rested upon certain passionate convictions they held concerning the nature of the Indians and the laws that should be devised for them by the crown. These convictions were held by men so powerful and so persistent that the crown was persuaded to permit four remarkable experiments during the critical years after Montesinos opened the struggle for justice in America by his sermons on Hispaniola in 1511.

Part II

Spanish Experiments in America

INTRODUCTION

Why Did Spain Experiment?

THIS chapter and the next four will deal with the social experiments which the Spanish crown authorized during the first half-century of the conquest in order to determine the correct administration of the New World. Each experiment asked a question and found for Spain an answer.

1. Could the Indians learn to live like Christian Spaniards?

2. Was it possible to colonize the New World peacefully with Spanish farmers?

3. Could the faith be preached by peaceful means alone? And lastly,

4. Could the encomienda system, by which Indians supported Spaniards, be abolished?

Before plunging into these four very closely related stories which at times require, for clarity's sake, to be kept in their separate channels almost by main force, we may ask how it came about that the Spanish crown took this elaborate experimental means to find its policy.[1]

For once the answer is essentially simple. Besides the driving force of the reform party, we cannot understand the experiments without recognizing the great quickening of thought and of life in general which the opening up of a wonderful new continent stimulated. As Samuel Johnson truly said, "the discovery gave a new world to European curiosity." How inevitable it was that that nation should be most profoundly stirred which held sovereignty over these distant and unknown lands!

Upon the Spanish people—legalistic, individualistic, firm in their allegiance to the crown and to the church, but within the traditional framework of both, and accustomed to plain speaking—the impact of the discovery of America was terrific. The ferment of invention which bubbled up—sending to the king hundreds of laboriously worked out plans for contrivances to drive ships through the seas, improve navigation, extract gold from rivers and lakes, mine silver and gold, gather pearls—and, above all, the rush to participate as sharers in the glory and gain: all these were one reaction to the impact.

The eager religious-philosophical outpouring by theologians and jurists on both sides of the Ocean Sea, the great wealth of thinking and writing on the problems of conversion and Indian capacity, and the rush to participate in the spiritual conquest were another reaction to the New World. Spaniards were apparently too busy fighting Moslems during the Middle Ages to compose many theoretical treatises on political problems. But with the enemy finally driven out in 1492 and with the many opportunities for theoretical discussion offered by the discovery of America, Spain became in the sixteenth century the home of the most illustrious scholastics since the thirteenth-century Thomas Aquinas. Robert Blakey has well described the ensuing development of political theory:

There was no country in Europe in which politics, as a science, underwent a more general investigation and scrutiny . . . than in Spain. . . . We find many elaborate treatises on the abstract principles of government, displaying freedom of inquiry and a degree of talent and learning which would do honor to any country . . . and . . . in no part of human speculation has there been manifested more logical skill in arranging and a greater ability in handling general principles, than in the scientific works of Spaniards on politics and jurisprudence. . . . The discovery of the American continent called forth new principles of administrative science, and territorial right. . . . Hence it is that we find so many works in Spain and Portugal treating of colonial matters; embracing everything connected with the military and civil administration of the newly created governments of the west, and of all those general principles of policy which the parent states thought it expedient to lay down relative to their colonial territories.[2]

The importance of this mass of treatises for the story of the struggle for justice will be developed in later chapters of this book. Is it any wonder that the king, on the receiving end of this avalanche of conflicting theories and plans, and responsible to decree the administration of the new lands in accordance with Christian principles, was moved from time to time to give royal sanction to one experiment after another?

Practical consequences hung upon the answers to every theoretical question. For example, if the Indians were rational beings, could they with justice be deprived of their lands and made to work or pay tribute? If the Carib Indians were cannibals, did not this unnatural vice make necessary their enslavement by Spaniards? Under what conditions could "just war" be waged against the Indians? By what title or titles did the king of Spain exercise dominion in the New World? How much religious instruction should be given the Indians before baptism and, once converted, had this multitude of newly won souls the right to participate in all the sacraments? Las Casas, for instance, insisted that Indians be properly catechized before baptism, and sternly opposed mass conversion, practiced by many of the Spanish missionaries, particularly Friar Marcos Ardón, who is supposed to have baptized over a million natives in Guatemala.[3]

An issue of great importance to the Holy Office of the church was whether the Inquisition ought to "protect" Indians as well as Spaniards from the "disintegrating spirit of heresy." Fortunately for the Indians they were, generally speaking, untouched by the Inquisition on account of their *rudeza e incapacidad*. Friar Diego de Landa's torture of Indians in Yucatan suspected of idolatry shows what might have happened throughout Spanish America. Finally, must Indian children be taught Latin and instructed in the subtleties of Thomas Aquinas, or should they be drilled in a simple program of "reading, writing, and 'rithmetic"?

But always the central problem was to determine the capacity of the Indians.

In judging this capacity the Spaniards never doubted that their own standards were the logical ones to apply. The capacity to *live like Spaniards* was therefore the matter to be adjudged. The absence among the Indians of motives which the Spaniards acknowledged, such as love of gold and wealth, inspired astonishment and contempt in all but a few Spaniards. Always the effort during the experiments was to examine the Indians' ability to live under Spanish institutions of government and religion.

The tragic failures which attended these efforts to impose Spanish and European culture upon New World natives do not surprise us today. Modern anthropology and psychology have so permeated our thought that we understand the clash of alien cultures somewhat better than those sixteenth-century Spaniards and know why the experiments had to end as they did. What is remarkable about them is the driving force and the vision of the ecclesiastics who, equipped with only the love of God and the idea of the brotherhood of man, so powerfully persuaded the monarch of imperial Spain that he repeatedly gave them a chance to try a better way of conquest than simple military usurpation.

Chapter IV

COULD THE INDIANS LEARN TO
LIVE LIKE CHRISTIAN SPANIARDS?

The Jeronymite Interrogatory

ALTHOUGH the Laws of Burgos had affirmed in 1512 the principle of the encomienda whereby the Indians served Spaniards in Hispaniola, the Clarification of the Laws of Burgos in the next year recognized that some Indians who had learned enough from contact with Spaniards to be capable of becoming Christians, and politically developed enough to govern themselves, could be set free at the discretion of the royal judges. The reaction of the colonists, who were presumably to lose the services of the Indians set free under this provision, can be imagined. It was hardly to be expected that a pattern so early established as Indian servitude to Spanish masters could be easily disrupted. Nevertheless by 1516 Cardinal Jiménez de Cisneros, who had been harassed by Las Casas, now in Spain working with other ecclesiastics for Indian freedom, on the one hand, and by colonial officials and the energetic representatives of colonists working for enslavement of the Indians on the other, decided to order a thorough investigation of the Indian problem which would serve as a sound basis for all Indian policy. To this end he summoned three reluctant Jeronymite friars from their monastic retreats, supplied them with copies of the numerous opinions already given on the subject, and provided them with minute and lengthy instructions. The last article of this formidable document directed them to discover whether any Indians could be found capable of living by themselves, and to set free all such Indians. At the same time the Cardinal bestowed on Las Casas the high-sounding title "Protector of the Indians" and sent him back to America. Caught between the open hostility of some of the colonists and royal officials and the zeal of Las Casas, who reached Hispaniola shortly after them, the friars soon realized that they must advance cautiously.

In April 1517 they conducted their official enquiry and took down a quantity of information, some publicly, some in secret, from the twelve oldest inhabitants and the ecclesiastics. Of the seven questions put to each witness, the third struck at the heart of the matter:

Does the witness know, believe, or has he heard it said, or observed, that these Indians, especially those of Hispaniola and women as well as men, are all of such knowledge and capacity that they should be given complete liberty? Would they be able to live *políticamente* as do the Spaniards? Would they know how to support themselves by their own efforts, each Indian mining gold or tilling the soil, or maintaining himself by other daily labor? Do they know how to care for what they may acquire by this labor, spending only for necessities, as a Castilian laborer would?

The hundred closely written pages of replies to this and the other questions contain significant information for anyone interested in the contact of races. Not one of the colonists considered the Indians capable of living in freedom. Marcos de Aguilar was willing to admit that continuous contact with Spaniards might make it possible for the Indians or their children to live alone, but, as Juan Mosquera deposed, many Indians were so steeped in vice that they did not even wish to see Spaniards and fled to the hills at their approach! Jerónimo de Agüero complained that the Indians refused to dig gold or till the soil except for large rewards. And yet they seemed to have no sense of value, for an Indian would trade his best shirt or only hammock for a mirror or a pair of scissors! At times they even gave their possessions away for nothing to those who asked for them. Whoever saw a Castilian laborer as simple as that?

Licentiate Christóbal Serrano corroborated this opinion of Indian prodigality and considered that, inasmuch as Indians showed no greediness or desire for wealth (these being the principle motives, according to the licentiate, impelling men to labor and acquire possessions), they would inevitably lack the necessities of life if not supervised by Spaniards. It was difficult to inculcate habits of honesty and sobriety, stated Juan de Ampiés, because when Spaniards beat them or cut off their ears as punishment, the guilty ones were not held in less repute by their fellows! Pedro Romero, wise with the experience of fourteen years of marriage to an Indian, agreed with the other colonists, but wanted the officials to be on the outlook for those with capacity for freedom, and felt that if some Indians petitioned for liberty and presented "legitimate reasons," they should be granted their freedom.

Miguel de Pasamonte, veteran Treasurer of the King in Hispaniola, presented an interesting bit of evidence on the early social history of the Indies when he opposed giving Indians their freedom on the ground that it would be dangerous because of the friendships between the Indians and the large number of Negroes on the island. Gonzalo de Ocampo conceded that the Indians must have had ability of a sort because they had raised crops, built houses, and made clothes before the Spaniards arrived. The Indian chieftains, likewise, appeared to him to have a good method of keeping together and protecting the people under their administration, but in all other matters neither Indians nor chieftains manifested sufficient ability to live like Spaniards.

The Dominican Bernaldo de Santo Domingo alone of the ecclesiastics boldly declared the Indians ready for liberty and presented a memorial containing an idealistic description of life in the town where the freed Indians were to live, ruled by their own officials and assisted toward the good life by friendly Spaniards.

The consensus of opinion among the colonists was well expressed by one Antonio de Villasante, a resident of Hispaniola since 1493. He deposed that he was more familiar than any other Christian with Indian customs and languages in Hispaniola, and emphatically believed that neither men nor women knew how to govern themselves as well as the rudest Spaniards. If allowed to run free, the Indians would revert to their former habits of idleness, nakedness, drunkenness, improvidence, gluttony, dancing, and would patronize witch doctors and eat spiders and snakes. Moreover, the colony would face economic ruin. As Lucas Vázquez de Ayllón concluded, far better that they should become slave men (*hombres siervos*) than remain free beasts (*bestias libres*).

The opinions of the colonists, it is only fair to say, were in part derived from their experience. Some could remember the announcement made by Columbus to the Indians, almost a quarter of a century before, that they were free vassals of the Catholic Kings and that their chieftains could keep their liberty on paying annually a fixed tribute of gold for themselves and their people. This had not worked because the chieftains asserted that their subjects did not want to mine gold and would not obey orders to do so. The attempt to place responsibility on the freed Indians themselves by requiring each one to pay annually a small gold tribute had likewise failed, although at first the Indians appeared pleased with the arrangement. Later they complained that the amount was too large. Finally, as Diego de Alvarado deposed, they stopped digging entirely, began to drink and dance together, and were suspected of plotting to wipe out the Spanish settlement.

Perhaps what had most impressed the colonists was the experience of Governor Nicolás de Ovando, who had launched a small experiment himself to test the capacity of the Indians to live like Spaniards. Though nothing in the royal instructions had authorized this social experiment, about 1508 Ovando had put at liberty the two most capable Indian chieftains he could find, Alonso de Cáceres and Pedro Columbus. These Indians had lived near Spaniards for some years, knew well how to read and write, were married, and appeared to be more intelligent than other natives. Ovando granted them Indians so that they might live like Spaniards, and favored them in every possible way.

The colonist Juan Mosquera, who as *visitador* had frequently observed the development of Ovando's experiment, informed the Jeronymites that, during the six years (1508–14) the Indians were at liberty, they neither tilled the land assigned to them nor raised pigs. Nor were they able to feed and clothe themselves, much less their dependents, by the produce of their united labor. When Albuquerque made the first general allotment of Indians in 1514, Mosquera added, these chieftains were deprived of their repartimientos. Thus the first sociological experiment in America ended, and the chieftains later died, concluded Mosquera, "in poverty and without honor."

In the face of this avalanche of fact and opinion against the Indians the Jeronymites refused to put at liberty any except one single Indian, who, by his peaceful inclinations and evident ability, appeared to be ripe for freedom. All others were collected into villages under administrators and friars. Though the three friars had not succeeded in setting aright affairs in the Indies, they had amassed a body of evidence on Indian life which was to be cited more than once in later controversies.

The Experiments of Rodrigo de Figueroa

When the successor to the Jeronymites, Rodrigo de Figueroa, arrived, fewer Indians remained to experiment upon. Their concentration in villages by the Jeronymites had favored the spread of a smallpox epidemic which had carried off a large number. Las Casas had left Hispaniola for Spain in 1517 to escape arrest for opposing the decisions of the Jeronymites, and proceeded to campaign feverishly at home for Indian liberty. The death of the regent Jiménez de Cisneros in November 1517 interrupted his protestations, but he at once worked his way into the favor of the Flemish advisers of the young King Charles.

The story of how he forced the Indian problem upon the notice of Charles reveals him as an agile and effective negotiator. His earnest, sincere, and single-minded efforts impressed most of those who had dealings with him, and his insistence on the ability and virtues of the natives helps to explain why the crown was unwilling to drop the enquiry whether Indians could live by themselves as free men. Partly because of the continual exhortations of Las Casas, and partly because such opponents as Fonseca thought one more investigation would quiet once and for all the clamorous Indian champions, the King ordered Judge Rodrigo de Figueroa to make a further investigation in Hispaniola of Indian capacity. That this decision was not merely a local regulation for Hispaniola may be seen by the fact that Antonio de la Gama, newly appointed judge in Puerto Rico, was given an identical order on March 3, 1519.

The voluminous instructions given Figueroa for Hispaniola, dated December 9, 1518, include a succinct summary of the whole controversy. Figueroa was to see that certain officials and all persons living in Spain were deprived of their encomiendas in Hispaniola, to grant all capable Indians their liberty, and to send the King the signed opinions of all "disinterested persons" in the colony on the problem of Indian liberty.

On his arrival in 1519, Figueroa found Hispaniola in a desperate plight, with only one thousand colonists and those disgusted with their lot, and the Indians fast melting away. As his instructions stipulated, he entered into lengthy consultations with the Jeronymites, Franciscans, Dominicans, the officials, and colonists, and found the general opinion solidly against Indian liberty. Some Indians he nevertheless put at liberty, including a few who had been mining gold for the King. Immediately the royal officials entrusted with collecting the King's revenue from mined gold (the *quinto*, or royal fifth) objected that it would not be one third as great as that of the previous year, and they feared that the establishment of the villages of free Indians would undermine the discipline of Indians digging gold for encomenderos. But these doubters were far away in Hispaniola while Las Casas followed the King and court all over Spain proclaiming the virtues of the Indians and the cruelty of the Spaniards.

Thus, in May 1520 Figueroa was instructed to give the Indians their freedom "with all convenient speed." In order to prevent the chaos which might arise from too precipitate action, Figueroa was to begin with the Indians taken away from nonresidents. In addition, Indians left alone by the death of their encomenderos were to be set free. In order better to instruct the Indians in the political way of life some good Spaniards, especially laborers, were to be placed among them and were to teach the Indians how to work. The freed Indians were to be provided with bread, meat, and the proper implements for work until they raised crops of their own. Apparently even free Indians were thought to need some supervision, because priests and an administrator were assigned to each village. If Figueroa found other Indians capable and desirous of living in these villages, they were to be included even though their encomenderos objected. Antonio de la Gama was ordered on July 12, 1521, to carry out the same program in Puerto Rico. Thus gradually but steadily Indian freedom was to be achieved in America, according to its advocates in Spain.

The reply of Figueroa to the charges against him is the most important material we have on this experiment. In this apologia Figueroa describes his efforts in 1519 to carry out his instructions by setting up three villages of free Indians regardless of the unfavorable predictions of friars and colonists. The Indians proved indeed utterly incapable, though he took the greatest interest in their welfare, visited the villagers frequently to exhort them to greater effort, and wrote letters to them when other duties forced him to be absent. He himself had carefully chosen the village administrators and duly warned them that they were responsible for teaching the Indians how to mine gold and how to work their fields. He had watched closely in order to detect any signs of capacity, regretted that he found none, and concluded by recommending that the experiment be abandoned and the Indians returned to service under Spaniards.

He made, however, one more experiment. Francisco de Figueroa, evidently one of the numerous Figueroa relatives the colonists had objected to, was given sixteen Indians to determine whether they could mine gold without help from Spaniards. Supplied with food and the proper tools, these Indians were taken to the mines and kept there for about two months. According to Figueroa, the Indians showed more interest in eating food than in mining gold. During the whole period, the sixteen Indians produced a grand total of less than twenty-five pesos of gold, a trifling amount compared with the cost of the food they had eaten. Not one of the many colonists who hastened to present evidence before Judge Lebrón approved these experiments or considered that any benefit had resulted from them. Thus closed another chapter in the history of Spanish experiments to determine the capacity of the American Indian, and Figueroa departed for Spain with the *importunidades, pasiones,* and *murmuraciones* of angry colonists ringing in his ears.

The Experiencia in Cuba

The last act of the Indian liberty experiments was played in Cuba during the decade 1526–35. The decision to probe yet once more into this tender question represented a victory of theory over past experience.

The decision of 1526 to experiment further ran counter to many official depositions sent about that time to the Council of the Indies by such weighty persons as the Dean of Tierra Firme, the veteran colonist Francisco de Barrionuevo, and the historian Oviedo, all of whom gave an unfavorable view of Indian character. Oviedo in fact strongly urged the Council to grant Indians to the Spaniards in perpetuity.

These opinions bring new evidence to light on some of the prevailing attitudes toward the Indians. Barrionuevo, for example, felt that the law permitting Indians to hold the municipal offices of *alcalde* and *alguazil* should be revoked, and also advised the revocation of the law prohibiting Spaniards from beating Indians or calling them "dogs." Barrionuevo deemed it God's will that the island natives died so easily and stated that it was not on account of their maltreatment by Spaniards. In all his twenty-four years' experience in the Indies, he had known many cases of Indian women married to Spaniards or reared in convents who acted like Spaniards for a while. But after their husbands died or after they left the convents, they would go back to the mountains and revert to their old habits. Barrionuevo also stated that he had known the chieftains set at liberty by Governor Ovando in 1508 and had seen how inattentive they were in church and in other ways how they demonstrated their accustomed bestiality rather than Christianity. Once, one of them on a Sunday cast off all his clothing piece by piece and went home stark naked. Later when Barrionuevo served the King on the island of San Juan he had seen Indians wash off the baptismal water from their heads and then exclaim, "Now I am a Christian no longer!"

The Dean of Tierra Firme supported Barrionuevo on all these points and added other illustrations. He deposed that the Indians lived like animals and had little ability or discretion. He admitted that if the Indians were instructed every day by Christians some good might result, particularly among the children. But they should not be given their liberty. Their memory was so feeble that if they did not repeat the Ave Maria every day they forgot it. The historian Oviedo concurred with all these sentiments and outdid himself in applying strong and depreciative adjectives to describe Indians.

Wherever lay the responsibility for the royal decision to continue experimentation, on September 14, 1526, Pedro Mexía, the Franciscan Provincial in Hispaniola, was ordered to proceed to Cuba where "there is greater need for remedy than in other places."

In Cuba he was to put at liberty all Indians then without encomenderos as well as those whose encomenderos should die in the following six months. The hope definitely persisted in Spain that at least some of the Indians were capable of improvement, as may be seen from the royal provision of November 9, 1526, that twelve of the most capable Indian children in Cuba were to be sent to Spain for education. Once instructed in the Christian and Spanish way of life, they were to return as missionaries to their own people.

Probably no worse time or place could have been chosen. Governor Guzmán and Bishop Miguel Ramírez, charged with putting the royal theories into practice, were both grasping individuals with only a faint interest in the welfare of the Indians. The culture level of the Cuban natives was low, earlier expectations that they would prove more intelligent than the natives of Hispaniola having proved unfounded, and few Spaniards believed the Indians worthy of liberty. Though never mentioned in the letters and reports sent to Spain, the constant depreciation of Indian character and the thorough-going skepticism prevalent among Spaniards concerning Indian capacity must have helped to make the Cuban experiments the resounding failures that they proved to be. Modern students of the capacity of underdeveloped peoples report that the attitude society adopts is of great importance. For example, the majority of well-to-do South Africans have believed that the "poor whites," who constitute the larger part of the European population of the Union of South Africa, are really incapable of progress. Hence their efforts to help have been halfhearted and largely ineffective. The progress of Negroes in the United States toward full participation in our national life has been delayed by a similar disbelief in their capacity on the part of whites.

Another explanation for the failure in Cuba was that the home government, occupied as it was with the problems resulting from the conquest of Mexico and the opening up of Peru, was unable to give much attention to the course of events in Cuba. A serious native uprising of 1528 embittered the already difficult relations of colonists and natives. The epidemic of 1530 struck down a third of the Indians and made Spaniards more than ever loath to release a single one of the survivors. The story of Cuba's troubles, as depicted in the existing documents, becomes a tale of avaricious ghouls disputing over an already well-stripped body. This was the Cuba where the final attempt to test the Indians was made.

Probably this Cuban experiment illustrates better than most the truth uttered by the Italian humanist Peter Martyr, who was a member of the Council of the Indies during most of the early battles for Indian liberty:

All these instructions have been thought out by prudent and humane jurisconsults and sanctioned by religious men. But what of that? When our compatriots reach that remote world, so far away and so removed from us, beyond the ocean whose courses imitate the changing heavens, they find themselves distant from any judge. Carried away by love of gold, they become ravenous wolves instead of gentle lambs, and heedless of royal instructions. . . .

Guzmán collected about one hundred natives left alone by the death of their encomendero, harangued their chieftains on the King's interest in their salvation and on his desire for them to enjoy a "different liberty," and then withdrew, giving the chieftains a few hours to decide whether they would choose the experiment or preferred to live as before under new encomenderos.

Whether the Indians thought anything would be better than their previous servitude or were attracted by the novelty of the new plan, we do not know. At any rate, the chieftain Diego, after having discussed the issue with the people, formally declared before Guzmán and the omnipresent notary that he and his subjects wanted to live alone, to cultivate their own crops, to dig gold for the King, to serve God and the Holy Virgin, and to pay tithes to the church. Or at least so said the interpreter, Pedro Ribadeneyra. The other Indians decided similarly, and Guzmán sent them off to start the *experiencia* near Bayamo, a healthful town about twenty-five leagues from Santiago, but cut off from Spanish settlements by a dangerous road. Once arrived at Bayamo the supervisor, Francisco Guerrero, was made responsible for teaching the subjects of the experiencia how to live like "Christian laborers in Castile."

The original instructions, given by Governor Guzmán to Guerrero on April 3, 1531, are preserved and reveal an imposing list of duties for which the supervisor was theoretically responsible. He must prevent his charges from communicating with other Indians, presumably to prevent contamination and to permit the experiment to unfold itself in a sort of social vacuum. The Indians must be taught to raise cotton, maize, chickens, and pigs as a Spanish farmer would. Guerrero must also see that they carried on their tasks regularly and did not become idlers or vagabonds. With the fruits of this labor they must dress and feed themselves as well as pay the tithe to the church and a tax to the King. He must make them stop their idolatrous ceremonies and witchcraft. Once purged of these errors of the devil, they were to be taught the elements of Christianity.

In this work of conversion Guerrero was to employ such methods as seemed suited to their nature. Though instructed to celebrate Mass daily, he was permitted to excuse Indians from this service at his discretion. The natives must be allowed to indulge in their dances, under the provisions of the King's law, but Guerrero was to prevent their using paint or masks in their terpsichorean frenzies. One's imagination falters in the attempt to visualize the ancient Indian dances performed in the garb of "Christian laborers of Castile" under the watchful eye of the administrator!

Such were the formal instructions given by an uninterested governor to an unscrupulous administrator. Guzmán thrust the whole responsibility upon Guerrero and never once visited the Bayamo village. Guerrero's exploitation of the natives makes one understand why the Flemish courtiers surrounding King Charles and battening on the remunerative offices in the Spanish government referred to the Spaniards fondly as "their Indians." According to a deposition sent to the Council of the Indies, Guerrero visited the village seldom, spent little time indoctrinating the natives or teaching them "how to live like Castilian laborers." He commandeered the natives for service in his own house, took an Indian woman named Isabella away from her husband, and kept her "for his own evil purposes." When the Indians managed to raise a crop the administrator invited all his friends to a feast. Whenever he felt the need of relaxation, there were always partridges and pigeons to be hunted and plenty of Indians enjoying "a different liberty" to accompany him as servants.

In 1532 a new and more honorable governor named Manuel Rojas sent out one Vadillo, a royal official, to investigate the village. It was a sad sight, he reported, for many Indians had died, others had fled, and those remaining were restless and hungry. Of the Indians still alive, Vadillo saw two whom he considered capable of living by themselves. Administrator Guerrero confided to Vadillo later that of those two he himself believed only one ready for liberty. Then, as sometimes occurs today, there was no complete agreement, among the social experimenters, either on the techniques to be used or the value of the results obtained. Vadillo and Guerrero agreed so heartily, however, on the incapacity of the Indians that Governor Rojas advised the Emperor that though it might be "convenient for the royal conscience" to make one more attempt with a selected group, probably little would come of it. The most satisfactory solution, Rojas suggested, was to give liberty only to those Indians petitioning for this privilege who could prove their ability to use freedom wisely. The reply came promptly from Spain. Rojas was ordered to make yet another trial with carefully chosen Indians.

The last experiment ran its course and differed in no essential from the previous attempts. The new supervisor fell ill and was absent for eight months, during which time many of his charges scattered and the experiencia languished. The Governor received no help from the officials ordered from Spain to assist him and he finally reported in December 1535 that he believed the Indians in no way capable of living by themselves and recommended that they be given to some Spaniard in Bayamo.

What did these sixteenth-century "guinea pigs" think of their "different liberty"? Unfortunately no records exist of the Indians' reactions to the experiments. We may, however, get some light from one incident recorded by the Governor. Rojas reported that after an Indian couple had attempted unsuccessfully to secure the release of their daughter from Bayamo, they secretly stole her away by night to their mountain home, hanged her and then themselves. This early American tragedy may have been caused either by hatred for the experiment itself or by the native's deep-rooted aversion to leaving his home. Earlier in Hispaniola one chieftain had sworn with all his subjects to drink the fatal juice, *agua de yuca*, if the provision of the Laws of Burgos collecting them into villages were carried out.

A curious tale, related by Oviedo, may be referred to at this point as the sole example we have of an Indian experiment made to determine the nature of the Spaniard. The natives of Puerto Rico, having heard that the white men with horses could not be killed, decided to look into this important matter before declaring war. A small party of unarmed Indians made friends with one of the Spaniards and took him for a walk to point out the natural beauty of their island. On reaching a river, the strongest of the Indians submerged the Spaniard for a few minutes. Hauling the lifeless Spaniard to the bank, they waited to see him spring to action and began laughingly to explain to the wet body that it was all a joke. For three days the experimenting natives remained by the body "until it began to smell," whereupon they concluded that Spaniards were mortal and went to war against them.

Even though the experimental villages had failed, how fared the plan of Rojas to set free those able Indians who petitioned for liberty? The royal order announcing this plan had been duly promulgated in Santiago in December 1533. The next year, while Rojas visited the mining camps, he announced the plan to the Indian miners, explaining in great detail the duties of a freed Indian.

One would like to know how Rojas and the Provisor, who had been detailed to assist him, reached their decision on the cases presented to them at Bayamo early in 1535. It was before the era of intelligence tests. Rojas and the Provisor had only those primitive instruments—their own intelligence plus their own prejudices—to enable them to separate the sheep from the goats.

An Indian named Diego and his wife had been awaiting examination for many days at Bayamo where the petitioners for liberty had been directed to meet their judges. He was found able to live alone *políticamente,* but deficient in religious instruction; it was thus necessary to put him and his wife in the experimental village rather than to give them complete liberty. Cascarro, an Indian belonging to Rojas himself, was discovered to be of "good and holy intention," moderately well instructed in the faith, but stupid in all other matters, for which reason he too was commanded to live among the Indians of the *experiencia* in the hope that he would correct his defects. The same decision was made concerning Alonso Cabezas and his wife. Three other natives came to petition, but on learning the conditions, departed, and could not be found, though Rojas had them searched for. Finally one Indian came who was clearly able to live alone and declared that he wanted to be free along with his wife. Rojas was willing to grant him his freedom, but knowing "that his wife was old and therefore impossible to reform," stipulated that Diego alone could be free. On hearing this sentence, the Indian turned away and did not return to ask for liberty again. The government was at last persuaded that nothing could be gained by further attempts to make the Indians live like "Christian farmers in Castile." [1]

Nowhere, during or after these experiments, was there any recognition in official or ecclesiastical circles that the attempt to impose Spanish institutions upon the Indians might be just as deadly to them as the firearms and hunting dogs of the conquistadores.

Chapter V

COULD THE NEW WORLD BE COLONIZED PEACEFULLY WITH FARMERS?

The Meaning of Las Casas' Attempt to Establish a
Colony as an Alternative to the Encomienda System

THE first proposal by Bartolomé de Las Casas which won royal approval failed completely when put to the test. His plan, which was the culmination of several years of agitation at court, was to colonize in 1521 the northern coast of Venezuela, then called Tierra Firme, with Spanish farmers who would till the soil, treat the Indians kindly, and thus lay the basis for an ideal Christian community in the New World. The colony was such a complete and humiliating failure that Las Casas retired to a monastery, entered the Dominican Order, and for almost ten years kept himself apart from affairs of this world.

Yet the story of the various colonization projects and of this utopian experiment, as it was fought for in the council chambers of Spain and eventually carried out on the hot sands of the Venezuelan coast, may have the same value for the modern student of colonial policy that a post-mortem examination has for the surgeon whose patient has died on the operating table.

This attempt has often been dismissed as a harebrained scheme dreamed up by a pure but impractical visionary. A closer examination of the experiment will show that Las Casas had not only the weaknesses of human nature to contend with in his colonists but also the animosity and determination of the conquistadores that he should fail. At any rate, the question Las Casas attempted to answer was not a stupid one, and it was a hardheaded and far from naïve royal administration which gave permission for the experiment to be made.

The vision which guided Las Casas was of a new world in which Spanish farmers—transplanted with tools, seeds, and supplies furnished by the King; their native industry, farming ability, and firmness in the faith being their own contribution—would take root in America. They would till the soil of Tierra Firme and live side by side with the Indians there in such a way that their faith and their skill and industry would insensibly be absorbed by the natives, and an

54

ideal Christian community would come into being. The poor and lowly peasants of Spain would enjoy an opportunity to improve themselves in America, these industrious people would develop the King's newly discovered lands, thus increasing royal revenue, and above all the natives would be Christianized, not brutalized or despoiled of their wives and property. The practice of bringing sturdy folk who would do their own work, if extended throughout Spain's empire, would make unnecessary the encomienda system by which Indians labored for Spaniards. The experiment was as bold in its own way as two other great deeds which occurred about the same time—the circumnavigation of the world by Magellan's men and the victory over Montezuma and his hosts by Cortés.

Before turning to Las Casas' experiment, however, we must mention earlier attempts at colonization and follow the growth of his design for the Indies, which eventually led him to believe that justice for the Indians depended upon the systematic colonization of the New World with Spanish farmers. Otherwise this experiment in Venezuela is merely a curious incident in the conquest and cannot be seen as the truly important step it was in the history of Spanish groping for a policy which would ensure justice for the Indians.

Las Casas was by no means the first advocate of a planned immigration to build up a healthy, prosperous society in Spain's America. Columbus himself in a letter to the crown written in 1493 had recommended that two thousand farmers be sent out. Although the crown was eager to have such persons go as colonists,[1] the men who actually went to Hispaniola during the early years, as previously pointed out, were usually ex-soldiers, seedy noblemen, adventurers, or convicts.

Occasionally royal orders and provisions during those first years of Spain's rule in America reveal that the need for sober colonists was recognized, at least by those responsible for making policy. For example, a contract was signed September 5, 1501, between the crown and Luis de Arriaga to colonize four towns in Hispaniola with fifty settlers each, although this project led to no important results.[2]

But during the early years of the conquest no consistent effort was made by the government to attract farmers to the New World. True, in 1511 ordinances were promulgated by which the red tape required for permission to emigrate was cut somewhat, and immigrants were relieved of paying certain taxes.[3] And in 1513 King Ferdinand ordered Pedrarias Dávila to take farmers with him to Darién to experiment with the cultivation of spices, wheat, and barley.[4] Certain privileges were offered to these farmers, but apparently few were attracted and Dávila's expedition was notorious for its relentless pursuit of gold and Indians. No stress was placed on the need for farmers in the colonies to build up a citizenry not dependent on Indians for support until Las Casas became convinced of the injustice of the encomienda system.

Las Casas therefore went to Spain, obtained support from the crown, and returned to Hispaniola as "Protector of the Indians" but, as described in the preceding pages, became disgusted with the Jeronymites and returned to Spain to fight at court for Indian liberty. He brought with him in 1517 a remarkable document which was the culmination of all his thinking on the problem of Indian-Spanish relations since his great awakening in 1514. During these years, he had come to feel that a new pattern was needed. The encomienda system by which Indian labor was given to Spaniards must go. But what could replace it?

"The Indians Are Free Men and Must Be Treated as Such": The Utopian Memorial of 1517

The friends of the Indians developed two approaches. One declared that some Indians, at least, were ready for self-government like Spaniards, an approach described in the preceding chapter. The other advocated the development of Spanish-Indian communities where Indians might absorb the Spanish way of life. The second approach is most clearly expressed in the document Las Casas took with him to Spain in 1517, evidently presented to the King by a number of ecclesiastics but written in the hand of Las Casas.[5] This represents a fresh and indigenous Spanish Renaissance attitude and is to be distinguished from the ordinances set forth by Bishop Vasco de Quiroga in his will in 1565 to govern the Indian communities of New Spain, which were obviously inspired by Sir Thomas More's *Utopia*.[6] This radical and thoroughgoing blueprint of 1517 for the government of the Indies was apparently worked out by Las Casas and the Dominicans associated with him without benefit of advice or assistance from anyone.

The proposal is simple but revolutionary. The first of the fourteen remedies specified as necessary provides that all arrangements by which Indians work for Spaniards are to be suspended, at least temporarily. The second remedy recommends that Indians not be given to individual Spaniards, but that a community be established by the King in each town and city of the Spaniards in which all the Indians are to be held in common. They are to be worked in common and governed by salaried supervisors according to certain rules and regulations.

The third remedy is that forty farmers with their wives and children be sent to each town as permanent residents. There were plenty of needy persons in Spain who would be interested in making a permanent home in the New World under proper conditions, argued Las Casas. Each farmer would be given five Indians with their families to live under his tutelage. They would work together and share the profits in a brotherly way, after the King's portion was set aside. Thus would the Indians prosper and learn, rather than die. The Indians would want to work when they saw the Spaniards working, and their sons and daughters would intermarry.

Thus will the land be made fruitful and its people multiply, because they will plant all manner of trees and vegetables. Your Majesty's revenues will be increased, and the islands ennobled and be, therefore, the best and richest in the world. And if as time goes on the Indians should prove themselves able to live alone and govern themselves, and serve Your Majesty in the same way as your other vassals do, this is provided for in the laws.

Certain other remedies are set forth in this document. An ecclesiastic is to be placed in each island to protect the Indians and punish any Spaniards who mistreat them; no Spaniards who have been in the Indies are to have anything to do with the execution of these plans; Indians are not to be punished for their wrongdoings in the same way as Spaniards. Twenty Negroes or other slaves are to be put in the mines in place of the Indians from each community; no priest is to be allowed in these towns unless he is properly educated to preach correctly in Indian questions and other matters; Indians are not to be moved from one island to another; and "the books on Indian questions by Dr. Palacios Rubios of the Royal Council, and Master Matías de Paz, formerly professor in Valladolid, are to be printed and sent to the islands so that Spaniards there may realize that Indians are men and are free and must be treated as such." [7]

After describing several other subsidiary remedies, including the establishment of the Holy Inquisition, "inasmuch as two heretics have already been discovered and burned there," the memorial proceeds to set forth in minute detail the life proposed for these Indian communities.[8] After the Indians have rested sufficiently, they are to be divided up among the towns of the Spaniards near the mines. Each Indian community is to have a hospital in the shape of a cross, with space for fifty beds in each of the four sections, and in the middle an altar so that they may all see Mass from their beds. If Indians need animals, land, or anything else, the Spaniards are to loan them half of what they have, and thus the harm done earlier to the Indians will be rectified. The best pasturage is to be given the Indians, even if it is all at present in Spanish hands, and no Spaniard connected with these Indian communities may have anything but the gold or crops he himself produces.

Satisfactory living arrangements must be provided for the Indians or they will die; and they are not to dig for gold until after their fields are cared for. Then follows a careful statement on the officials required to administer all this: the head supervisor to oversee all, priests to instruct the Indians in religion, bachelors in grammar to teach, physicians, surgeons, and druggists to serve them, lawyers to represent the Indians in legal matters, overseers, miners, fishermen, swineherds, men to run the hospitals, boatmen—in fact, a galaxy of officials to perform almost every conceivable need the Indians might have.

The food to be provided for the Indians is minutely detailed. Indians are to be taught to sit on benches and eat from tables, not allowed to sit on the ground and eat like dogs. Nor may they sleep on the ground, but must carry their hammocks wherever they go. Hospital care for ailing Indians is also described, even a sort of ambulance service: "two or three beasts of burden are always to be kept on hand at each hospital to be sent out to bring in sick Indians when necessary."

Finally, inasmuch as the principal end of all this is the salvation of the Indians, various observations and rules are made concerning their education and conversion. To bring this extraordinary proposal to a close, a budget is given showing that the seventy-four officials needed for this project on each island would cost 6,600 *castellanos* per year. The estimated cost of beasts of burden, cows, spades, axes, and sheets for the hospital beds is also stated. If these things are not done, concludes the memorial, the land of the Indies already discovered will be lost to Spain as well as the lands to be discovered. While this noble utopian plan was never approved by the King or court, it reveals significantly not only what Las Casas and his Dominican companions were aiming at as they carried on their negotiations in Spain to save the Indians, but also the existence of a strong strain of paternalistic and humanitarian thought existing side by side in the Spanish character with the dominant imperialistic attitude.

The First Colonization Plan for America, 1518–19

Even before this memorial was considered in Spain, word came from Hispaniola that the Dominican friars there had come to the conclusion that land must be set aside specifically for the conversion of the Indians, far from the sight and sound of Spaniards interested only in gold. The first suggestion of this idea, which became a basic tenet of Las Casas, appears in a letter sent by the Dominican Provincial in Hispaniola, Pedro de Córdoba, to Las Casas, requesting the latter to obtain authorization for one hundred leagues on the coast of Tierra Firme near Cumaná to be set apart for Franciscans and Dominicans so that they might preach the faith without hindrance.[9] If one hundred leagues could not be provided, Las Casas was to ask for ten leagues or at least an island. Córdoba added that if none of these requests were granted, he would recall the Dominicans from those parts, for it was no use preaching "when the Indians see those who call themselves Christians acting in opposition to Christian ideals." No such grant of land was made because the Bishop of Burgos strongly opposed the idea, but on September 3, 1516, a royal instruction had ordered that no one was to go to the Pearl Coast of Tierra Firme where the Dominicans were preaching because "it is their express wish to try to convert the Indians before they have contact with the Spaniards." [10]

Here we see first expressed the passionate conviction of the friars that if only they could work on the Indians unhampered by gold-thirsty Spaniards, the conversion of the New World would be a simple matter. We shall return to this theme when the attempt to convert the fierce natives of Guatemala by peaceful means alone is described in the next chapter. It suffices to say here that the Dominican Pedro de Córdoba's idea of 1516 anticipated that famous Vera Paz experiment which took place some twenty years later in Guatemala.

The death of Cardinal Jiménez de Cisneros, who had been a powerful and enlightened supporter of Las Casas, again retarded his campaign. When young King Charles arrived in May 1517, Las Casas at once addressed himself to the task of winning the confidence of the new monarch's influential Flemish advisers. Many years later, in his *History of the Indies*, Las Casas set forth the story of this successful diplomatic campaign in loving and exuberant detail, with himself set firmly in the center of the stage.[11]

Even though Las Casas did not obtain the grant of land Córdoba had requested, he did present a specific plan, apparently in 1518, which shows that he had fastened upon Tierra Firme as the most suitable territory for a fresh start in the Indies and that he had adopted Córdoba's idea that the conquistadores must be kept away from the Indians if Christianization and the colonization of the land were to proceed. This plan is disclosed in a letter to the King signed by Las Casas as "General Representative of the Indians." [12] The King ought to establish in Tierra Firme, "the best and richest territory in the Indies," ten fortresses, one every hundred leagues. In each fortress there should be placed one hundred Christians, governed by a captain strictly enjoined from making excursions against the Indians and committed to pacifying them. A bishop is to be appointed for every hundred or one hundred and fifty leagues, and many Dominicans and Franciscans are to be despatched to Tierra Firme "because one friar is worth more than 200 armed men." The expense of all this will not be excessive, declared Las Casas, and can easily be met by taking a part of the gold and pearls seized by those Spaniards who have so cruelly treated the Indians and scandalized the country.

Las Casas then urged a colonization plan for the Indies as a whole. Any laborer who wants to go to the New World, even a foreigner, should be encouraged to do so by an offer of good land, low taxes, and prizes for those who produce silk, pepper, cloves, ginger, wine, and wheat. Those who establish sugar mills are to be assisted with loans and permitted to introduce twenty Negroes. Thus will the land flourish, the royal revenue increase by leaps and bounds, and the New World be populated, "and not destroyed as is now the case."

The King was being advised on all sides that laborers must be sent to the Indies. About this time Las Casas advocated the introduction of Negro slaves, as had been previously suggested in the utopian memorial of 1517, because he felt they could withstand the heavy work required by the Spaniards better than could the Indians. He soon repented of this, realized that it was as unjust to enslave Negroes as Indians, and washed his hands of all such proposals.[13]

The Jeronymite Bernardino de Manzanedo advised, in February 1518 on his return from Hispaniola, that "the fundamental way to populate the land is for many farmers and artisans to go there," as did a memorial by a Dominican who advanced the interesting idea that fines should be levied on Spaniards who harmed the Indians, and that these fines should be used to help the natives who were left and to populate the Indies with married Christian laborers from Spain.[14] The Bishop of Ávila recommended the same, the citizens of Hispaniola submitted detailed plans to populate the island, and the Licentiate Alonso Zuazo did likewise, urging that laborers should be encouraged from all parts of the world, only excepting Moors, Jews, and newly converted Christians.[15]

These recommendations, plus the tireless activity of Las Casas and the support of the Flemish advisers of the King and Cardinal Adrian, led to the royal order of September 10, 1518, on the "Privileges and Liberties granted to Farmers who go to the Indies." [16] This order was the first fruit of the efforts of Las Casas during three years of intense effort and led directly to the first serious attempt at planned colonization in the New World.

The First Attempt of 1518–19

The "Privileges and Liberties granted to Farmers who go to the Indies" were designed, the order explained, "to develop the land, provide an opportunity for improvement to those who live in poverty in Spain despite their unremitting labor, and to occupy the new found lands so that foreigners will not do so." The inducements offered by the King were: free passage from their homes in Spain to see the New World, free medical care and medicines, free land, animals, seeds, and all else needed to support them until their crops had matured, freedom from taxes for twenty years except the tithe for the church, assistance from Indians to build their new homes, and prizes to the farmers who produced the first dozen pounds of silk, cloves, ginger, cinnamon, or other spice, the first fifteen pounds of pastel, and the first quintal of rice or of olive oil.

The King made this order effective at once and instructed Juan López de Recalde, his treasurer in the House of Trade in Seville, to grant these privileges and liberties to any farmers who appeared there for passage to the New World.[17] Recalde was to receive the farmers sent by Las Casas and others who had been charged "with inciting laborers to go to the Indies," was to explain the contents of the instruction, the richness of the land, and the privileges. This royal official was also to ensure that each farmer had the necessary seed and plants—wheat, barley, beans, lentils, rice—that some knew how to produce silk, that they had the necessary implements to till the soil and, finally, that the captain of their ship handled them well and "that no ill-treatment or discourtesy befell them."

Shortly afterward on September 20, 1518, Las Casas also managed to get a royal order authorizing them to establish villages of free Indians in the New World, who were to live by themselves in an orderly "political way like Spaniards." [18] These Indians were to pay tribute like other vassals and were not to be given to Spaniards in encomienda. A typical Las Casas touch, which shows his shrewd practicality in certain matters, was the instruction of September 20, 1518, to the royal judge in Hispaniola that Las Casas was to be the first person allowed to speak to the Indian chieftains on the subject of their liberty and their living like Spaniards in villages by themselves. Las Casas wanted no one to muddy the water before he arrived!

But the "Representative of the Indians" turned his immediate attention toward rounding up farmers to go to the New World. He knew that Spanish peasants would have to be induced to leave their homes for an unknown land. Lest their local officials and feudal lords should attempt to hinder those who showed some interest, Las Casas obtained a royal order, making known to "officials, judges, gentlemen, good men of every city and town" the purpose of the plan to send farmers to the Indies and stating clearly that no impediments were to be placed in the way of those who wished to go.[19] Many other royal orders were issued to help put the plan into effect, including an instruction to bishops to have their priests support the project in their sermons.[20] Magistrates were instructed to decide quickly concerning lawsuits involving farmers who wished to emigrate.[21]

On October 12, 1518, Las Casas and one Captain Luis de Berrio began their work as agents for the colonization scheme. In the *History of the Indies* Las Casas gives his version of this first attempt made in Europe to recruit sturdy workers for American lands. They went from town to town in Castile, making speeches on the advantages of the plan to the townspeople assembled in the church, and were probably the first of the many colonization agents who roamed over Europe extolling the riches and pleasures of life waiting in America.

But the feudal lords of Spain were ill-pleased at this interference with their laborers. In Berlanga, for example, where seventy of the two hundred inhabitants signed up to emigrate, although they did so secretly for fear of their lord, the powerful Don Iñigo Fernández de Velasco, he nevertheless did hear of it and ordered Las Casas out of town. Even four of the well-to-do men of the town had signed to go overseas in order to have their sons "grow up in a free world." The same preliminary success and eventual failure attended their efforts in Rello, under the rule of the Count of Coruña, where twenty of the thirty inhabitants signed up including two brothers over seventy years of age who also wanted to "leave their sons in a free and pleasant land." The hostility of the lords prevented Las Casas, despite this interest by the townspeople, from securing all told more than a handful of farmers to adventure in the New World.[22]

Presently dissension arose between Las Casas and his colleague Berrio, who wanted to leave Castile and try recruiting in Andalusia where his wife lived.[23] When Las Casas opposed this, Berrio set off alone and signed up a group described as "the scum of the earth" by Las Casas, who returned to court with his tale of opposition by the feudal lords. These had no intention of allowing their peasants to leave the land, no matter how urgently farmers were needed in America. It was scarcely to be expected that they would react differently, for they regarded these recruiting agents as troublesome fellows who could do only harm and stir up difficulties.

The skepticism Las Casas found prevalent at court with respect to his plan to recruit laborers and his disheartening experience in recruiting induced him to drop this project in April 1519. Not so Captain Berrio, who managed to round up, after great delays and difficulties, some fifty families consisting of 207 persons who sailed from San Lúcar on April 15, 1520, to establish their homes in America.[24] The House of Trade in Seville, acting on royal instructions, supplied them with tools, ornaments, and "a thousand kinds of seeds as well as plants, which they carried with them aboard ship in large earthen jars." On reaching Hispaniola they all promptly fell ill, most of their plants were lost, and some of the women and children died.[25] Although Las Casas heard of their misfortunes and prevailed upon the King to send wheat and wine to succor them,[26] absolutely nothing resulted from this first attempt at colonization. The King and his advisers, as

well as the friends of the Indians, came to realize that the emigration
of any considerable number of farmers from Spain simply could not
be achieved.

The Battle for the Tierra Firme Agreement, 1519–20

Las Casas, however, continued to strive for his great objective—
the freedom and salvation of the Indians. Chapter after chapter of his
History of the Indies is filled with the passionate story of his battles
in the period from April 1519, when his recruiting activities ended,
until May 1520, when the King at last gave him a grant of land in
Tierra Firme.[27] All his hopes were now centered on establishing villages of high-minded Spaniards in the thousand leagues along the
northern coast of South America.

The first big gun in this campaign was fired at Barcelona in 1519
when King Charles was presiding there for the first time over the
Council of the Indies. Bishop Juan de Quevedo of Tierra Firme declared to Charles that the Indians were slaves by nature, in accordance
with the Aristotelian concept, and this brought forth a counterblast
from Las Casas. Here, too, Las Casas came to know, and to dislike,
Gonzalo Fernández de Oviedo, the first official historian of the Indies.
Oviedo, who had lived for a number of years in the New World, had
not found the Indians as mild and virtuous as Las Casas painted them;
he was also seeking a grant of land. Oviedo was granted the land he
asked for, Santa Marta, but not the authorization for the one hundred
noblemen of the Order of Santiago he requested, his concept of colonization being distinctly aristocratic. He mocked at Las Casas' prefer-
ence for simple farmers and later gave an ironical account of the
whole experiment, though to his own cost, because Las Casas was
able to prevent Oviedo's history from being printed.[28] Indeed, it did
not appear until the middle of the nineteenth century.

This new proposal of Las Casas took account of the fact that any
plan must provide royal revenue if it were to win support. To com-
bine profit with peaceful preaching, Las Casas conceived the idea of
forming a new order of knighthood, whose members would be known
as Knights of the Golden Spur. These knights were to be as different
from the aristocratic lords requested by Oviedo as were King Arthur's
Knights of the Round Table from the ordinary, swashbuckling medieval knights. They were to number fifty men, each to furnish two
hundred ducats and thus provide for the expenses of founding the
colony. They were to wear a dress of white cloth, marked on the breast
with a red cross, similar to the cross of Calatrava, but with some additional ornamentation—all designed to distinguish them in the eyes
of the Indians from all other Spaniards. These Knights of the Golden

Spur were to operate in a territory of one thousand leagues along the coast of northern South America. In return for this concession Las Casas promised the King prompt and increasing revenue, the establishment of towns, and conversion of the Indians.

The Bishop of Burgos, Juan Rodríguez de Fonseca, an old enemy of Las Casas, promptly brought all his influence to bear against the project. Diego Columbus, son of the discoverer, rallied to the support of Las Casas and wrote a powerful plea to the Grand Chancellor of King Charles, Don Mercurino Arborio de Gattinara, as did Las Casas. The eight preachers of the King entered the fray, declared against encomiendas, and proposed that salaried governors be appointed to make sure that the Spaniards taught the Indians agricultural matters.[29] If this were done, the eight preachers—probably under the spell of the Representative of the Indians—felt that the Indians would prove themselves within a short time *noble y política* people. Perplexed by this impressive difference of opinion among experts, the King decided to name a commission of thirty or forty of his most trusted and eminent advisers to reach a decision. This alone was considered a great victory by Las Casas, who reflected upon the goodness of a God who had brought it to pass that a poor priest like himself, without wealth or high position and persecuted by Spaniards who believed that he was destroying the nation, could have his plan considered by some of the greatest and wisest heads in the land.[30]

Francisco López de Gómara, the contemporary historian who liked Las Casas no better than did Oviedo, suggested that Las Casas' promises to send back many pearls may have had something to do with his victory.[31] When a friend expressed surprise that the colonization plan was so drawn up that it would yield temporal gain, Las Casas had an answer. The move was a purely opportunistic one as Las Casas later confessed in a sorrowful and realistic spirit:

From the moment that I saw they wanted to sell the faith and consequently Jesus Christ, and they struck Him and buffeted Him and crucified Him, I agreed to buy it, proposing many profits and temporal gains for the king, in the manner you have seen.[32]

The opposition to the colonization plan was bolstered up during these days by unfavorable reports from Hispaniola on the Figueroa experiment, described in the preceding chapter. The backstage negotiations, however, were important too and illustrate the relentless nature of both sides. According to Las Casas, Bishop Fonseca conspired with Oviedo to have petitions submitted to the King offering to assure greater revenues than Las Casas for the very same territory. Another junta was called and Las Casas again had his plans approved. Fonseca then composed a secret memorial listing all possible objections—they came to thirty—why the land should not be granted to Las Casas. With the greatest difficulty Las Casas obtained permission to see the memorial, and then only in the chambers of the Lord Chancellor. By four or five nights of feverish labor, Las Casas responded to each charge and convinced the Chancellor, who advised the King to ignore the offers of Oviedo and others and to accept the Las Casas proposal.[33]

An opinion rendered by an unknown royal official at that time, still gathering dust in the Archivo General de Indias, reveals the kind of opposition Las Casas faced. This official, in summarizing his opinion of Las Casas' proposal for the benefit of King and Council, pointed out that Las Casas had no personal knowledge of the land he proposed to colonize, that he had neither the authority nor the experience in governing men required by the enterprise he proposed. The official concluded: "there is no assurance whatsoever that the proposal will succeed, it conflicts with the privileges of persons now in Hispaniola, and there are other weighty and secret reasons against Las Casas which lead me to recommend disapproval of his plan." [34] Nevertheless Las Casas fought on and defended his colonization plan inside and outside the Council.

The last seven days before Charles embarked at La Coruña in May 1520 to assume his imperial duties in Germany were devoted to Indian problems. The climax occurred when Cardinal Adrian, later to be pope, made a "very solemn and learned speech, proving by natural reasons, by the authority of the divine law and of the holy fathers, and by human and ecclesiastical laws that the Indians should be brought to a knowledge of God by peaceful means and not by Mohammedan methods." This stirring address turned the tide, and on May 19, 1520, the King and Council decided "that the Indians were free men, ought to be treated as such and induced to accept Christianity by the methods Christ had established." [35]

The way was now clear for favorable action on the colonization plan and on the same day the King concluded an agreement with Las Casas which granted the right he had fought so stoutly to win—permission to colonize a stretch of coast from the province of Paria to Santa Marta, a distance of about two hundred and sixty leagues, with territorial rights extending down to the Strait of Magellan. It was a great victory and forty years afterward in 1560 when Las Casas was writing the portion of the *History of the Indies* which deals with it, he still savored the taste of triumph and recalled the joke he and Cardinal Adrian had cracked in Latin over the outcome.[36]

In return for the colonization rights received from the King, Las Casas guaranteed to pacify and convert the Indians of Tierra Firme, to organize them into villages so that within two years the King would have at least ten thousand taxpaying vassals, to explore the land and report on its economic possibilities—all this without cost to the crown. For his part the King permitted Las Casas to select the fifty men to accompany him and conceded many other privileges, including coats of arms for the fifty Knights of the Golden Spur, and the right to name towns, provinces, rivers, and coasts of the territory. Likewise the farmers to go with Las Casas from Spain were to receive the equipment, privileges, and exemptions granted those who had been recruited earlier.[37]

The Representative of the Indians had thus won a resounding victory at the Spanish Court, and King Charles surrounded by his Flemish courtiers, "with loud music from clarions and flutes and with great demonstrations of joy, then weighed anchor and departed, leaving unhappy Spain oppressed with sorrows and misfortunes."[38]

The Reality in America

If royal orders and detailed instructions from Spain had been heeded, Las Casas would have had much less difficulty establishing his colony in Venezuela. For in the summer months of 1520 during his final preparations, Las Casas obtained from the crown letters of recommendation to practically every important official in the New World, royal and ecclesiastical, urging support and assistance for the project.[39] Most essential of all, it was specifically ordered that no one on any pretext whatever was to capture any Indian or take any Indian's property or treat any Indian badly, "especially in the territory under the administration of Las Casas." All this was solemnly proclaimed on July 30, 1520, in Valladolid, some thousands of miles and months of travel away from the tropical lands of America where this high policy was to be put into effect.

The story of his ill-fated expedition, recorded with relentless detail by Las Casas in his *History of the Indies,* is very like a Greek tragedy. Writing forty years after the event, Las Casas remembered and could not forbear telling that he had to borrow money in Seville before he himself could leave Spain, because all his funds had been exhausted in moving about during his campaign for royal approval, and that some friends made up a collection of trinkets to take along for the Indians.[40] According to one historian, Pedro Gutiérrez de Santa Clara, it was a motley crew that Las Casas assembled at Seville. These farmers

had forgotten their spades and their cows, and began to fancy themselves gentlemen, especially on Sundays and holidays, when they sallied forth with many feathers in their colored caps, and the Reverend Father in their midst. At last they all embarked in Sevilla, together with their women and many effects which they considered convenient to bring along: many biscuits, much wine, and hams, as well as many other gifts of one kind or another, all at the expense of His Majesty.[41]

On November 11, 1520, Las Casas departed from San Lúcar with seventy carefully selected laborers and, after a good voyage, arrived in Puerto Rico early in February 1521.[42] Here he learned that the Indians of the Chiribichi and Maracapana coast (part of Las Casas' territory) had killed some of the Dominican friars who had been preaching there.[43] As retribution the Audiencia of Santo Domingo had determined to send a punitive expedition against the Indians to make war "with fire and sword," and to enslave them. It was a vicious circle in which Las Casas found himself imprisoned, because the Dominicans had been killed as a result of the previous enslaving expedition of Alonso de Hojeda along the Tierra Firme coast. The armada was even then in Puerto Rico and about to sail, reported Licentiate de Gama to the King in February 1521 in the same letter in which he announced the imminent departure of Ponce de León for the coasts of Florida.

Las Casas exhausted every means to stop the armada. He flourished the royal orders in the face of Captain Gonzalo de Ocampo, who was unmoved. Leaving his farmers in Puerto Rico, he bought a boat, hurried to Hispaniola, and raged before and against the audiencia without effect.[44] The royal officials refused to proclaim the royal order banning Spaniards from going to the territory Las Casas wished to colonize. Indeed, Spaniards were at that very moment returning from Tierra Firme with newly captured Indian slaves.

Finally a compromise was arranged, however, which showed that Las Casas was more of a realist than he has usually been considered. When he was convinced that he could not keep Spaniards out of his territory, and when the Spaniards saw that Las Casas could facilitate their access to Tierra Firme, a trading company was formed with the crown, royal officials, and Las Casas all holding stock. The armada being formed in Hispaniola to wage war against the Indians was to be turned over to Las Casas, with one hundred and twenty of the three hundred men gathered for the expedition. Las Casas was to colonize peacefully, the friars were to preach the faith, and the Spaniards were to barter with the Indians and have recourse to war only when Las Casas certified that the Indians were cannibalistic or unwilling either to receive the faith or be friendly with the Spaniards. It was a sorry and impossible alliance, Las Casas recognized later, but it was a desperate effort to salvage some part, no matter how small, of his original plan.

Distrustful of this new arrangement, Las Casas finally left Hispaniola in July 1521 for Puerto Rico, only to find all his "modest and industrious farmers" gone off with other Spaniards to rob and assault Indians.[45] So he set out alone to Tierra Firme where Captain Ocampo was punishing and enslaving Indians. The town established by Ocampo was almost destitute, the near-by Indians had fled, the Spaniards were starving, and none of them wanted to stay with Las Casas to colonize by peaceful means.

He was left behind with a few servants and persons paid to accompany him when the other Spaniards sailed away. The Franciscans near-by in Cumaná received him joyfully with song and prayer. They had constructed a monastery of wood and straw, had developed an "orchard with wonderful oranges, a small vine yard and vegetable garden, very fine melons and other agreeable things." Las Casas ordered a house built for his little group near the friars.

But there was no peace. Spanish vessels stopping to fill their water casks at the near-by mouth of the Cumaná River provided an opportunity for Indians to get wine.[46] When drunk, they took up arms against the Spaniards, using poison-pointed arrows. Las Casas now began "to drink deeply at the well of bitterness." He made violent but unsuccessful representations before the Alcalde of Cubagua from which the Spanish vessels had set out. Finally, the Franciscans persuaded him to leave his group and return to Hispaniola to plead their cause before the royal officials there.

Within two weeks after his departure the Indians attacked the settlement and killed one of the Franciscans and five of Las Casas' group.[47] Thereafter the Spaniards descended upon Tierra Firme in a series of slaving expeditions. According to Miguel de Castellanos, who accompanied Las Casas as his treasurer, more than six hundred Indians—boys, girls, men, and women who lived along the coast set aside for peaceful colonization—were captured and taken to Hispaniola as slaves in two months' time.[48] Meanwhile, the vessel bearing Las Casas lost its way and took two months to accomplish what was normally a week's voyage. When he learned the grievous news on arriving in Hispaniola, he considered it God's punishment for his having entered into the trading company arrangement with the profit-minded Spaniards.

It was the last straw. Las Casas wrote a long account of the whole episode to the King, which has not yet turned up in any archive, and awaited a reply.[49] During this period of deep dejection he talked much with his friends in the Dominican monastery of Hispaniola, particularly with Domingo de Betanzos, who urged him to become a friar.[50] Las Casas pondered on this and then requested admission to the Order of Preachers. The news was received joyfully by everyone on the island—by royal officials and other Spaniards, as well as by ecclesiastics, though for vastly different reasons. The friars saw in Las

Casas a powerful ally in their attempts to protect and Christianize the Indians, while the Spaniards were pleased because they thought that Las Casas, as a friar, would be henceforth less turbulent and troublesome to them. Both factions were to some extent right.

For almost ten years after assuming the robe of the Order of Preachers, Las Casas did not disturb the Spaniards as they continued their conquest of the New World. Little is known of him in these years. He seems to have devoted himself to meditation, to the study of political theory, and to history. Henceforth his writings, whether letters, memorials, or treatises, were heavily buttressed with quotations from the Scriptures and from all manner of authorities, learned and divine. Las Casas believed in the power of the pen, and it is no accident that the picture by which he is best known to the world shows him seated at a writing table with quill in hand.

During this period two of his most important writings were undertaken in the Dominican monastery overlooking Puerto Príncipe in Hispaniola. The bulky treatise defending the Indians, the *Apologetic History,* in which he asserts that the New World natives fulfill every one of Aristotle's conditions for the good life, was begun here. Here he also began his most substantial work, the *History of the Indies,* during those dark days after the complete failure of his plan to colonize Tierre Firme by peaceful and Christian means.

But his entrance into the Order of Preachers did not permanently dampen Las Casas' fiery zeal, nor did he ever lose his faith in the importance of planned, peaceful colonization. In 1529, toward the end of his first ten years as a Dominican, he sallied forth to negotiate a truce with the troublesome native chieftain Enriquillo and converted him by peaceful means, thus foreshadowing the Vera Paz experiment in Guatemala a few years later.[51] His reputation for zeal and integrity had not decreased among the ecclesiastics, for on August 7, 1529, we find the Dominican Julián Garcés and the Franciscan Juan de Zumárraga recommending that he be called to join them in Mexico where able friars were urgently needed.[52] We know that by 1533 he had returned to the world, for the royal judges in Hispaniola complained to the King in that year that he was refusing absolution to encomenderos.[53] In one case they reported, Las Casas had prevailed upon a Spaniard on his deathbed to leave all his worldly goods to the Indians as restitution, much to the dismay of his expectant heirs. About the same time he sent to the Council of the Indies a memorial urging another peaceful colonization plan—with detailed statements on laborers, fortresses, friars, profits for the King—all in the familiar pattern. And he assured them:

Every day you will see the fruits of this just government. This, gentlemen, is *just* government. This is the right path, and the foundation by which you

should govern and the foundation which the King our Lord must establish
in order to take just possession of these lands, and to hold these kingdoms
justly.[54]

The Aftermath

The colonization plan had failed, partly because the conditions
stipulated by Las Casas as necessary to launch the project did not exist. As long as he did not have full control of the territory to be colonized, other Spaniards with different interests and attitudes toward
the Indians were bound to create situations which made peaceful
relations impossible. Las Casas, however, never abandoned the idea
that peaceful means alone would convert the Indians, and he put it
into practice in Guatemala some fifteen years later in the remarkable
Vera Paz experiment to be described in the following chapter. As if
to prove the validity of Las Casas' doctrine, records exist in the Archivo General de Indias which tell how certain Indians of Tierra
Firme turned Christian a few months after Las Casas left this region,
because of good treatment.[55] Again, however, the cupidity of other
Spaniards intervened, for it was charged that these very Indians were
shipped to Hispaniola and there sold.[56] Exactly the same story with
exactly the same result was told by Bishop Vasco de Quiroga concerning the experience of certain Flemish or German Franciscans in
Tierra Firme about a decade later. These Franciscans had gone to a
region where no Christians had been before. Their preaching was
well received, the Indians were converted and baptized without any
force being used, and the Indians freely supplied the friars with food
and other necessities. Then Spanish soldiers arrived in ships and captured the Indians, and the ecclesiastics were forced to flee. Some years
later, in the seventeenth and eighteenth centuries, the Jesuits proved
conclusively that an Indian community could be established and
maintained in their famous Paraguay "Reductions," the spirit and
methods of which had been anticipated in the memorial sent to the
crown in 1518 by Las Casas.

Contemporary Spaniards had no good word to say for any attempt
to provide by peaceful colonization an alternative to the encomienda
system by which the natives throughout the New World served their
European conquerors. As late as the beginning of the seventeenth
century, opponents of Las Casas took the trouble to deride it,[57] and
most Spaniards probably agreed with Francisco Eraso who declared
in 1551:

The plans of the ecclesiastics to establish villages and from them go forth
to Christianize the Indians are doubtless made with good intentions, but it
is clear that such proposals are worthless and that no fruit would come
of such attempts in many years.[58]

The cause of these successive failures was simply that Spaniards willing to risk their lives and fortunes in the New World were not interested in becoming farmers, even if they had been such in Spain, but men of wealth and position. Cortés well expressed this feeling when he refused a grant of land made to him in 1504 on his arrival in Hispaniola: "But I came to get gold, not to till the soil like a peasant." [59]

Colonization remains to this day, however, the hope of almost every Spanish-speaking nation of the Americas. And Las Casas, by emphasizing the need for hard-working farmers to exploit the rich new lands rather than the Indians, anticipated the famous dictum of the Argentine statesman Juan Bautista Alberdi, "To govern is to populate." [60]

Chapter VI

COULD THE FAITH BE PREACHED
BY PEACEFUL MEANS ALONE?

The Only Method of Attracting All People
to the True Faith

THE most successful experiment Bartolomé de Las Casas ever tried was his attempt in 1537 to convert the Indians of Guatemala by peaceful means alone. This experiment, like all his work on behalf of the Indians, was solidly based on an idea, which was expounded at length in a treatise entitled *The Only Method of Attracting All People to the True Faith,* recently printed in Mexico for the first time.[1] This treatise is considered one of the three great writings of Las Casas and will shed glory on his name as long as the Spanish conquest of America is studied. The principal ideas in this dissertation have long been known through the summary made by Antonio de Remesal in the early seventeenth century, although the manuscript itself appeared to have been lost. So believed Joaquín García Icazbalceta, and it was only due to the efforts of another great nineteenth-century Mexican scholar, Nicolás León, that a fragment of the treatise was discovered and saved for posterity. Although the manuscript thus rescued from oblivion seems to include all essential concepts of the original treatise, the work now known to us contains only chapters five, six, and seven of Book I.

The Doctrine

The doctrine enunciated by Las Casas in this treatise, the first of his many polemical writings, was simple enough. He quoted, as did Pope Paul III in the bull "Sublimis Deus," the words of Christ "Go ye and teach all nations," and agreed with the Pope that the American Indians were included.[2] As the Pope declared in Rome in that momentous pronouncement on June 9, 1537, at about the time that Las Casas was preaching the same doctrine in Guatemala:

The sublime God so loved the human race that He not only created man in such wise that he might participate in the good that other creatures enjoy,

72

but also endowed him with capacity to attain to the inaccessible and invisible Supreme Good and behold it face to face . . . all are capable of receiving the doctrines of the faith.

The enemy of the human race, who opposes all good deeds in order to bring men to destruction, beholding and envying this, invented a means never before heard of, by which he might hinder the preaching of God's word of salvation to the people: he inspired his satellites who, to please him, have not hesitated to publish abroad that the Indians of the West and the South, and other people of whom we have recent knowledge should be treated as dumb brutes created for our service, pretending that they are incapable of receiving the Catholic faith.

We . . . consider, however, that the Indians are truly men and that they are not only capable of understanding the Catholic faith but, according to our information, they desire exceedingly to receive it. Desiring to provide ample remedy for these evils, we declare . . . that, notwithstanding whatever may have been or may be said to the contrary, the said Indians and all other people who may later be discovered by Christians, are by no means to be deprived of their liberty or the possession of their property, even though they be outside the faith of Jesus Christ; and that they may and should, freely and legitimately, enjoy their liberty and the possession of their property; nor should they be in any way enslaved; should the contrary happen it shall be null and of no effect.

By virtue of our apostolic authority, we declare . . . that the said Indians and other peoples should be converted to the faith of Jesus Christ by preaching the word of God and by the example of good and holy living.[3]

Las Casas was much more specific than Pope Paul III in the application of this doctrine to the New World. In the treatise he declared that wars against the Indians were unjust and tyrannical; hence the gold, silver, pearls, jewels, and lands wrested from them were wrongfully gotten and must be restored. Not only was force unlawful to subdue and convert them; it was also unnecessary. Once the Indians accepted Christianity the next and inevitable step would be for them to acknowledge the king of Spain as their sovereign.

To those who have read the mighty fulminations and sulphurous adjectives of Las Casas in his *Very Brief Account of the Destruction of the Indies* or in the *History of the Indies,* the mild language and eloquent exhortations of the treatise on peaceful preaching will come as a pleasant shock. It would almost seem that he was making a special effort to practice what he preached. He rarely mentions the Indies, but pitches his argument on a high level where only universal truths are considered.

Las Casas uses the first four sections of chapter five of the treatise to explain the simple truth that all peoples on the face of the earth have been called by God to receive the faith as a free gift. Although it is true that men everywhere differ from each other, it is clearly impossible for a whole race or nation—no matter how stupid or idiotic

—to have absolutely no capacity to receive the faith. Manifestly the New World natives are included among the nations of mankind, particularly when one considers that the Indians are mostly intelligent beings, and that a high proportion are endowed with exceptional understanding, as their accomplishments in the mechanical and liberal arts attest.

Las Casas then enters into the heart of the matter, which is that "the way to bring into the bosom of the Christian faith and religion men who are outside the church must be a method which persuades their understanding and which moves, exhorts and gently attracts the will." The preacher, however, is not sufficient cause himself to engender a desire for the faith, since it is God who moves the spirit of man to accept His truths. Miracles also help, and some matters are not to be understood but are accepted only on faith—which makes it essential that those persons preaching Christianity act in such a way as to inspire the infidels to accept these matters on faith.

But over and over again Las Casas returns in the thirty-six long sections of this chapter to his central idea that the preaching must be carried on peacefully. He exhausts his readers with the many and expressive adjectives he employs to describe the proper method. It must be bland, suave, sweet, pleasing, tranquil, modest, patiently slow, and above all peaceful and reasonable. Moreover, following St. Augustine, faith depends upon belief which presupposes understanding. This emphasis upon understanding was later to bring Las Casas into conflict with ecclesiastics who favored rapid and wholesale baptism of the natives, without too many questions asked or catechisms learned. The question became so hotly debated in the Indies that the crown referred it to Francisco de Vitoria, the renowned Dominican theologian at Salamanca.

The infidels were to be given plenty of time to ponder upon the truths presented to them and no pressure, let alone force, applied to hasten their acceptance of the faith, for, according to Las Casas, haste or violence repels rather than attracts those who are not yet Christians. Indeed, preaching to the infidels is a difficult art which must be carefully studied. Above all the minds of the listeners must not be occupied by sadness, sorrow, or anger—as would be the case were force used—if they are to be led to accept the new ideas. Las Casas shows a remarkable understanding of the human heart and a sound appreciation of psychological truths when he states:

Anyone who proposes to attract men to a knowledge of the true faith must avail himself of the force of habit and repetition. That is to say, he must as frequently as possible propound, explain, distinguish, determine, and repeat the truths which they appreciate in the faith. He must also induce, persuade, plead with, supplicate, follow, attract, and lead by the hand those individuals who are to embrace the faith. If the missionaries proceed in this manner, the infidel will welcome an opportunity to learn the faith which he is told about, and he will accept it more easily, and will come to look upon it as wholly reasonable. Therefore, it will not be hard for men, even for idolaters and infidels, to abandon their infidel rites and the superstitions of their depraved religion. And once they have received the true faith and true religion, perhaps lukewarmly or as a pretense, they will sincerely change in spirit and begin to live with fervor and enthusiasm and advance until they achieve a real understanding.[4]

The argument now shifts to another tack. Las Casas begins with Adam and shows that since the beginning of time the holy fathers have exhibited a paternal spirit in dealing with their fellow men. The books of prophecy testify abundantly on this point, for they show that the faith was taught—and here we see a good example of the expressive mildness of Las Casas' writing in this treatise—"as rain and snow fall from heaven, not impetuously, not violently, not suddenly like a heavy shower, but gradually, with suavity and gentleness, saturating the earth as it falls."

This method, too, was established by Christ who ordered it to be observed by his apostles. Although the method was usually effective, if peaceful means did not work they were merely to leave. Thus Christ conceded to the apostles only license and authority to preach the faith to those who desired to listen to it. They were not to force or molest those who did not, nor were they to punish those who ejected the apostles from their cities. As He declared, "I send you forth as lambs among wolves."

Las Casas then sets forth the conditions under which preaching to the infidels can be successful. The mere enumeration of them explains clearly why Las Casas aroused such astonishment and opposition among conquistadores and even some ecclesiastics, for the infidels must be convinced that the preachers are not moved by a thirst for wealth or by a desire to acquire dominion over them, and the preachers must live such exemplary lives and manifest such love, charity, and affability toward the Indians as will cause "to grow in the Indians the desire to listen to them and to hold their teachings in great reverence." On each of these points, Las Casas marshals a multitude of authorities and illustrations, particularly from the writings of St. John Chrysostom.

The argument now becomes historical. Las Casas shows that peaceful persuasion was the ancient method of the church, and refers particularly to the spiritual conquest of Spain and England. Here occurs one of the few specific references to the Indies that Las Casas permits himself in the whole treatise. How different from these early spiritual conquests has been the way Spaniards brought to Montezuma and

Atahualpa the knowledge of Christ! But this is all that Las Casas says on a topic which later provoked all the torrents of his wrath.

Finally, the decrees of the church and especially the bull "Sublimis Deus" of Paul III, which is quoted in full, are cited to reënforce the argument. Las Casas comes to a triumphant end of the thirty-six sections with a detailed summary of all that has gone before and chapter five comes to an end after 281 pages of close argument.

Chapter six is much shorter—a mere ninety-two pages—and is devoted to setting forth and immediately dismissing the warlike method of preaching the faith. To those who hold that infidels should first be subjected, whether they wish it or not, and then preached to, Las Casas replied that this means war. And war brings with it these ills:

The clash of arms, sudden and furious attacks and invasions; violence and grave disturbances; scandals, deaths, and slaughter; rape, plunder, and destruction; the separation of parents from their children; captivities; the robbing of kings and natural lords of their estates and domains; the devastation and desolation of innumerable cities, palaces and towns; all these evils fill the world with tears and lamentations, with sad groans and with all manner of mournful calamities.[5]

Peace, on the other hand, is wholly desirable and Las Casas refers to Jesus' order that one should always enter another's house with the salutation "let there be peace in this house." Furthermore, says Las Casas, "peace is such a great good that nothing which men long for is more beautiful, more precious, more pleasing, or more useful." [6]

War is a new method, is irrational, unnatural, and not in consonance with human nature. Moreover it is against Christ's instructions and intentions as well as those of the apostles.[7] War violates the commandment which charges every man to love his neighbor as himself, is an indecent and infamous act which at most can affect material things and not the spirit, and of all methods "the most miserable and criminal, full of every kind of evil and cruelty, a method adopted by robbers and the most impious of men. It will lead infidels to depreciate religion and avoid those who are preaching the faith." [8] Clearly, therefore, warlike methods to establish a kingdom or to propagate Christianity "are incompatible with either the goodness of Christ or the royal dignity." Instead there must be used "the sweetness of His doctrine, the sacraments of the church, and mercy which will bestow many benefits with graciousness, gentleness, charity, and peace." [9]

Those who wage war saying that they are not forcing the infidels to accept the faith but are merely removing the obstacles which prevent the preachers from explaining the faith are making—Las Casas asserts—absurd and foolish claims, for they arouse lasting resentment and effect no conversions except those feigned for fear of worse evils.

The final chapter, seven, reveals that Las Casas was not indulging in all this theological discussion for its own sake. Inasmuch as wars against the natives are "unjust, iniquitous, and tyrannical," those who wage them commit mortal sin and are obliged to make restitution to the infidels of all that they lost in the wars. Spaniards who have killed an infidel should be responsible for the maintenance of the wife and children of the murdered Indian during all the time he might have lived. Ecclesiastics who have employed or permitted the use of force in preaching the faith or instructing the Indians are also guilty of sin.

Las Casas closes the last book of his treatise with an exhortation from St. Prosper to win souls by gentle means, by tender compassion rather than with imperious force.[10]

The Vera Paz Experiment in Guatemala, 1537–50

If the treatise on *The Only Method of Attracting All People to the True Faith* were simply one of the many theoretical works written concerning America, such a lengthy description of its doctrine would scarcely be justified today, even though it was composed by Bartolomé de Las Casas. But the ideas set forth in this bulky volume are important because they led to the famous Vera Paz experiment carried on in Guatemala in the years 1537–50 by Las Casas and his fellow Dominicans. When this audacious friar quoted in the pulpit the doctrine later elaborated in the treatise, the Spanish colonists living in Santiago in the kingdom of Guatemala were hugely amused. As one chronicler describes it, "even though the book was written in an elegant Latin," the colonists laughed at it and at its author. The Lord had delivered this troublesome fellow into their hands, or so the colonists believed, and their contempt took the form of urging Las Casas to put into practice his proposal to convert the Indians by peaceful means alone. They were very certain that even if Las Casas should escape with his life, his failure would be so resounding that they would henceforth be spared his absurd and annoying sermons.

The Spanish authorities provided an opportunity for the theory put forward by Las Casas to be tested, and may be said to have approached the problem in an experimental mood. But neither party to the controversy in Guatemala felt any doubt whatsoever of the outcome. Certainly Las Casas did not consider the proposal to be an experiment at all, but a demonstration of God's truth.[11] Las Casas strongly emphasized the fact that Christ did not rest content with uttering His truths, but insisted on putting them into practice in the world about Him. As one of Las Casas' favorite authorities, St. John Chrysostom, had declared:

Men do not consider what we say but what we do—we may philosophize interminably, but if when the occasion arises we do not demonstrate with our actions the truth of what we have been saying, our words will have done more harm than good.[12]

The moment for action in America had arrived and Las Casas selected for his demonstration the only land left unconquered in that region, the province of Tuzutlán—a mountainous, rainy, tropical country filled with fierce beasts, snakes, large monkeys, and, to boot, lacking salt. The natives living there were ferocious, barbarous, and impossible to subjugate—or at least so believed the Spaniards, for three times they had tried and as often had returned, "holding their heads," from this province which they forthwith named Tierra de Guerra, "Land of War."

To this province and to this people Las Casas offered to go, to induce them voluntarily to become vassals of the King of Spain and pay him tribute according to their ability; to teach them and to preach the Christian faith, and all this without arms or soldiers. His only weapon would be the word of God and the "reasons of the Holy Gospel."

The two requests Las Casas made were modest, and Governor Alonso Maldonado speedily granted them: that the Indians won by peaceful methods should not be divided among the Spaniards but should depend directly upon the crown, with only moderate tribute to pay, and that for five years no Spaniards except Las Casas and his brother Dominicans should be allowed in the province, in order that secular Spaniards might not disturb the Indians or provoke scandal.

Having concluded this agreement with the Governor, Las Casas and his companions—Friars Rodrigo de Andrada, Pedro de Angulo, and Luis Cáncer—spent several days praying, fasting, and undergoing other spiritual disciplines and mortifications. Then they carefully planned their approach and began by composing some ballads in the Indian language of the Tierra de Guerra. These ballads were virtually a history of Christianity, for they described the creation of the world and the fall of man, his exile from Paradise, and the life and miracles of Jesus Christ. Las Casas then sought and found four Christian Indian merchants accustomed to trading in the Tierra de Guerra and patiently taught them by heart all the verses, and trained them, moreover, to sing them "in a pleasing manner."

At last, in August 1537, the Indians set out alone with their merchandise, to which Las Casas had added some Spanish trinkets, such as scissors, knives, mirrors, and bells, which had proved popular with the natives. The merchants went directly to the great chieftain of the tribes in the Tierra de Guerra, a warlike person, highly respected and feared by all. At the end of the day's trading, one of the merchants called for a teplanastle, an Indian stringed instrument, and the group proceeded to sing all the verses they had learned. The novelty of the situation, the harmony of instrument and voices, and the new doctrine —especially the statement that the idols they worshiped were demons and that their human sacrifices were bad—excited great wonder and admiration among the Indians.

For the succeeding eight nights the merchants repeated their performance, gladly acceding to requests from the audience to sing some well-liked part over and over again. When the Indians wanted to know more, they were told that only the friars could instruct them. But what were friars? The merchants thereupon described them: men dressed in black and white robes, unmarried, their hair cut in a special fashion—men who wanted neither gold, feathers, nor precious stones, and who day and night sang the praises of their Lord before beautiful images in churches. Only these holy men—not even the great lords of Spain—could instruct the Indians, and the friars would come most willingly if invited. The chieftain was content with all that he had been told and sent his younger brother to ask the friars to come and teach them, instructing him, however, to observe secretly whether the friars behaved as well as the merchants alleged.

We may be sure that Las Casas and his associates passed some anxious days before their trusted merchants returned bringing with them the envoy and his retinue. They accepted joyfully the presents sent by the chieftain and, while the envoy was visiting the town, conferred and decided to send only one emissary, the Friar Luis Cáncer, a devoted and experienced missionary who knew Indian languages well. So the Indians, loaded down with Spanish trinkets, returned to their Tierra de Guerra, taking with them Friar Luis. On entering the chieftain's territory, he found triumphal floral arches raised and great fiestas prepared to welcome him. The chieftain himself received Cáncer with the greatest respect and veneration and ordered a church built at once. He was an interested spectator at the first Mass celebrated there and was particularly impressed by the friar's vestments and cleanliness, for his own priests went about in filthy clothes, their hair matted with blood, and their temples were no more than sooty, dirty hovels. Assured by his brother that the friars really followed the customs described by the merchants, and his fear of armed invasion quieted by the news of Governor Maldonado's order, the chief decided to become a Christian and urged all his people to do likewise. He was the first to tear down and burn their ancient idols. Thus was won the first soul in the Tierra de Guerra.

Cáncer hastened back to Santiago where Las Casas and the other friars rejoiced to hear the news of the success of their peaceful method. When the rains ceased in October 1537, Las Casas and Pedro de Angulo went into the Tierra de Guerra and there witnessed an example of the steadfastness of their chieftain in the faith. He refused to permit the usual sacrifices of parrots and other birds and animals at the wedding ceremony of his brother (the envoy), in spite of great opposition in Cobán, the chieftain of which was the bride's father. The faithful chieftain also rebuilt the church which some of his disaffected vassals had burned and arranged for the friars to visit other parts of his land, where they made many converts.

Naturally all this was a bombshell to the Spanish colonists in Guatemala who had hoped for such a complete disaster that Las Casas would never again dare to write or talk on the subject of peaceful conversion or restitution to the Indians of their property. The documents do not enlighten us on the events of the year 1538 in the Land of War, but it is obvious that in November 1539 Las Casas was still stronger than his detractors, for Pedro de Alvarado, the most important conquistador and then Governor of Guatemala, wrote in that month to the King that Las Casas was about to leave for Spain to bring more ecclesiastics, and strongly praised his work, as did the Bishop.

This official support, plus Las Casas' own eloquence and experience, had its effect. During the year 1540 a perfect flood of royal orders was issued in Spain designed to forward the peaceful conversion of the Indians. On October 17 alone, a dozen such orders were issued. The Franciscans were instructed to provide Las Casas with Indians under their care who, like the merchants, had musical talent; the royal officials were charged with punishing all Spaniards who flouted the Governor's order to stay out of the Tierra de Guerra; Maldonado's agreement with Las Casas was solemnly reaffirmed. Money also was provided, and the King concluded by requesting various Indian chieftains—Don Juan, the first convert, Don Gaspar of the village of Chequiciztén, Don Miguel of Chichicastenango, and Don Jorge of Terpanatitán—to continue to aid in the conversion of the surrounding Indians. Subsequently Don Miguel, Don Gaspar, and others received coats of arms for this important work.

It would be gratifying to those who believe in the ultimate triumph of justice in this world to be able to report that henceforth all went smoothly in Guatemala; but the facts are otherwise. For ten years the colonists and the ecclesiastics fought like cats and dogs over the peaceful preaching of the faith. In the course of the struggle the municipal council of Santiago informed the King that Las Casas was an unlettered friar, an envious, passionate, turbulent, most unsaintly fellow who kept the land in an uproar and would, unless checked, destroy Spanish rule in the New World; furthermore, that the so-called "peaceful" Indians revolted every day and killed many Spaniards. But royal orders continued to flow from Spain supporting Las

Casas and his fellow Dominicans. And the Land of War was officially christened "Land of True Peace" amid the sardonic laughter of the colonists.

Las Casas returned to Guatemala in 1544 as bishop of Chiapa, a region which included the Land of True Peace. The battle waxed so hot with the colonists that a special royal investigator was sent to Guatemala in 1547 to look into the alleged mistreatment of the Dominicans by the Spanish colonists, and he reported that much evidence could be found to support the charge. For a time Bishop Las Casas himself had to flee to Nicaragua to escape his irate parishioners, whom he had excommunicated right and left, including the judges. The fight to preach the faith peacefully went on—even after Las Casas' resignation as bishop in 1550 at the age of seventy-six.

The end of the experiment is chronicled in a sad letter sent by the friars to the Council of the Indies on May 14, 1556. They were writing, says the report, in order that the King might clearly understand what happened. For years the friars had worked strenuously despite the great heat and hardness of the land—they had destroyed idols, built churches, and won souls. But always "the devil was vigilant" and finally he stirred up the pagan priests who called in some neighboring infidel Indians to help provoke a revolt. The friars and their followers were burned out of their homes and some thirty were killed by arrows. Two of the friars were murdered in the church and one sacrificed before a pagan idol. One of those to die was Friar Domingo de Vico, a zealous, learned missionary, who was able to preach in seven different Indian languages. When the Spaniards in Santiago were asked by the friars for help to punish the infidel Indians, they unctuously declined, citing the royal order forbidding them to interfere with the Indians or to enter the territory. Subsequently the King ordered the punishment of the revolting Indians, the Land of True Peace became even poorer, and the possibility of winning the Indians by peaceful means alone faded away.

Later Attempts at Peaceful Conversion

The original movers of the Vera Paz experiment never wavered in their conviction that all people, including Indians, could and should be brought to the faith by Christian, peaceful means. Las Casas held no monopoly of the idea, but the significance of his achievement lies in the fact that he alone worked out in advance a most complete and theoretical justification for the policy and then, when challenged, dramatically and for a time successfully, demonstrated the validity of his idea. It is impossible to prove that all the many subsequent attempts to preach the faith peacefully after Vera Paz were inspired by Las Casas and his fellow Dominicans.[13] Sometimes their influence was explicitly recognized but often there was no reference to it.

Many Spaniards continued to feel that "the voice of the gospel is heard only where the Indians have heard also the sound of fire arms," while others took the following related view:

To handle them gently, while gentle courses may be found to serve, it will be without comparison the best; but if gentle polishing will not serve, then we shall not want hammerors and rough masons enow, I meane our old soldiours trained up in the Netherlands, to square and prepare them to our Preacher's hands.[14]

Against such attitudes Las Casas fought all his life. Despite opposition, his ideal of peacefully bringing to the faith the natives of the marvelous new world discovered by the Spaniards lived on. The doctrine, so carefully buttressed up by such a wealth of citations in *The Only Method of Attracting All People to the True Faith,* was never wholly forgotten, despite the failure in the Land of True Peace. Other friars in other parts of the Spanish empire in the New World were inspired by this treatise and by the Vera Paz experiment to follow the same ideal in their own territory.

Chapter VII

COULD THE ENCOMIENDA SYSTEM
BE ABOLISHED?

The Meaning of the New Laws

THE fourth and last great experiment undertaken by Spaniards in the first half-century of their conquest was the most daring of all, and the one least likely to succeed. The colonization attempt of Las Casas had failed, the experiments to test the capacity of the Indians had not discovered any natives able to live alone as free subjects of the King, but the preaching of the faith by peaceful means alone was proceeding well—at least in 1542. On November 20 of that year, Emperor Charles V cast aside the advice of some of his oldest and most important advisers and, following the recommendation of Las Casas and other Dominicans that the encomienda system be abolished, promulgated the famous New Laws. These New Laws revoked or limited the right of Spaniards to service and tribute from Indians, who would ultimately be put under the crown and administered by paid royal officials along with the other natives known as "crown Indians." This radical step led to a near revolt in Mexico, a serious rebellion in Peru in which the Viceroy was killed, and provoked grave unrest throughout the empire. Why did the Emperor approve these New Laws?

To Bartolomé de Las Casas, whose constant and vociferous efforts on behalf of the Indians were largely responsible for the passage of these laws, the answer was simple and clear. The existence of the encomienda made invalid the just title of the king of Spain to the Indies, and stigmatized him as a tyrant instead of a true lord,[1] for true lordship required either that the people of the land spontaneously subject themselves to the rule of Spain or that the King, given jurisdiction over them at the behest of the Pope, use it for the sole purpose of benefiting those people. The encomienda system, which virtually enslaved the Indians according to Las Casas, was from no point of view beneficial to them. Therefore, since it negated the king's just title, it must be wiped out.

Lack of Adequate Materials for a Study of the Encomienda System

To the historian today, however, who pores over the extensive but still fragmentary records available for a study of this decisive crisis in the history of the New World, the reasons for the King's decision to reverse his earlier attitude toward the encomienda are not so clear.

The history, if it could be written, of the system by which Spaniards commandeered Indian labor in the New World would certainly contribute greatly to our understanding of this important part of the story of Spain in sixteenth-century America. But adequate sources do not now exist in usable form for writing such a history, and no completely satisfactory monograph has appeared on the subject as a whole. This is not to say that no significant studies have been made.[2]

One would like to know, however, what sort of life the encomendero led in that "solid mansion of stone or other durable material" which he was supposed to build in the town nearest his encomienda. No diaries kept by encomenderos have come down to us, whether because time has destroyed them or because they were never written. Spaniards have always shown a marked reluctance to reveal themselves in autobiographical works. For a knowledge of how well Indians were indoctrinated into the faith by encomenderos, one may dredge about in the replies to Philip II's questionnaire, and—if he has faith in such official, statistical compilations—may find important bits of information on encomiendas.[3] France V. Scholes, who has probably made more archival investigations on encomienda history than any other scholar, feels that much interesting and valuable material could be assembled.[4] This would include manuscript sources such as *probanzas* of services of the conquistadores, encomienda lawsuits, and the records of the judicial enquiries into the official actions of every important royal administrator in America—the *residencias* and *visitas*—which exist by the ton in the Archivo de Indias. Perhaps in years to come some earnest young student will take pleasure in disproving the statement hazarded here on the paucity of sources for the encomienda by locating and organizing this material!

Travelers often provide fresh and valuable descriptions of foreign lands, but not so for sixteenth-century Spanish America. In the crucial period before 1550 few if any foreigners were able to break into the jealously guarded Indies and those few who did later manage to do so—such as the Englishmen Robert Tomson, John Chilton, Job Hastings, Henry Hawks, and Miles Philips—were so busy keeping themselves alive and safe from the Inquisition that they had neither leisure nor opportunity to observe the workings of the encomienda system. The Italian Girolamo Benzoni wrote a book on his experiences in the Spanish colonies,[5] but it does not inform us sufficiently on the encomienda system to be compared with Edward Young's *Travels in France,* which gives a foreigner's picture of life there on the eve of the Revolution, or Frederick Olmstead's *A Journey in the Seaboard Slave States,* with its picture of slave society in the Old

South just before the outbreak of the Civil War. Nor have we economic records of the encomienda system comparable to the plantation data found on the Old South and printed by Ulrich B. Phillips.[6] The plantation system and the encomienda were not, of course, similar institutions but they were both basic to the life of their times, and the contrast in the sheer amount of our knowledge on them is startling. One would not expect to find exactly the same kind of information on the encomienda as for the plantation, but the lack of adequate economic data on the encomienda, particularly before 1550, is marked.

The lack of biographical materials is particularly regrettable. A number of conquistadores wrote histories or at least reports of their deeds, but no encomendero seems to have done so, nor is there a biography of any encomendero.

Doubtless many manuscript materials have been lost, particularly local records that were never sent to Spain. Officials in New Spain were ordered on December 10, 1531, to keep a sort of ledger in which the audiencia was to strike a balance of good and bad conduct on each encomendero every two years and send the score to Spain.[7] None of these accounts has come down to us. Royal orders abound, of course, for Antonio León Pinelo plowed through over five hundred volumes of them in preparation for his standard *Tratado de confirmaciones reales* (1630), and even then did not utilize all available legal records.[8] But the intimate and varied source materials needed for a real history of the encomienda system simply do not seem to exist, or, if they do, are not known to historians. Until recently the very definition of encomienda was in doubt, and there were also disputes as to whether the institution was indigenous to America or transplanted, a question now partly settled by Robert S. Chamberlain's researches which clearly reveal that in certain respects the Spanish and the American practices were very close.[9]

Most disturbing of all, no comprehensive Indian records are available to tell how the Indians felt about the encomienda. Indian declarations against the system, of course, exist, and we may safely suppose that it was a horror to some of them, but the documents available do not provide a complete story. And the Indians put under the crown, instead of being commended, still await their historian. Today a book as revealing as Eileen Powers' *Medieval People* simply cannot be written about the men and women who formed a part of the encomienda system. Under such disadvantages, historians draw conclusions at their peril. Only a brief and generalized sketch of the early history of the encomienda will be given here as background for the New Laws.

The Development of the Encomienda System to 1542

The early regulations drawn up for the encomienda and its official sanction in 1512 under the Laws of Burgos have been already described as specific results of the first cry for justice in America by Friar Antonio de Montesinos. The Burgos regulations were extremely precise and humane, but they proved unenforceable. The fruitless Jeronymite rule of 1518 followed, succeeded in turn by more disputes, more meetings in Spain. By now Las Casas had entered the battle and had impressed upon the King's preachers the miserable condition of the Indians, and the injustice and evil effects of the encomienda system. Miguel de Salamanca, the oldest and most authoritative of the preachers, presented a memorial which has been preserved in the *History of the Indies* of Las Casas. This statement contains the substance of all the subsequent attacks against the encomienda.

The greatest evil which has caused the total destruction of those lands and which will continue, unless a remedy be found, and which is neither just nor can it or ought it be allowed in reason, is the encomienda of the Indians as it now exists, that is to say, being allotted for life in order that, working as they are worked, all the profit deriving from their work goes to those who hold them in encomienda; wherefore this form of encomienda and the manner in which it is executed is contrary to the well-being of the Indian Republic; also it is against all reason and human prudence; also it is against the welfare and service of our Lord the King and contrary to all civil and canon law; also it is against all rules of moral philosophy and theology; also it is against God and his will and his Church.[10]

Although the Council received this memorial civilly, and the King, on May 20, 1520, decreed that the Indians ought to be free and be treated as freemen, the memorial does not appear to have had any direct effect. It is true that in 1523, the King ordered Cortés not to commend Indians "because God created the Indians free and not subject," but this law was not obeyed and, after many discussions, the encomienda was legalized in 1526 for New Spain, with the proviso that no encomendero was to receive more than three hundred Indians.[11]

When the first audiencia was sent to Mexico in 1528, the crown offered to make encomiendas permanent and to give the Spanish holders lordship and jurisdiction over the Indians in a certain form that was to be stated at the time of making the grants.[12] The crown veered around sharply during the next two years, and in 1530 gave the second audiencia strict instructions to establish the office of corregidor, a royal official who was to administer Indians placed under the crown.[13] The crown's promise of 1528 was not redeemed, although petitions by conquistadores for formal grants of Indian fiefs poured into the court continuously.

The disputes continued, although Las Casas during these years was living quietly in a convent in Hispaniola and the battle was carried on by other Indian defenders.

The stoutest opponent of the encomienda system at the time was the Bishop of Santo Domingo, Sebastián Ramírez de Fuenleal, who was later to take part in the great battle of the New Laws in 1542. Now as president of the Audiencia of New Spain he recommended that royal officials be put in charge of the Indians and that conquistadores be given a regular pension. If the encomenderos complained that the land would therefore be depopulated and lost to the crown, Bishop Ramírez advised the Empress on February 2, 1533, she could safely disregard such predictions, for Spaniards desirous of encomiendas had been making them since the conquest began.[14]

The advice of this principal royal official in New Spain was not followed. Shortly after the conclusion of the last experiencia in Cuba, in 1536, the famous Law of Inheritance for Two Generations was passed, which permitted encomenderos to pass on their encomiendas as inheritance to their legitimate descendants or to their widows for one life.[15] The law thus encouraged the hope that a permanent inheritance for the conquistadores and their families might soon be secured. Now voices were raised for grants in perpetuity, and even for a law which would hand over to the Spaniards, forever, civil and criminal jurisdiction over the Indians. Just at this juncture Las Casas arrived in Spain, fresh from the triumphs of peaceful preaching in the Land of True Peace in Guatemala, and determined that an even greater triumph must be achieved: the encomienda system itself must be destroyed.

The "Eighth Remedy" of Las Casas and His "Very Brief Account of the Destruction of the Indies"

These were years of great ferment in Spain on Indian affairs. The bull of Pope Paul III, declaring the Indians free and capable of receiving the faith, had just been issued. The problem of the basis for the just title of the king of Spain to the Indies was being aired throughout the land, and so many memorials and treatises were written on the subject that the King "was discomfited thereby." [16]

Las Casas reached Spain in 1539 determined, according to one author, either to win real assistance for the Indians or to abandon his work for them to labor in other mission fields.[17] It was at this time that his denunciation of the slapdash methods used by some ecclesiastics to baptize thousands of Indians without proper religious instruction so disturbed the court that the noted Friar Francisco de Vitoria and some of the other foremost theologians of Salamanca were called upon to render an opinion on the matter.[18]

Las Casas was more concerned, however, to make sure that there would be Indians left to baptize. For two years he haunted the court and Council of the Indies, advocating the abolition of the encomienda system, which he believed to be the principal enemy of the Indians. The President of the Council, Cardinal Loaysa, remained unmoved by the charges and denunciations of Las Casas. Emperor Charles V was absent from Spain during this period, but returned in 1542, and almost immediately ordered that special meetings be held to consider Indian matters, an action which some believed was caused by Las Casas' influence with the Emperor's Flemish advisers. During the years 1542 and 1543 Las Casas was much at court, seems to have had a hand in all decisions of the Council of the Indies, and as usual composed two special treatises to forward his cause.

The first treatise was entitled *Remedies for the Existing Evils, with Twenty Reasons Therefor,* a stern condemnation of the whole encomienda system.

In this juridical treatise, the following propositions were the most significant ones:

The pope intended to do the Indians a favor, not harm, by his donation to the king of Spain. The Indians are free, and do not lose this liberty by becoming vassals to the king of Spain. Inasmuch as the Indies are far away, no partial prohibition of encomiendas or attempts to regulate them by law will succeed. A general order must be issued, in such wise that it cannot be contravened.[19]

The other treatise written by Las Casas during these years was the famous—or infamous—*Very Brief Account of the Destruction of the Indies.*[20] This denunciation of Spanish treatment of the Indians caused oceans of words to flow in the sixteenth and succeeding centuries, including our own. This bloody description of the Spanish conquest, translated into all the principal European languages and illustrated with gruesome pictures, served as the choicest weapon of anti-Spanish propagandists everywhere. Even today it seems to have a Lorelei-like attraction for Hispanophiles who wish to combat the black legend of Spanish cruelty in America, and the revisionists quote Las Casas so frequently in their attacks on his writings that they help to spread ever more widely his accusations.[21]

At once there sprang up persons to challenge Las Casas' statistics—for he claimed some fifteen or twenty millions of Indians had perished —and to complain that he gave a most unbalanced picture of Spanish deeds in the New World in the first half-century after Columbus. His vehemence in 1542 has been matched by the vehemence of other Spaniards who have been denouncing him these four hundred years.

It is not possible to present here an essay on the comparative cruelty of Europeans in America which would do justice to this large theme.[22] No one today would defend the statistics Las Casas gave, but few would deny that there was considerable truth in his main charges. One Mexican writer, who has devoted himself to analyzing the *Very Brief Account*, concludes that the detractors of Las Casas have shrewdly exploited his numerical errors without ever disproving his essential truths.[23]

Other Spaniards than Las Casas charged their countrymen with cruelty. The secret investigation against Viceroy Antonio de Mendoza contained this accusation:

After the capture of the hill of Mixtón, many of the Indians taken in the conquest of the said hill were put to death in his presence and by his orders. Some were placed in line and blown into bits by cannon fire; others were torn to pieces by dogs; and others were given to Negroes to be put to death, and these killed them with knife thrusts, while others were hung. Again, at other places, Indians were thrown to the dogs in his presence.[24]

Friar Motolinía, certainly no friend of Las Casas and author of one of the bitterest and most sarcastic letters ever written against him, stated in the *History of the Indians of New Spain* that "countless" natives were destroyed in labor at the mines, that service in the mines of Oaxyecac was so destructive that for half a league around it the Spaniards could not walk except on dead men or bones, and that so many birds came to scavenge that they darkened the sky.[25] The royal official Alonso de Zurita stated that he had heard many Spaniards say that in Popayán province the bones of dead Indians were so thick along the roads that one could never lose the way.[26] Governor Francisco de Castañeda in Nicaragua reported that Spaniards on horseback hunted down Indians and lanced them, including women and children, at the slightest provocation or with no provocation whatsoever.[27]

The historian Pedro Cieza de León, who participated in the Peruvian campaigns, wrote:

I know from my experience gathered during a long residence in the Indies that there were great cruelties and much injury done to the natives, such as cannot be lightly stated. All know how populous the island of Hispaniola was, and that if the Christians had treated the natives decently and as friends there would certainly be many there now. Yet there remains no other testimony of the country having once been peopled than the great cemeteries of the dead, and the ruins of the places where they lived. In Tierra Firme and Nicaragua also not an Indian is left. They asked Belalcázar how many he found between Quito and Cartago, and they desired to know from me how many now remain. Well, there are none. In a town which had a population of ten thousand Indians there was not one. When we came from Cartagena with Vadillo I saw a Portuguese, named Roque Martín, who had quarters of Indians hanging on a perch to feed his dogs with, as if they were those of wild beasts. In the Realm of New Granada and in Popayán they did things so ruthless that I would rather not mention them.[28]

Some of the most telling descriptions of Spanish cruelty were embedded in royal orders, so much so that the seventeenth-century jurist Solórzano was ordered to remove from the manuscript of his *Política Indiana* some of the royal orders on mistreatment of Indians to prevent notice of these things reaching foreigners.[29] Anyone who reads widely in the chronicles and reports left by Spaniards will find information supporting and supplementing many of the accusations made by Las Casas in 1542.

The diseases brought by Spaniards took heavy toll of the Indians, the dislocation of Indian life and customs caused grave difficulties, as any anthropologist today would expect and as Las Casas realized in the sixteenth century, and the filthy habits of the Spaniards may have also helped to destroy the bath-taking natives of the New World.[30]

There appears to have existed in Europe, long before Las Casas wrote, a disposition to believe in the cruelty of Spaniards in their conquests. About 1522, for example, a short anonymous account of Yucatán appeared in German with a woodcut which shows three evil-looking men dressed like Europeans engaged in chopping up babies. And the cosmography of Sebastian Münster has an American scene depicting a man and woman dismembering a human being on a table, while another cut shows the man sitting comfortably on a stool beside a slow fire, over which he turns a spit thrust through a headless body.[31] The famous De Bry illustrations, which spread far and wide the denunciations of Las Casas even to those who could not read, therefore had predecessors which tended to paint the same dark picture of Spanish action in the New World.

The above recital of gruesome details is not made to blacken the history of Spain in America or to add soot to the black legend, but rather to provide necessary background for a consideration of the New Laws, the ordinances by which Charles V tried to abolish the encomienda system. Certainly one of the documents which helped to produce an atmosphere in which it was possible to secure royal approval for such a radical innovation was the *Very Brief Account of the Destruction of the Indies*. As Antonio de León Pinelo emphasized in his *Tratado de confirmaciones reales*, an impressive seventeenth-century treatise dedicated to the task of proving the justice of the encomienda system, the bad treatment of the Indians by the Spaniards was the cause of the whole dispute. And to those who denounce Las Casas as an "insensate fanatic," who singlehanded destroyed Spain's reputation, the conclusion of the late Pelham Box still is a valid answer:

The implication that but for the Apostle of the Indians Spain would have escaped the hostility of jealous neighbors is too naïve to be discussed. No power possessing a rich empire can hope to escape envy. . . . If he [Las Casas] exaggerated on details he was right in fundamentals and his truth is not affected by the use hypocritical foreigners made of his works. . . . It is not the least of Spain's glories that she produced Bartolomé de Las Casas and actually listened to him, however ineffectively.[32]

The New Laws

The "Laws and ordinances newly made by His Majesty for the government of the Indies and good treatment and preservation of the Indians," formally approved by Charles V at Barcelona on November 20, 1542, have been, as Henry Stevens declared, "at once the pride and humiliation of Spain," and merit detailed description.[33] They include the first regulations to establish procedures for the Council of the Indies, as well as ordinances on the Indians.

The individual laws provided for such matters as that the Council of the Indies should meet every day, that the servants of the President or Council members should not be attorneys or officials before the court, that those officers should not accept bribes or engage in private business, that they should take especial care for the preservation and increase of the Indians, and also laid down a number of specific rules on the conduct of business that came before the Council.

Then follow detailed regulations so sweeping and so strongly in favor of the Indians that Las Casas himself might well have drafted them. The audiencias were commanded "to enquire continually into the excesses and ill treatment which are or shall be done to them by governors or private persons, and how the ordinances and instructions which have been given to them and are made for the good treatment of the said Indians have been observed." It was further commanded "that henceforward, for no cause of war nor any other cause whatsoever, though it be under title of rebellion, nor by ransom nor in any other manner can an Indian be made a slave, and we desire that they be treated as of the Crown of Castile, since such they are." Indians "who until now have been enslaved against all reason and right" were to be put at liberty. Indians were not to carry loads unless absolutely necessary and then only "in such a manner that no risk of life or health of the said Indians may ensue." No free Indian was to be taken to the pearl fisheries against his will, "for since these fisheries have not been conducted in a proper manner, deaths of many Indians and Negroes have ensued."

Most grievous of all, in the estimation of the conquistadores, were the provisions regarding encomiendas. Those who held Indians without proper title were to lose them; those who held unreasonable numbers of Indians in Mexico—and these persons were listed by name— were to have some taken away, and those who had ill-treated their Indians were to be deprived of them, especially "those principal persons" involved in the disturbances of Pizarro and Almagro in Peru. The climax was reached, for the encomenderos, by the laws taking Indians away from all royal officials and prelates, and prohibiting all future grants of Indians. As it was stipulated in Law No. 35, "Henceforth no encomienda is to be granted to anyone, and when the present holders of encomiendas die, their Indians will revert to the crown." [34]

Indians thus taken away and put under the crown were to be well treated and instructed, and the first conquistadores and married settlers were to be preferred in appointments to royal offices in the Indies. New discoveries were to be made according to certain rigid rules, no Indians were to be brought back as loot, and the tribute to be assessed on newly discovered natives would be fixed by the Governor. Finally, Indians of the islands of San Juan, Cuba, and Hispaniola "are not to be molested with demands for tribute, or other services . . . but must be treated in the same manner as the Spaniards who reside in the said islands."

The reaction of rage and astonishment among the conquistadores was instantaneous and inevitable, for by these laws the property of every encomendero was diminished and the future of his family made insecure. All the most powerful officials, royal and ecclesiastical alike, were similarly disadvantaged. It was particularly galling to the colonial Spaniards who, as encomenderos, had developed secure and honored positions in the New World, that the Spaniards at home should have contrived these laws which, if enforced, would reduce the position and security of the very men who, in their own opinion, had contributed most to Spain's glory in the New World.

Why Were the New Laws Decreed?

No ordinance Spain passed for the government of the Indians was more important than the New Laws, yet we do not know the full story of their enactment and their revision. Certain manuscript records have recently been found, however, which throw some light on these significant events in the history of America. These manuscripts contain the opinions of nearly all the members of the junta before the

New Laws were passed, and also given by the same advisers before they were revoked. They embody, therefore, the attitudes of the Emperor's principal advisers before and after the event.[35]

An analysis of these opinions shows the majority of junta members definitely opposed to the encomienda system as then functioning, although a minority made various counterproposals and the experienced President of the Council of the Indies voted against the hasty abolition of the system.

It must be emphasized that Las Casas was not the only friar agitating at this time for reform in the Indies. The Franciscan Jacobo de Testera had arrived for this same purpose in 1540 with a warm letter from Archbishop Zumárraga recommending him and Las Casas for their zeal and devotion to the protection of the Indians. The Dominicans Juan de Torres and Pedro de Angulo were also present at court working for the Indians.

The court likewise had other information on cruelty to Indians than that furnished by Las Casas in his *Very Brief Account of the Destruction of the Indies*. It appears from manuscripts in the Archivo General de Indias that one of the most respected members of the Council, Gregorio López, was sent early in 1543 to Seville to inspect the India House and make a special investigation there on the "liberty of the Indians." This document sheds little light on their liberty, but it does show that many persons were ready to depose what they knew concerning the ill-treatment being meted out all over the Indies. Here may be found the statements dated June 23, 1543, of Luis de Morales, who had earlier submitted an extensive individual report, Rodrigo Calderón, Licenciado Loaysa of the Mexican Audiencia, the Bishop of Tierra Firme, Diego Alemán, Pedro de Aguilar, and others.[36] Spain must have rocked with complaints on cruelty to Indians, for the Spanish Cortes of 1542 in Valladolid petitioned the King to "remedy the cruelties which are committed in the Indies against the Indians to the end that God be served and the Indies preserved and not depopulated as is now the case." [37] The royal reply was noncommittal: "We shall provide as it may be convenient," but this petition shows that some defender of the Indians must have been circulating among the representatives at the Valladolid Cortes, in that fateful year of 1542, and had left no stone unturned.

While the parliament was going on record against cruelty to Indians, and the special junta was deliberating on the abolition of the encomienda system, Charles V ordered an inspection (*visita*) of the Council of the Indies itself, which indicated that something was felt to be wrong there. Professor Ernest Schaefer, author of the standard monograph on the Council, is not certain why the visita was held, and his most diligent search has not turned up the records of this inspection.[38] One contemporary writer asserted that Las Casas was responsible for having the visita made, but the few records existing in the archives are silent on this point.[39] Apparently the Council was suspended from June 1542 until February 1543. During the course of the visita it was discovered that Dr. Beltrán, the oldest member, had accepted gifts of money from Cortés, Hernando Pizarro, and Diego de Almagro, for which he was fined and dismissed. The Bishop of Lugo, who opposed the abolition of the encomienda, was likewise fined, dismissed, and exiled to his bishopric. The Emperor also lost confidence in Cardinal Loaysa, President of the Council, on account of various complaints which were not made public because of his exalted position. Charles V called in the Bishop of Cuenca, Sebastián Ramírez, who was stoutly opposed to encomiendas, to assist the Cardinal in Indian affairs.[40] The Emperor probably had been suspicious of the Council for some time, since he had received a secret report in 1541 charging that Pizarro had sent bribes to several members to win them to his side in pending disputes.[41]

Charles V called on Las Casas and his faithful friend Friar Rodrigo de Andrada to appear before the Council, which was instructed to hear them because of their great experience and knowledge.[42] Throughout the tense period when the New Laws were being considered, Las Casas appears to have been active and influential. The Emperor conferred another distinction on him by nominating Las Casas as bishop of Chiapa.[43] A few months later the additions to the New Laws were made, and the complete text was printed on July 8, 1543. Las Casas' authority was now so great that, according to one account, he was responsible for the visita, and "nothing was determined in the Council except by his direction, for the Emperor had ordered that he enter the Council." His influence was such, asserted this same author, that the Emperor accepted everything that Las Casas said and was prepared to leave Peru to the Incas, until Friar Francisco de Vitoria counseled him not to do so, lest Christianity perish there.[44]

Contemporaries saw the hand of Las Casas guiding Charles V and even winding this experienced ruler around his little finger.[45] That the tough-minded Charles was frightened or hurried into precipitate action merely by Las Casas seems unlikely for, as the historian Ranke said, "there never was an instance of his having been forced into anything by violence or danger." [46] The vigorous representations of Las Casas against the injustices he saw in the encomienda must have had great weight, however, with a monarch who already distrusted the Council of the Indies, whose members were accused of having accepted bribes from the lords of the Indies, these very men who stood to gain from encomiendas and were loudly clamoring for them.

Las Casas continued to press for more protection for the Indians throughout the remainder of 1543 and the early months of 1544. By spring he came to believe that their legal rights were so firmly established in Spain that his presence was no longer necessary at court. He must have known that representatives of conquistadores in Spain had hastily sent copies of the laws they hated to the New World and were grimly biding their time while waiting for the explosion they knew would come. Perhaps Las Casas expected this too and wished to be in the thick of the fight in America.

At any rate Las Casas finally decided to accept the bishopric of Chiapa, in which lay the Land of True Peace. On Passion Sunday of 1544, this veteran of the Indies was consecrated bishop in the Church of St. Paul, in the "Very Noble and Very Loyal City" of Seville. Las Casas had been born here, and now it was from this same city that he set forth at seventy years of age to continue his labor for the Indians of Chiapa. He would be among friends, for in this bishopric his Dominican brothers were successfully putting into effect one of his great dreams, preaching the faith to Indians by peaceful means alone. Behind him lay, as he thought, his most spectacular victory over the forces of selfishness and ungodliness. The New Laws had been decreed, despite all the influence the conquistadores and their friends could muster against them, and these laws foreshadowed the eventual death of the encomienda system. The Dominican friar Bartolomé de Las Casas had set in motion as revolutionary a change in American society and in the administration of Spain's great empire overseas as his contemporary Nicolaus Copernicus had achieved in astronomical circles with his *De revolutionibus orbium coelestium,* printed in the same year as the New Laws.

The Encomienda Is Not Abolished After All

The ink was scarcely dry on the printed New Laws before the Franciscan Jacobo de Testera was back in Mexico informing the Indians of the great victory won by himself, Las Casas, and other champions of the Indian cause at court. The City Council discussed in solemn session on July 23, 1543, the disturbing news that

the French Franciscan Jacobo de Testera had arrived from Castile, and had permitted a great multitude of Indians to come out to receive him. These Indians bestowed gifts upon him and performed other services, erecting triumphal arches, sweeping clean the streets he was to pass and strewing upon them cyperus and roses, and bearing him upon a litter—all this because he and other Franciscans had informed the Indians that they had come to free the Indians and restore them to the state they enjoyed before they were placed under the rule of the King of Spain. These statements had excited the Indians and they went forth to receive Friar Testera as though he were a viceroy.[47]

The hopes of the Indians must have faded almost as quickly as the roses with which they welcomed Testera bearing his glad tidings. The Visitador Tello de Sandoval, sent to Mexico to enforce the New Laws, suspended the more rigorous ones as soon as he arrived in Mexico City, on account of the tremendous protests that reached his ears. In Peru the situation was even more dangerous, since the Viceroy Blasco Núñez Vela had arrived in Lima with the New Laws just as the revolt of Gonzalo Pizarro was well under way. Benito Juárez de Carvajal captured the Viceroy himself in the battle of Anaquito, decapitated him, and carried his head by the hair until this became inconvenient, when he put a string through the lips and thus bore it along happily, "calling it to the attention of everyone he passed." [48]

With the Viceroy's head on a string, there was no possibility of enforcing even the current laws, much less the New Laws. Indeed, Pizarro's advisers urged him to assume the kingship of Peru, marry an Inca princess, grant encomiendas in perpetuity, and enact judicious laws for the effectual protection of the Indians.[49] The history of this revolt is well known, and need not be repeated here.

Equally well known is the campaign waged by the Spaniards in Mexico against the New Laws. Tello de Sandoval, sent to enforce them, took down a quantity of information from royal officials, colonists, and ecclesiastics which showed that opinion was overwhelmingly against them. Perhaps most important of all, many unfavorable opinions and depositions on the matter were sent by friars of all the orders to the King and Council of the Indies. Indeed, the provincials of the Augustinians, Dominicans, and Franciscans made the long journey from Mexico to Spain to inform the King on "necessary remedies," and to demonstrate that the highest dignitaries of the missionary orders in closest contact with the Indians were solidly behind the conquistadores. The City Council of Mexico City despatched two special representatives, Alonso de Villanueva and Gonzalo López, who presented in June 1545 a long memorial advocating suspension of the New Laws and perpetuity of encomiendas. Many of these petitions, letters, and memorials have been printed and are familiar to students of this subject.

The separate opinion of the special groups convoked by the Emperor to reconsider the New Laws have not been published, however, with one exception, but are preserved in the Archives of the Indies through the diligence of some clerk who made copies of them, probably for the use of Charles V.[50] Evidence presented directly to this group has also been preserved. A number of Spaniards fresh from Mexico gave their first-hand account of the parlous state of affairs there; one witness, Juan Díaz de Gibraleón, a merchant who had lived eight years in Mexico with his wife, had returned to Castile because of the New Laws and did not intend to risk his business further in the New World. He had himself seen more than one hundred married Spaniards likewise bring back their wives and property to Spain because, under the New Laws, conquistadores and others were not able to buy goods and business was at a standstill. Many other witnesses deposed that they had returned or would return unless the situation were remedied. One even stated that seven or eight hundred discontented persons had returned to Spain on the same ship as himself.

When the witnesses were asked how many Spaniards had Indians and how many did not, none of them knew. They were all voluble, however, in replying to the question whether Spaniards who held encomiendas helped those who did not. The encomenderos gave their less fortunate countrymen food and clothing, ran the reply, which presented a rather idyllic picture of all needy persons receiving aid until after the New Laws were announced, when the encomenderos were forced to turn out their guests.[51]

The special representatives, Villanueva and López, also made a summary statement on June 9, reminding the King that the opinions, petitions, letters, and other statements all clearly indicated that it would be to the manifest advantage of the Indians, the King, and God that Indians be given in perpetuity to Spaniards.[52] The various religious orders having already presented their formal opinions, these representatives felt it was not right that individual ecclesiastics be allowed to present their views. Doubtless they had in mind Las Casas and others who defended the liberty of the Indians, for they warned the King particularly to look well to the quality of every person wishing to be heard in these matters. They admitted that in the islands during the early years of the conquest some excesses had been committed and some Indians badly treated. But things were different in Mexico now, and those who emphasized the poor treatment given to Indians had forgotten the good that had been done for them in Mexico. The representatives concluded by pointing out that Spaniards, not Indians, supported the ecclesiastics, and that those who proposed to support conquistadores by paying them pensions instead of granting them encomiendas did not suggest where the necessary money was to be obtained.

A large body of material which the Visitor Sandoval collected from the ecclesiastics in Mexico was also abstracted and summarized for the King and Council of the Indies.[53] The formal opinions of the Augustinians, Dominicans, and Franciscans have been printed, but not so the individual statements by the friars, as recorded in the summary presented as a part of the evidence against the New Laws in Spain in June 1545. Various questions were asked the witnesses, but they all boiled down to this: Do you not think the New Laws dangerous to the Indians, the Spaniards, and the King, and will benefits not flow from perpetuity of the encomienda system?

The witnesses were men of quality and of long experience in the Indies. All replied as one man to the questions put to them. Yes, the New Laws were dangerous, and encomiendas should be granted in perpetuity. Friar Domingo de la Cruz, Dominican Provincial for nine years in Mexico, urged perpetuity so that the good work the friars had commenced would not be interrupted by the departure of the Spaniards. In his opinion the Indians would not work even if paid for it and even if the audiencia ordered it. He also foresaw an Indian rebellion, for the Indians no longer feared horses. The poor and less favored Spaniards, now supported by encomenderos, would have no place to go. The Dean of Oaxaca and Friar Hernando de Oviedo made similar depositions, the Dean emphasizing the danger of revolt by fickle Indians poorly grounded in the faith.

Dr. Cervantes, Treasurer of the Cathedral of Mexico and over nine years a resident there, felt that it would be better if Indians were slaves, for then they could not revolt. Indians had been told after the New Laws were passed that henceforth they would no longer be slaves even if they rebelled, and that they might now do what they liked—which scandalized him. Juan González, Canon of the Cathedral of Mexico and thirteen years a resident, made a similar deposition. If Indians rebelled they should be justly enslaved; otherwise the Spaniards would kill them and their souls would be lost.

Essentially the same opinions on the New Laws were given by Bishop Juan de Zumárraga, the Augustinian Provincial Juan de San Román, the Dean of Mexico, the Commissary General of the Franciscans, and a number of other ecclesiastical dignitaries. Bishop Juan de Zárate, Friar Domingo de Betanzos, and Friar Andrés de Moguer replied at great length, practically composing treatises on the subject. One and all strongly urged the revocation of the New Laws.

The royal advisers, therefore, had a quantity of reports and information as they sat down to consider the revocation, and practically all of it was against the New Laws. The individual opinions of these advisers shows with what care they studied the difficult question before them.

The Duke of Alva, having seen the reports and interviewed ecclesiastics from Mexico, and having heard details on the revolt in Peru, advised the King to suspend the New Laws and "wholly content the Spaniards by promising perpetuity," but this perpetuity should be given without jurisdiction, "so that the Spaniards there should always need some favor from the king of Spain." He opposed pensions for conquistadores. The Indians should be definitely subjected to

Spaniards but treated well and not made to give personal service.[54]

The Cardinal-Archbishop of Toledo opposed granting encomiendas because of their destruction of the Indians, but agreed that some gratification should be given the conquistadores. The New Laws should not, therefore, be revoked, but their execution should be stayed until the colonists and conquistadores were given assurance that they would be rewarded according to their merits and services.[55]

Licenciado Salmerón, newly appointed member of the Council of the Indies, held that the New Laws were neither just nor practicable, but considered that only the most important Spaniards should be given Indians in perpetuity. The others should be granted them for a period of two lives only, so that the hope of further rewards from the king would ensure competent management. When Mexico was well populated, the need for making these grants, which he called *juros*, would probably cease. Salmerón worked out in great detail the conditions under which these juros should be granted to Spaniards who would be called *jurados* and would swear fealty to the king; they would bear arms and be ready to serve on horseback in putting down revolts; one or more would be stationed in each town at the time the Indians paid tribute—and in other ways they would serve their king.[56]

Dr. Juan Bernal, Licenciado Gutierre Velázquez, and Licenciado Gregorio López, all members of the Council, presented a joint opinion favoring permanent pensions for conquistadores and their dependents and moderate pensions for two lives for other Spaniards according to their merit. Conquistadores should have no direct authority over the Indians and should not even collect tribute, but should be paid their pensions by royal officials after the ecclesiastics had been provided for. If the conquistadores died without legitimate heirs, the juros would be returned to the crown. Each pension would be granted by means of a special letter from the king embodying these various conditions, among which was the interesting provision that the conquistadores were to hold no pensions, rents, or other property in Spain, "so that they will identify themselves with the land." Special officers should be sent to the Indies to determine how large these pensions should be and to make certain that the tributes levied on the Indians were moderate and just. These three councilors still appeared to support the principle underlying the New Laws.[57]

Dr. Guevara recommended that information be requested at once on the qualities and merits of the encomenderos, on the length of time they had held Indians, and on their treatment of them, and whether their Indians paid more tribute than those under the crown. Meanwhile, the New Laws should not be enforced.[58]

The Count of Osorno favored perpetuity with only civil jurisdiction and also wanted information on the number of Spaniards possessing Indians. He also proposed a rather complicated plan by which the encomenderos would receive a steadily decreasing proportion of the tribute, so that the crown would ultimately receive two thirds of the tributes and administer most of the encomiendas.[59]

The Comendador Mayor of Castile modestly stated that he had had little experience in Indian affairs. He noted that four of the five members of the Council of the Indies opposed giving Indians in perpetuity, and of these four, two had been in the Indies. On the other hand, witness the great trouble stirred up overseas by the New Laws. So, without venturing to give specific advice, he advised the King to take prompt action to content the conquistadores so that Spain would not have to conquer the Indies twice—once from Indians and again from Spaniards.[60]

The President of the Royal Chancellery of Valladolid, Bishop Sebastián Ramírez de Fuenleal, adhered to his original opinion that the New Laws were just. The trouble had been caused, he believed, by individuals and did not arise from injustice or damage from the laws. He recommended that the heir of a conquistador receive two thirds of his tribute as an entailed estate. If other colonists should merit similar treatment, let them have it.[61]

The Comendador of León advised suspension of the laws and that encomiendas be given in perpetuity to the most worthy Spaniards, whether or not they were conquistadores. He opposed requiring personal service from the Indians and urged that only just tribute be collected from them.

The Cardinal of Seville, García de Loaysa, who had also served as president of the Council of the Indies for twenty-one years, adopted a sort of "I told you so" tone, referred to his unsuccessful efforts in 1542 to dissuade the King from passing such dangerous laws, and harked back to previous discussions of the Council on the same problem in 1527 and 1535. He still strongly supported encomiendas granted in perpetuity, which he believed would ensure conversion of the natives, increase of royal revenue, and peace for the Indies.[62]

All these opinions and deliberations of the royal advisers were faithfully reported by Prince Philip to Emperor Charles V, who was absent in Germany on imperial affairs.[63] The representatives from Mexico went there, too, to press their case in person. Likewise an Augustinian friar, possibly the Provincial from Mexico, Juan de San Román, paid a personal visit to Charles which is supposed to have been instrumental in turning the tide.[64] According to another interpretation, Charles V was offered twenty-one million *pesos de oro* for the revocation of one of the New Laws, and similar amounts for others, presumably by the representatives from Mexico.[65] At any rate, on October 20, 1545, at Malines, Charles did revoke Law No. 35, which was the heart of the matter: it prohibited the granting of encomiendas and required all encomiendas to revert to the crown at the death of the encomendero.[66] By this single stroke, Charles V reversed the policy he had so strongly approved less than three years before. The encomenderos won a complete victory on this vital issue, and a royal decree was also promulgated specifically reëstablishing the right of succession of their wives and children. The law requiring all suits concerning Indians to be heard by the King in person was likewise revoked, although this revocation was itself soon revised to provide that encomienda cases should go to Spain for adjudication, with the audiencias merely transmitting testimony.

But this was not all. The provincials of the three orders and one of the representatives from Mexico kept after Charles, and succeeded in persuading him to revoke, in February 1546, the law which removed Indians from encomenderos who had treated their charges badly and from persons involved in the Pizarro-Almagro fight in Peru.[67] The New Laws relating to the encomiendas were crumbling fast, although certain provisions, such as the removal of encomiendas held by prelates, governors, and other royal officials, were carried out and the laws relating to them never repealed. The decision of the crown to continue the encomienda, however, meant that the reform group had been beaten on their most important proposal.

The aggressive delegation from Mexico was not satisfied even with this, for they desired above all to secure perpetuity for encomiendas, and continued to bombard Charles with "reasons which were just." He was now moved to act. In a most equivocal royal order of April 1546, at Ratisbon, Viceroy Antonio de Mendoza of Mexico was informed of the pressure being exerted on behalf of the encomenderos, instructed to make a careful census of the needs and merits of all conquistadores, and empowered to grant Indians, without civil or criminal jurisdiction over them, as he "saw convenient, neither more nor less than I would do if I were there, giving to every person what is proper so that all are remunerated, contented, and satisfied." [68] Any viceroy who could have accomplished this feat in a land seething with as much discontent as Mexico would indeed have been a worthy representative of Charles V in any part of his empire!

The moment had now arrived for the City Council of Mexico to strew roses in their turn. On December 16, 1546, the members discussed the triumph which had made possible the continuance of the encomienda system, and voted to set aside the second day of the Christmas holiday for a general rejoicing throughout the land. A bull fight was arranged to take place in the lesser plaza of Mexico City, also dances in the ancient knightly style, and the major-domo of the town was authorized to buy the necessary vestments for one hundred knights, to have these lordly raiments dyed in sets of orange and white and blue and white, and to procure trumpets for the *fiesta,* "all at the expense of the town treasury." [69]

Concluding Reflections on the New Laws

As is true for many of the great crises in history, no dogmatic conclusion should be drawn with respect to the passage and modification of the New Laws of 1542. The necessary documents are not all available, and although the sources that do exist are copious in quantity they are generally ex parte statements produced by two of the best organized and most effective pressure groups that ever conducted lobbies at the Spanish court. Neither Las Casas nor his opponents had much to learn from modern artists in this field. Certain aspects of the struggle which culminated in the revocation of the laws which looked toward the eventual abolition of the encomienda system are, however, worthy of remark.

The unanimity of the religious orders in Mexico and of the majority of individual friars against the New Laws is impressive. Las Casas, of course, never altered his opinion in the least and even sent a hot blast from Mexico to the King in 1545 in which he recommended that those who urged the revocation of the laws be drawn and quartered.[70] But the King could hardly have ignored the clamor for revocation raised by so many royal officials, conquistadores, and ecclesiastical dignitaries. The church by now had an economic stake in the encomienda system, and its continuance was almost as vital to friars as to conquistadores.[71] The Dominicans of Nicaragua frankly confessed to the audiencia that they felt they simply could not live without Indians and must leave the land if their Indians were taken away by the New Laws.[72]

To this consideration must be added the effect of the revolt in Peru and the threat of disorders in Mexico. The organized, persistent, and aggressive labors of the lay and ecclesiastical representatives from Mexico must also be recognized as an important element in the complex of forces which combined to force a revision. The work of these representatives was made much easier and more fruitful by the absence of Las Casas from the court. It is even possible that this absence was a purposeful exile, engineered by those who feared his presence in the Council chambers in Spain, though no evidence exists to prove it.

Besides reflecting these pressures of interests and personalities, the debate over the New Laws and their revocation reveals another important aspect of the problem—the struggle between the feudalists and the regalists—which may have been the determining factor in the royal decision. The feudalists favored the encomienda system because it maintained society as organized in the Old World. There was a fighting class, a praying class, and below them the mass of laborers to do the work. The Mexican historian Zavala points out that the Dominican Domingo de Betanzos represented well the feudal viewpoint when he maintained in 1541 that if the Indians were placed directly under the lordship of the king, instead of being given in encomiendas to the Spaniards, all the colonists of the Indies would be on the same level and all equal in their poverty, which he considered directly contrary to the concept of a well-ordered commonwealth.[73]

During the debate over the New Laws this feudal concept was directly challenged by those who feared that the granting of encomiendas in perpetuity with civil or criminal jurisdiction would seriously diminish thereby the king's power in the New World. This regalist attitude was taken by several of the advisers whose manuscript opinions have been described. Unless the king retained full jurisdiction and was able to grant encomiendas as acts of royal grace or as rewards for meritorious service to the crown, these advisers foresaw that the New World would become a group of loosely organized feudal principalities and not an empire under the rule of the king of Spain.

Another group of Spaniards favoring the regalist viewpoint, though without much opportunity to press their views politically, were those without Indians, the "little men" of the New World, who never were important enough to receive Indians, yet who were not content to sink back into the old feudal system in which they were merely hewers of wood and drawers of water. They wanted to enjoy revenues from the Indians, too.

An interesting chapter in the social history of Spanish America remains to be written on this group of Spaniards without encomiendas. Such emphasis has been placed on the thirst of conquistadores for gold that the wealth of the Indies always has been popularly supposed to be greater than it really was. The exaggeration has obscured the fact that a poor element always existed in the New World. The crown recognized this problem as early as July 30, 1512, when a royal order to Diego Columbus authorized the appointment of Bachelor Bartolomé Ortiz as "Representative of the Poor in the Indies" and established as his salary the services of seventy Indians.[74]

Not all Spaniards, of course, could be granted Indians, even when the King approved the system. There simply were not enough Indians to go around. Naturally those left out when the plums were distributed became disgruntled and critical of this discrimination. Alonso García, for example, on February 1, 1545, complained to the King from Guatemala that the governors in those parts were most

unjust in their division of Indians.[75] García was evidently an old set-
tler who had been overlooked and resented it.

A sharp division seems to have existed between those who held encomiendas and those who did not. In Chile the "have-nots" were not
represented on the Town Council of Santiago until 1577, and even
then they won their battle only by carrying the matter to the Viceroy
in Lima.[76] The figures of the official chronicler López de Velasco reveal how few encomenderos there were and how stratified society in
the Indies had become by about 1573. According to this census, only
four thousand of the hundred and sixty thousand Spaniards in the
Indies were encomenderos. Of the two thousand Spanish families
living then in Lima, only thirty held encomiendas.[77]

The controversy over the New Laws shows that even in 1542
this stratification of society had proceeded far enough so that it was
recognized as an important problem to be taken into account and
attacked. The group of Spaniards without encomiendas did not, however, generate much political pressure, and probably had little to
do with the King's decisions. The final decision to ratify the existing system of encomiendas was reached as a compromise among the
humanitarian, the feudalist, and the regalist points of view.

The laws against cruelty to the Indians never were revoked, and
the laws abolishing personal service were reaffirmed several times in
the first few years after 1545.[78] The desire to placate the conquistadores, to reassure the ecclesiastics, and at the same time to maintain
for the King his preëminence by retaining the hope of royal patron-
age, doubtless was largely responsible for the revocation of the laws
that were withdrawn. The wisdom of this decision, from the stand-
point of the crown, became clear in the subsequent development of
the encomienda struggle, which had a long and troubled history.
Tense situations developed in America, but few revolts of consequence, and the King maintained his position as an all-powerful
monarch to whom the various factions fighting for favor presented
their problems for resolution.

Would the New Laws have really benefited the Indians as much
as Las Casas believed, if the crown had stood firm against all the pressures to change them? Would the Indians, if taken away from individual Spaniards, have been better treated under the administration of
royal officials? The change would have been merely a change of masters, says Robert Levillier, the Argentine historian.[79] Of course, no
one knows the true answer to this question. We do know that the
New Laws provoked the greatest battle of the century, indeed of
the whole colonial period, on Indian problems, and that important
ecclesiastical and lay figures felt that the enforcement of the laws
would mean the ruin of the New World. It is also certain that the final

decision of the crown to reverse itself and to permit the encomienda to continue not only terminated the fourth and last experiment carried on by Spaniards during the first half-century of the conquest of America—it also terminated the period of experimentation in Indian affairs. No further attempt was made to change radically the basic laws and basic institutions that had been established in these fateful fifty years, although one final and tremendous effort was made to halt the conquest itself, which will be described in the following chapter.

Part III

The Development of the
Struggle for Justice
1550–1600

INTRODUCTION

THE struggle for justice did not end with the failure of the four experiments just described, which were all carried out in the first half of the sixteenth century. The battle continued throughout the last fifty years of this vital exuberant period in Spanish history, and although Las Casas died in 1566, the ideas he stood for lived on to harass and infuriate his countrymen. The third and last part of this book is devoted, therefore, to the story of the struggle as it developed from 1550 to 1600.

The greatest single event in the history of just war in America, the celebrated Valladolid dispute of 1550 and 1551, is the subject of the first chapter. Friar Antonio de Montesinos had demanded in 1511 that the colonists of Hispaniola tell by what justice they waged war against the defenseless Indians, and the question had never been answered to the satisfaction of the reform group. Now the venerable Las Casas, ripe with theological study and experience of almost half a century in America, waged scholastic combat at the Spanish court against Juan Ginés de Sepúlveda, humanist and royal historiographer, in an attempt to prohibit such wars.

Las Casas and his supporters had failed to have the encomienda system suppressed, as we have seen in the last chapter. The next logical step, from their viewpoint, was to have all further wars and conquests stopped, so that the evil of Indian slavery could grow no larger. This was the real issue at Valladolid, though sometimes it has been beclouded by the very weight of theological authorities used and by the complexity of the hairsplitting arguments. The disputation was inconclusive, and the conquests were not stopped. But the effort to have war waged justly, if it must be waged at all, went on unrelentingly for the rest of the century and the battle spread even to the newly opened-up Philippine Islands.

At the same time the allied question of the basis for the just title of Spain to the New World was also involved and discussions about it continued to give Spaniards difficulty. It will be remembered that King Ferdinand had been sufficiently moved by the sermons of Montesinos to order half a dozen theologians and jurists to prepare replies for his benefit.

Since that time hardly a year had passed without someone in Spain or the Indies composing a treatise on some aspect of the struggle for justice.[1] Friar Francisco de Vitoria, whose four-hundredth anniversary was recently celebrated, and Las Casas both left imperishable writings on the subject. It became a favorite topic for discussion in the halls of the University of Salamanca and wherever justice-loving men gathered in Spain. We must realize however that the battles on the legitimacy of Spain's rule did not always take place in university circles or hushed council chambers. The struggle also took place in America and directly influenced events there. The final chapter, therefore, tells the story of the dispute as it developed in Peru during the rule of Viceroy Francisco de Toledo.

Chapter VIII

"ALL THE PEOPLES OF THE WORLD ARE MEN"

Development of Regulations for Conquistadores to 1550 [1]

The immediate result in America of the question on just war asked by Montesinos was the formulation of the Requirement in 1513. For about a decade this document seems to have been used fairly regularly, though no one seems to have been entirely satisfied. To establish a better policy, the crown placed the question before the newly organized Council of the Indies. The Dominican Cardinal Loaysa, President of the Council, was moved by the clamor of those who thought the conquest was not proceeding according to Christian principles to order a special session of that body in 1526, over which Emperor Charles V himself presided as it met in the Alhambra.

The arguments used before by Enciso when the Requirement was under discussion triumphed again. For the "Ordinances on discoveries and good treatment of the Indians" which were speedily promulgated on November 17, 1526, ordered that when captains of the King discovered or conquered a territory they were to proclaim immediately to its "Indians or inhabitants that they have been sent to teach them good customs, to dissuade them from vices such as the practice of eating human flesh, and to instruct them in the holy faith and preach it to them for their salvation." [2] The King explained that this order was necessary because of the many abuses committed against the Indians. The long list of specific wrongs cited covers several pages of small print and shows that the spirit of Las Casas was at work even though he was cloistered at the time in a monastery thousands of miles away.

This 1526 decree further ordered that every leader of an expedition officially licensed to make discoveries in the Indies must take along a copy of the Requirement and have it read by interpreters "as many times as might be necessary." Furthermore, every expedition must carry at least two ecclesiastics approved by the Council of the Indies as a regular part of their company. These ecclesiastics were to instruct the Indians in religious matters, to protect the natives "from the rapacity and cruelty of the Spaniards," and in general to ensure that the conquest was carried out justly. The contract of any conquistador who waged a war unjust in the opinion of the ecclesiastics attached to his expedition was to be revoked. War was to be waged only after the ecclesiastics had given their consent in writing. This sanction could only be given when the war was to be waged according to the method permitted by "the law, our Holy Faith and Christian religion."

The royal ordinance which put this policy into effect remained as standard for a generation and was never officially superseded by any other general law until Philip II issued his 1573 ordinance. The enactment of the 1526 law was fortunate indeed for historians, for the ecclesiastics were intelligent observers and left valuable records of their adventures as they accompanied Spanish expeditions to the New World. Whether the occasion was the discovery of the Amazon, a perilous descent into a smoking volcano of Central America, or the formal taking possession of some new island in the vastness of the Ocean Sea, a friar was usually on the spot to record for posterity a well-nigh priceless description of the occasion and his part in it.

The 1526 law remained on the statute books until superseded by the standard ordinance of 1573, but one important change was made at the time of the New Laws, when one of these famous ordinances took a further step away from the Requirement by stipulating that "Indians could not be enslaved by war or any other cause whatsoever."

This provision was never revoked as were some of the other New Laws. At least one conquistador, Juan Pérez de Cabrera, encountered such serious difficulties when the Audiencia of Guatemala insisted that he conduct his expedition in strict accord with the New Laws that he abandoned the conquest. By this time, however, the Requirement seems to have disappeared, and the subsequent development of regulations for the exploration and settlement of America reveals a steady retreat from the peremptory demands of the Requirement.

The "royal letter to the kings and republics of the mid-way and western lands" dated May 1, 1543, breathed a conciliatory spirit entirely alien to that of the Requirement. The papal history outlined in the Requirement was omitted and great stress was laid upon the spiritual duties of the kings of Spain resulting from their temporal overlordship. To fulfill these obligations, said the letter, the King was sending Bishop Juan de Zumárraga and other ecclesiastics to the midway and western lands. Perhaps because Las Casas and other Indian champions were then present at the Court of Spain, no mention was made of dire punishments to follow if the native kings did not receive the missionaries in the proper spirit. The whole message was couched in brotherly and friendly language, with the possibility of a refusal not even touched upon.

Likewise, President Pedro de la Gasca omitted the Requirement from his 1548 instructions to Captain Diego Centeno on conquests in the Río de la Plata region and those given June 18, 1549, to Captain Juan Núñez de Prado for the pacification of Tucumán. Ecclesiastics were to accompany both expeditions and were to be consulted on all important matters. The captains were particularly ordered to explain to the Indians that the Spaniards' chief aim was to teach them Christianity and good habits.

Although the letter to the "kings of the mid-way and western land" and the La Gasca instructions exhibited a wholly new spirit, Las Casas and other reformers were pressing for a wholesale revision of the standard 1526 law, which had permitted Indians to be declared rebels if they did not heed the Requirement. The practical significance of this was great, for, as late as 1550 the very year of the Valladolid disputation in Spain, conquistador Pedro de Valdivia on the far-off frontier of Chile reported to the King that he had cut off the hands and noses of two hundred Indian prisoners "because of their rebellion, when I had many times sent them messengers and given them Requirements as ordered by Your Majesty." [3]

The respectful attention given to the venerable Bishop of Chiapa by the Council of the Indies during the years 1549–51 is eloquent testimony to the power and prestige of his personality. Strengthened by the triumphant spiritual conquests in the Land of True Peace, whose story has already been told, Las Casas argued before the Council of the Indies that no more conquests ought to be authorized until a junta of theologians could determine whether such conquests were just and could devise a law for the guidance of future conquistadores which would better protect the Indians against ill treatment.

Prelude to Combat [4]

Las Casas was the more determined to force the issue to a conclusive decision because of the activities and increasing influence of Juan Ginés de Sepúlveda. The dispute really started in 1547, when Las Casas returned to Spain, after engaging in acrimonious discussions in Guatemala and Mexico on his treatise concerning *The Only Method of Attracting All Peoples to the True Faith.* He discovered that Sepúlveda, elegant and erudite humanist, had composed a treatise which sought to prove that wars against the Indians were just. The manuscript had been written under the high auspices of no less a personage than the President of the Council of the Indies, Cardinal

García de Loaysa of Seville, who had opposed the New Laws. When García de Loaysa learned that Sepúlveda had publicly announced his belief in the justice of the wars against the Indians, he encouraged Sepúlveda to write a book on the Indian problem, assuring him that "it would be a service to God and the king." Sepúlveda set to work at once and in a few days the resultant treatise, entitled *Democrates alter, sive de justis belli causis apud Indos,* was being circulated at court and, according to his own account, was approved by all who read it. Las Casas stated that the manuscript was rejected by the Council of the Indies, and therefore Sepúlveda prevailed upon friends at court to have the case transferred to the Council of Castile which, according to Las Casas, "was entirely ignorant of affairs of the Indies." It was at this moment that Las Casas arrived from Mexico, understood the gravity of the situation, and raised such an outcry that the Council of Castile referred the thorny matter to the universities of Alcalá and Salamanca where it was discussed during the spring and early summer of 1548. After "many and very critical disputes," states Las Casas, "the university authorities determined that the treatise should not be printed, for its doctrine was not sound."

It was a bold step for Las Casas to engage such a scholar as Sepúlveda in learned combat, for this humanist, who stepped forward to give comfort to Spanish officials and conquistadores by proclaiming the conquest just, supporting this view with many learned references, possessed one of the best-trained minds of his time and enjoyed great prestige at court.

His contributions to knowledge were recognized in Spain, and on the eve of the battle he had just completed and published his translation of Aristotle's *Politics,* which he considered his principal contribution to knowledge. Therefore when he began to compose the treatise which was to be "a service to God and the king," he was completely saturated with the theory of "The Philosopher," and particularly with the concept that certain men are slaves by nature.

Naturally the obdurate and effective opposition of Las Casas infuriated Sepúlveda, more accustomed to deference than contradiction, and he simply could not believe that his treatise *Democrates alter,* sponsored by such high authority, could be prevented from reaching the printer. He embarked upon a campaign of correspondence with various persons, including an acrimonious exchange with Friar Melchor Cano, but the universities remained adamant. Antonio Ramírez de Haro, Bishop of Segovia, also opposed his thesis. Then Sepúlveda wrote in refutation *Apologia pro libro de justis belli causis,* and sent it to Rome where it was printed in May 1550. Meanwhile he had also written, to win over the common people who did not read Latin, three apologias in Spanish, which he hoped to receive authorization

DR. JUAN GINÉS DE SEPÚLVEDA, PRINCIPAL OPPONENT
OF LAS CASAS IN THE DEBATE ON THE JUSTICE OF
THE WARS AGAINST THE AMERICAN INDIANS

to publish. Las Casas was on the alert, and also composed an apology in Spanish for the non-Latinists, to combat this attempt of his adversary to win a more popular audience in Spain.

While waiting for this permission, Sepúlveda reported to Prince Philip on his adversary in a letter dated September 23, 1549. "By falsehoods, by favors, and by machinations," the Bishop of Chiapa has managed to have his own way. Sepúlveda's books have been banned throughout Spain and the Indies. Any copies that have reached the New World are to be promptly confiscated. On the other hand Las Casas, "this quarrelsome and turbulent fellow," has written "a scandalous and diabolical confessionary" against Sepúlveda's treatise upholding the justice of the conquest. Although the Council has rebuked Las Casas, continues Sepúlveda, the gravity of the issue requires that the Emperor himself take cognizance of the dispute and support appropriate action. The whole case must be argued before the Council of Castile by the most learned theologians of the universities of Alcalá and Salamanca so that this troublesome question can be settled once and for all.

Conquests in the Indies Must Stop!

While Sepúlveda was pressing the authorities to approve his book pronouncing the wars against the Indians just, Las Casas was vehemently arguing that they were on the contrary scandalously unjust and that all conquests must stop if the royal conscience was to be kept unsullied. Moreover Las Casas had also worked up a defense against those who claimed that his theories denied the rights of Spain to the Indies, and presented his ideas in the form of thirty propositions in which he aimed to show his concept of the true title of Spain in the Indies, a subject which will be discussed in the next chapters. His attitude on the wars is clear. The Spanish sovereigns have from the beginning forbidden wars, conquests, and acts of cruelty. Hence, all the wars, invasions, and conquests that have been made, have been tyrannical, contrary to justice and authority. His formula is precisely what it always had been: Convert the Indians first by peaceful means and they will afterward become faithful Spanish subjects.

Las Casas now brought forward another breath-taking proposal which he had originally presented in 1543 to the Council of the Indies at the time of the New Laws agitation, a memorial which was recently discovered in a Bolivian monastery and printed. This was to make conquistadores up and down the Indies grind their teeth in rage and desperation, for he urged that the licenses of all expeditions then under way should be revoked and that no similar grants should be made in the future.

No action had been taken on this proposal, but the treatise written by Sepúlveda and combatted by Las Casas in the years 1548 and 1549 raised the issue again, and in an acute form. The first step was taken in a royal order of April 29, 1549, to the Audiencia of Peru on "The Manner in which New Discoveries are to be Undertaken." In this order great emphasis was placed upon the necessity of making the Indians understand the peaceful intentions of the Spaniards. Ecclesiastics were to explain that the Spaniards came only to seek the friendship of the Indians and their reduction to the service of God and the king, not to kill them or to seize their property. Spaniards were strictly enjoined from taking Indian women and were to pay for everything they took, even food, according to the prices set by the ecclesiastics—all this on pain of death and confiscation of their property. No force was to be used except in self-defense and that "moderately, according to the needs of the situation." Any infraction of any of these instructions was to be severely punished, "inasmuch as this matter is so important for the exoneration of the royal conscience and of the persons who undertake such conquests, as well as for the preservation and increase of these lands." This order, sent out under royal authority to Peru, might well have been drafted by Las Casas, and probably was.

A more drastic step was taken by the Council of the Indies on July 3, 1549, when it advised the King that the dangers both to the bodies of the Indians and to the King's conscience which the conquests incurred were so great that no new expeditions ought to be licensed without his express permission and that of the Council.[5] Moreover, concluded the Council, a meeting of theologians and jurists was needed to discuss "how conquests may be conducted justly and with security of conscience." This statement by the highest board in Spain on Indian affairs, which must surely become a milestone in the history of Spanish colonial theory, is worth quoting. The Council stated that, although laws had of course been issued previously to regulate the conquests,

we feel certain that these laws have not been obeyed, because those who conduct these conquests are not accompanied by persons who will restrain them and accuse them when they do evil.

The greed of those who undertake conquests and the timidity and humility of the Indians is such that we are not certain whether any instruction will be obeyed. It would be fitting for Your Majesty to order a meeting of learned men, theologians, and jurists with others according to your pleasure to discuss and consider concerning the manner in which these conquests should be carried on in order that they may be made justly and with security of conscience. An instruction for this purpose should be drawn up, taking into account all that may be necessary for this, and this instruction should be considered a law in the conquests approved by this Council as well as those approved by the Audiencias.

Friar Alonso de Maldonado also advised the King to hold a public enquiry and stated that he not only approved Las Casas' doctrine but had himself written a treatise "proving the injustice of the wars according to all law, natural and divine."

The King took the final step and ordered on April 16, 1550, that all conquests be suspended in the New World until a special group of theologians and counselors should decide upon a just method of conducting them.[6] On the same day another order was despatched which provided that before any conquest be licensed, the King was to be informed of the conditions proposed "in order that all may be done in a Christian fashion."

This stringent order was actually carrried out, at least in New Granada, the Chaco region, and Costa Rica. A close watch was kept to see that the order was obeyed, despite considerable pressure from colonists that new expeditions be permitted. Friars particularly were on the alert to make sure that violations of the law were called to the attention of the proper authorities.

Las Casas had won his point; the conquests were stopped. Both Sepúlveda and Las Casas agreed that there should be a meeting to decide whether or not the conquests were just, and this too was ordered by the King and Council of the Indies. Probably never before or since has a mighty emperor—and in 1550 Charles V was the strongest ruler in Europe with a great overseas empire besides—in the full tide of his power ordered his conquests to cease until it could be decided whether they were just.

The Two Sessions of the Judges, 1550–51

The King moved promptly in arranging for the disputation, for a "kind of civil war in the court" was being waged, some powerful figures siding with Sepúlveda and others with Las Casas. An official of the Council of Castile attempted to prevent the appointment of the Dominicans Domingo de Soto and Melchor Cano as judges—because of their previous declarations that war against the Indians was unjust—but was unsuccessful, as he was in his attempt to have Dr. Moscoso, who had approved *Democrates alter,* substituted. On July 7, 1550, the King ordered Cano and Soto as well as Friars Bartolomé de Miranda and Bernardino de Arévalo to meet at Valladolid in August to decide "upon the regulation which will be most convenient in order that the conquests, discoveries, and settlements may be made to accord with justice and reason." The other ten members of the congregation of fourteen were members of the Council of

Castile or of the Council of the Indies, and included such officials as Gregorio López, glossator of the well-known edition of the *Siete Partidas,* Gutierre Velázquez, Sandoval, Hernán Pérez de la Fuente, Ribadeneyra, and Briviesca. Unfortunately the great Dominican Francisco de Vitoria, in some respects the most able theologian of the century, had died in 1546. Had he lived, the Emperor would doubtless have named him a member of the group and another classic work from his pen might have been the result.

Interest in the struggle was sharpened by the personal rivalry between Sepúlveda and Las Casas, but the central issue was recognized as much larger and of national importance. It was simply: Was the current method of carrying on conquests in America just or unjust? As Domingo de Soto put the question in pointing out their duties to the members of the learned assembly:

The purpose for which Your Lordships are gathered together here . . . is, in general, to discuss and determine what form of government and what laws may best ensure the preaching and extension of our Holy Catholic Faith in the New World; . . . and to investigate what organization is needed to keep the peoples of the New World in obedience to the Emperor, without damage to his royal conscience, and in conformity with the Bull of Alexander.

The principal step Las Casas took to defend his position was to compose and present to Prince Philip a 550-page Latin treatise, which is his only major writing not yet published. This *Argumentum apologiae,* consisting of sixty-three chapters of close argument, was dedicated to demolishing the doctrine Sepúlveda had set forth in *Democrates alter.* Las Casas also seems to have worked out a summary, designed perhaps for those who might find it irksome to plow through his detailed argument with its multitudinous proofs.

The great debate began in the middle of August and continued until the middle of September 1550 before the "council of the fourteen" in Valladolid. On the first day of the session Sepúlveda spoke for three hours, giving a résumé of his book *Democrates alter.* On the second day Las Casas appeared, armed with his monumental treatise which he proceeded to read word for word seriatim, as he himself states. This scholastic onslaught continued for five days, until the reading was completed, or until the members of the junta could bear no more, as Sepúlveda suggested. The two opponents did not appear together before the council, but the judges seem to have discussed the issues with them separately as they stated their positions. The judges also carried on discussions among themselves.

It is no wonder that the bewildered judges requested Domingo de

Soto, an able jurist and theologian, to boil down the arguments and present to them a résumé for their more perfect comprehension of the theories involved. This he did in a masterly summary which was then submitted to Sepúlveda, who replied to each of the twelve objections raised by Las Casas. The members then scattered to their homes, taking with them copies of the summary. Before departing, the judges agreed to reconvene on January 20, 1551, for a final vote. The judges later considered that more time was required for a study of the important issue, the ecclesiastics became occupied with Lent, and the meeting had to be again postponed. Both Domingo de Soto and the Bishop of Ciudad Rodrigo, Pedro Ponce de León, a newly appointed member of the group, sought to avoid the meeting altogether and other theologians displayed a reluctance to appear. Finally, sharp official notes were sent to them reminding them that their presence was required and expected. Miranda, the Bishop of Ciudad Rodrigo, and Cano were excused because the Emperor sent them to the Council of Trent.

Most of the information available on this second session, which took place in Valladolid from about the middle of April to the middle of May, 1551, comes from the pen of Sepúlveda, who discovered, much to his disgust, that Las Casas had availed himself of the vacation period to prepare a rebuttal to Sepúlveda's reply to him. To this last blast Sepúlveda made no rejoinder "because he saw no necessity; indeed, the members of the junta had apparently never read any of the replies," but he appeared again before the junta and debated with the theologians the meaning of the bulls of Alexander VI. It was probably at this time that Sepúlveda composed his paper entitled *Against those who depreciate or contradict the bull and decree of Pope Alexander VI which gives the Catholic Kings and their successors authority to conquer the Indies and subject those barbarians, and by this means convert them to the Christian religion and submit them to their empire and jurisdiction.*

Sepúlveda stated that much of the discussion at this session revolved around the interpretation of the papal bulls of donation, that the Franciscan judge, Bernardino de Arévalo, strongly supported his case in the deliberations of the council, but that when Sepúlveda wished to appear again the other three theologians declined to discuss the issue again with him. At the end both Las Casas and Sepúlveda claimed victory.

The Argument

Unfortunately the records of the proceedings of this council have not been preserved. At least such an indefatigable investigator as

Friar Vicente Beltrán de Heredia has not been able to locate them after long and careful search. The arguments presented by the two opponents are therefore our chief sources for the dispute.

Sepúlveda, who appeared first before the judges, set forth his position by following very closely the argument previously developed in his *Democrates alter* in dialogue form. Leopoldo, "a German considerably tainted with Lutheran errors," takes the part of the man who believes the conquest unjust, while Sepúlveda speaks through Democrates who kindly but firmly demolishes Leopoldo's ideas and convinces him of the complete justice of wars against the Indians and the obligation of the king to wage them.

The fundamental idea put forward by Sepúlveda was a simple one and not original with him. Thomas Aquinas had laid down, centuries before that wars may be waged justly when their cause is just, and when the authority carrying on the war is legitimate and conducts the war in the right spirit and the correct manner. Sepúlveda applied this doctrine to the New World and declared it was lawful and necessary to wage war against the natives there for four reasons:

1. For the gravity of the sins which the Indians had committed, especially their idolatries and their sins against nature.

2. On account of the rudeness of their natures, which obliged them to serve persons having a more refined nature, such as the Spaniards.

3. In order to spread the faith which would be more readily accomplished by the prior subjugation of the natives.

4. To protect the weak among the natives themselves.

It will not be possible to reproduce here the authorities marshaled for and against Sepúlveda's four propositions. But one of the important points argued at great length before the fourteen long-suffering members of the junta as they sweltered through the September heat of Valladolid was the interpretation of the fourteenth chapter of St. Luke, wherein the Lord commanded his servant, "Go out into the highways and hedges, and compel them to come in, that my house may be filled." Sepúlveda maintained that this command justified war against the Indians in order to bring them into the Christian fold. Las Casas was obliged to tread warily when answering this argument for, if he maintained that force ought never to be used to advance the faith, how could certain past actions of various emperors and popes be justified to the Christian conscience? It is a notable tribute to his skill and to the prestige he enjoyed that never once in the long course of his career of controversy did he come within the grasp of the Holy Office of the Inquisition.

Las Casas stated that the words in St. Luke "compel them to come in" have two senses. If referring to the Gentiles, the passage does not mean external compulsion by means of war, but internal compulsion by the inspiration of God and by the ministry of his angels. To support this interpretation, Las Casas adduced the authority of St. John Chrysostom.

When the judges enquired of Las Casas how, in his opinion, the conquest should proceed, he replied that when no danger threatened, preachers alone should be sent. In particularly dangerous parts of the Indies, fortresses should be built on the borders and little by little the people would be won over to Christianity by peace, love, and good example. Here it is clear that Las Casas never forgot and never abandoned his plan for peaceful colonization that had been such a resounding failure in Tierra Firme.

To support his last reason—that war should be waged to protect the weak among the natives themselves—Sepúlveda described the cruelty practiced by the Indians, their cannibalism, and their use of human sacrifices in religious ceremonies. Las Casas replied to these charges with the same ammunition he had used when explaining that the Indians were "prudent and rational beings, of as good ability and judgment as other men and more able, discreet, and of better understanding than the people of many other nations." And Las Casas closed with the following blast which shows how intimately connected were the problems of just war and the just title of Spain to the Indies:

The Doctor [Sepúlveda] founds these rights upon our superiority in arms, and upon our having more bodily strength than the Indians. This is simply to place our kings in the position of tyrants. The right of those kings rests upon their extension of the Gospel in the new world, and their good government of the Indian nations. These duties they would be bound to fulfill even at their own expense; much more so considering the treasures they have received from the Indies. To deny this doctrine is to flatter and deceive our monarchs, and to put their salvation in peril. The doctor perverts the natural order of things, making the means the end, and what is accessory, the principal. . . . He who is ignorant of this, small is his knowledge, and he who denies it is no more of a Christian than Mahomet was. . . . To this end (to prevent the total perdition of the Indies) I direct all my efforts, not, as the doctor would make out, to shut the gates of justification and annul the sovereignty of the Kings of Castile; but I shut the gate upon false claims made on their behalf, and I open the gates to those claims of sovereignty which are founded upon law, which are solid, strong, truly Catholic and truly Christian.

Aristotle and the American Indians

The most important point discussed at Valladolid, certainly the most hotly disputed then and now, was the second justification propounded by Sepúlveda, the idea that the rudeness of the Indians' nature justified war against them, a concept that seems to come easily to most imperialistic nations, for they frequently invoke it. Sepúlveda declared that the Indians, being rude persons of limited understanding, ought to serve the Spaniards, and applied to the Indians Aristotle's theory that, since some beings are inferior by nature, it is only just and natural that prudent and wise men have dominion over them for their own welfare as well as for the service of their superiors. If the Indians failed to recognize this relationship and resisted the Spaniards, just war could be waged against them and their persons and property would pass to the conquerors.

This line of reasoning at once recalls to us the long and passionate history of the debate over the character of the Indians. It is no accident that the volume of manuscripts on the Valladolid dispute still resting in a Bolivian monastery includes a copy of the Jeronymite Interrogatory of 1517, which records the first official investigation into the nature of the Indians, as well as the formal deathbed repentance by Friar Domingo de Betanzos that he had ever said the Indians were beasts, a curious episode that took place in Valladolid a year before the disputation was held.

Sepúlveda had made clear in *Democrates alter* that he considered Spaniards had a perfect right to rule over the barbarians of the New World because of their superior prudence, genius, virtue, and humanity. These peoples "require, by their own nature and in their own interests, to be placed under the authority of civilized and virtuous princes or nations, so that they may learn from the might, wisdom and law of their conquerors, to practice better morals, worthier customs, and a more civilized way of life." The Indians are as inferior in these characteristics, he declared, as children are to adults, as women are to men. Indians are as different from Spaniards as cruel people are from mild people, as monkeys from men.

Compare then those blessings enjoyed by Spaniards of prudence, genius, magnanimity, temperance, humanity, and religion with those of the little men (*hombrecillos*) in whom you will scarcely find even vestiges of humanity, who not only possess no science but who also lack letters and preserve no monument of their history except certain vague and obscure reminiscences of some things on certain paintings. Neither do they have written laws, but barbaric institutions and customs. They do not even have private property.

Sepúlveda here manifested a strong nationalism, and was in fact the first great nationalistic writer in Spain, according to Rafael Altamira. For, boasted Sepúlveda, did not Lucan, Seneca, Isidore, Averroes, and Alfonso the Wise testify to the intelligence, greatness, and bravery of Spaniards, from the time of Numantia to Charles V? And did not the brave and resourceful Cortés, with a handful of Spaniards, subdue

Montezuma and his Indian hordes in their capital? The mere fact that these barbarians lived under some form of government by no means proved that they were equal to Spaniards. It simply showed that they were not monkeys and did not entirely lack reason. And, Sepúlveda concluded,

How can we doubt that these people—so uncivilized, so barbaric, contaminated with so many impieties and obscenities—have been justly conquered by such an excellent, pious, and most just king as was Ferdinand the Catholic and as is now Emperor Charles, and by such a most humane nation and excellent in every kind of virtue?

In his attempt to disprove Sepúlveda's contention that the Indians had no real capacity for political life, Las Casas brought into court his long experience in the New World and, as Domingo de Soto stated in his summary, described in large part the history of the Indies. In painting a rosy picture of Indian ability and past achievements, Las Casas drew heavily upon his own *Apologetic History,* a tremendous accumulation of material on Indian life and history which was the result of many years of labor. It probably was started as early as 1527 at the Dominican convent in Hispaniola during his early years as a friar, and finished some twenty years later just in time to use against Sepúlveda at the Valladolid dispute.

The history of human exaggeration shows few more interesting exhibits than the *Apologetic History* and such a curious and elaborately worked out conception deserves extended description, especially since it remains today one of the least known and least read of all his works. The book was designed to crush the contention that the Indians were semianimals, whose property and services could be commandeered by the Spaniards, and against whom war could be justly waged. This effort required some 870 folio pages with many marginal annotations, which perhaps explains why it is seldom read. Here he advanced the idea, which astonished the Spaniards of his day, that the American Indians compared very favorably with the peoples of ancient times, were eminently rational beings, and in fact fulfilled every one of Aristotle's requisites for the good life.[7]

Throughout this welter of fact and fantasy, Las Casas not only strives to show that the Indians fully meet Aristotle's conditions, but he also develops the idea that the Greeks and Romans were, in several respects, inferior to the American Indians. The Indians clearly are more religious, for instance, because they offer more and better sacrifices to their gods than did any of the ancient peoples. The Mexican Indians are superior to the ancient peoples in rearing and educating their children. Their marriage arrangements are reasonable and conform to natural law and the law of nations. Indian women are devout workers, even laboring with their hands if necessary to comply fully with divine law, a trait which many Christian matrons might well copy. Las Casas was not intimidated by the authority of the ancient world, and he maintained that the temples in Yucatan are not less worthy of admiration than the pyramids, thus anticipating the judgments of twentieth-century archaeologists. Las Casas concluded from a stupefying array of evidence that the Indians are no whit less rational than the Egyptians, Romans, or Greeks, and are not much inferior to Spaniards. Indeed, in some respects, they are even superior to Spaniards.

One wonders why Las Casas felt it necessary to construct this truly stupendous history on Aristotelian lines and to cite him so frequently in his writings. Was Aristotelian influence so great in Spain and at the court that such a feat was necessary to gain his point? At any rate it was fortunate for him that none of his political opponents pounced on the declaration he had made, when opposing the Aristotelian idea in 1519 before King Charles, that "Aristotle was a Gentile, and is now burning in Hell, and we are only to make use of his doctrine as far as it is consistent with our Holy Faith and Christian customs." And how fortunate for the judges, too, that Las Casas did not read the whole of the work, but presented them with a summary of his description of Indian character and achievements. To complicate the matter further, Las Casas declared flatly that Sepúlveda did not understand Aristotle; in fact, that he had absolutely misunderstood "The Philosopher" and his theory of slavery. As one studies the use made by both contestants of Aristotle's theory of slavery, the doubt arises whether either Las Casas or Sepúlveda had a firm grasp on the theory, even though each one was absolutely certain he understood it. Even today the theory has its obscurities and, as a modern interpreter declares, "it must be confessed that Aristotle in no place clearly indicates how a true slave may be known from a free man." [8] In the absence of any clear definition of a slave, both contestants interpreted Aristotle according to their own lights.[8a]

Perhaps it is appropriate here to point out that the Valladolid disputation has often been oversimplified as a clear-cut dispute between a Christian apostle and a Renaissance humanist of Aristotelian persuasion. On the other hand, one contemporary writer, Edmundo O'Gorman, finds a paradox in the Valladolid confrontation of the two antagonists and has announced that to his mind "all of Las Casas' thought is fundamentally Aristotelian, while Sepúlveda is just as much of a Christian as Las Casas." [9]

It is true that Las Casas in his argument appears to accept the theory of Aristotle that some men are by nature slaves. But the important point to be stressed is that he asserts vigorously that the Indians of the New World do not fall into this category—nor indeed does any nation of mankind, except as individuals. Las Casas does not contest the Aristotelian theory of natural slavery but believes that these slaves are few in number and must be considered as mistakes of nature, like men born with six toes or with only one eye. Such cases occur very infrequently, for the Creator would never have brought into being such monstrosities, "against the natural inclination of all the peoples of the world." From this basic concept Las Casas draws the following conclusion which is certainly Christian rather than Aristotelian and which has no counterpart in Sepúlveda's argument:

All the peoples of the world are men . . . all have understanding and volition, all have the five exterior senses and the four interior senses, and are moved by the objects of these, all take satisfaction in goodness and feel pleasure with happy and delicious things, all regret and abhor evil.

Las Casas has faith in the capacity for civilization of all peoples; he does not believe in a static and hopeless barbarism, but in social mobility:

No nation exists today, nor could exist, no matter how barbarous, fierce, or depraved its customs may be, which may not be attracted and converted to all political virtues and to all the humanity of domestic, political, and rational man.

To bring this about Las Casas would not enslave the Indians but would treat them as free human beings who would accept the faith if it were preached to them peacefully and not by warlike methods—an idea which harks back to 1537, the year Las Casas wrote *The Only Method of Attracting All People to the True Faith.*

Sepúlveda certainly did not share this view. He did recognize, as O'Gorman emphasizes, the possibility of eternal salvation for all men through Christianity. But the way for the Indians to become Christian is by slavery to the superior Spaniards who will thus communicate to them the true religion.

It is true that Las Casas did not at Valladolid attempt to defend the character of all peoples in the world, nor did he work there for any liberty except Indian liberty, but all through his writings he fought the idea that slavery was good for the men he saw in the New World, whether Indians or Negroes. He once, early in his career, advised that Negroes born as slaves in Spain should be brought to work in America to spare the Indians, but soon after declared that, since learning that the Portuguese had captured and enslaved them unjustly, he now believed "that it is as unjust to enslave Negroes as it is to enslave Indians, and for the same reasons." [10] But he was so intent on saving the Indians that his arguments at Valladolid and elsewhere rarely rose to the level of general theories but were usually contentions relating to justice for the Indians.

There is some truth, however, to the statement by Otto Waltz that Las Casas anticipated Rousseau by centuries in his emphasis upon equality and brotherhood of all mankind. Did Las Casas not cry that "all men, infidels and Christians alike, are rational beings," and "all men may become Christians, a religion which is adapted to all the nations of the world"? [11] This universal approach may be seen most clearly in the chapter of the *Apologetic History* entitled "How All Nations May Be Brought to a Good Way of Life," in which Las Casas roundly declared:

Thus we clearly see, by examples ancient and modern, that no nation exists, no matter how rude, uncultivated, barbarous, gross, or almost brutal its people may be, which may not be persuaded and brought to a good order and way of life and made domestic, mild, and tractable, provided the method that is proper and natural to men is used; that is, love and gentleness and kindness.[12]

The question raised at Valladolid was not merely the applicability of the Aristotelian doctrine to the Indians, but also by implication the validity of the doctrine itself. The first frontal attack on the doctrine by a sixteenth-century thinker, however, seems to have been made by Jean Bodin a few years after Las Casas died.

Sepúlveda, on the other hand, emphasized the fact that the tutelage of the inferior Indians by the superior Spaniards would result in their Christianization eventually. Here he was applying, in a Christian world, the Aristotelian doctrine that the superior governors should rule in the interest of the Indians. Otherwise the Spanish rule would be tyrannical. Thus Sepúlveda was neither a suave pagan supporting vicious doctrines, as some nineteenth-century writers claimed, nor a sixteenth-century Nietzsche, as a more recent writer states. Neither do we need to accept the dictum of a frankly enthusiastic biographer that Sepúlveda's theory of slavery reveals "the balanced sanity of a great mind," and, of course, he was not alone among his contemporaries in his support of Aristotle's doctrine of slavery. He represents that curious and not wholly amalgamated mixture of Aristotelianism and Christianity that is observed in the thought of many a Renaissance figure.

This much, however, is true. At a time when the conquistadores were bringing to the notice of the civilized world a whole new continent peopled with strange races, he chose to regard all these new peoples as an inferior type of humanity which should be submitted to the rule of the Spaniards. Without having seen them or observed their lands and civilization, he felt no hesitation in condemning them all as not quite men, above monkeys to be sure, but unworthy of being considered in the same class with the Spaniards.

The solemnity with which Aristotle's doctrine of slavery and its application to the complicated situation of the New World were debated at Valladolid is all the more remarkable in view of the diversity of races and cultures in America. Aristotle believed that the state ought to consist of a single race, for a single race is united in its customs and habits which makes for friendship between citizens by reason of their likeness one to another. Spanish America has never had such unity. As the liberator Simón Bolívar pointed out at the Congress of Angostura in 1819:

It is impossible to say to which human family we belong. The larger part of the native population has disappeared, Europeans have mixed with the Indians and the Negroes, and Negroes have mixed with Indians. We were all born of one mother America, though our fathers had different origins, and we all have differently colored skins. This dissimilarity is of the greatest significance.[13]

Las Casas' concern to prove the Indians superior beings even according to Aristotle's theories might be explained by his realization that "The Philosopher's" influence was too strong to be opposed with safety. And Sepúlveda may have inserted the phrases concerning the Christianization of the Indians because he saw that this would be necessary to get approval for his general thesis. Neither adversary was as frank and realistic as the scholar Fernando Vázquez de Menchaca, who was probably writing his treatise *Illustrious Controversies* in Valladolid at the very time that the justice of wars in the New World was being debated there. In the introduction to this work he struck a blow at Aristotle's theory of slavery by stating that "men try to cover their wars with a cloak of justice," and explained that the purpose of his treatise was to combat such efforts by studying the most fundamental controversies and perhaps remedy this "relaxation of the human spirit, which is almost always caused by the influence and work of those who wish to please powerful and illustrious princes." [14]

Later on, Vázquez de Menchaca is even more explicit, for he says that, although he has not had an opportunity to study the doctrine of those who believe that Indians who are not disposed to serve the king of Spain may be justly subjugated, the truth seems apparent to him.

The doctrine of these authors is an unadulterated tyranny introduced under the appearance of friendship and wise counsel, for the certain extermination and tyranny of the human race. Because in order to practice with greater liberty their tyranny, the sacking of cities, and violence, they exert themselves to justify this tyranny with fictitious names, describing it as a doctrine beneficial to those who suffer the vexations, whereas in reality never has there been heard or seen a thing farther from the truth and more worthy of scorn and derision.[15]

Las Casas took the easier way. He accepted but never attempted to defend or extend Aristotle's doctrine although he definitely worked within its framework. He lauded the virtues of all the Indians as though they were a single nation, and thus laid himself open to grave charges, since the Indian nations were in fact so diverse, being besides on different levels of civilization. As Roberto Levillier has pointedly asked: Which Indians of which regions were these theologians talking about?

Indians were the Tekestas and Tahinos of Duba, mild and hospitable; Indians, the cannibalistic Caribs; Indians, the primitive Otomí, who lived in caves; Indians, the savage Jívaros; Indians, the Uros, more fish than man, who lived in the waters of Lake Titicaca; Indians, the artistic Maya stone cutters and the Chibcha jewelry craftsmen and the wise Inca legislators and the delicate Yunga ceramic workers; and the Colla weavers; Indians, the heroic Aztecs, the cannibalistic Chiriguanaes, and the untamed Diaguitas and Araucanians; Indians, the timid Juri, the nomadic Iule, the sedentary Comechingon, the fierce Guaraní. Their intelligence, cruelty, and meekness varied as did the color of their skins, their languages, their rites, their theogonies, and the true owners were confused with those who subjected them to obedience. Neither in their juridical position, in their physical aspect, in their language, in their tastes, in their morality, nor in their creative capacities were they alike.[16]

Neither Las Casas nor Sepúlveda provided an answer to this question which seems to Levillier and the rest of us today so reasonable. Sepúlveda believed that as the Indians became better acquainted with Christianity and European habits, they should be granted greater freedom. But even conversion, he maintained, did not necessarily make an Indian the equal of a Spaniard or entitle him to political independence.[17] He could be quoted therefore in support of the perpetual encomienda, which was being pressed hotly on the crown at that time by the conquistadores through their representatives in Spain. In effect, Sepúlveda seems to have advocated a permanent mandate for Spain over the peoples of the New World.

Conclusion

The judges, exhausted and confused by the sight and sound of this mighty conflict, fell into argument with one another and came to no definite decision. Las Casas stated that "the decision was favorable to the opinions of the Bishop, although unfortunately for the Indians the measures decreed by the council were not well executed," and

Sepúlveda wrote to a friend that the judges "thought it right and lawful that the barbarians of the New World should be brought under the dominion of the Christians, only one theologian dissenting." The dissident was doubtless Domingo de Soto.

The facts now available do not support either contestant. The judges apparently scattered after the final meeting, and for years afterward the Council of the Indies struggled to get them to give their opinions in writing. As late as 1557, a note was sent to Friar Melchor Cano explaining that all the other judges had submitted their decisions and that his was wanted at once. These written opinions have never come to light, with the exception of Dr. Anaya's statement which approved the conquest in order to spread the faith and to stop the Indians' sins against nature, with the stipulation that the expeditions be financed by the king and led by captains "zealous in the service of God and the king who would act as a good example to the Indians, and who would go for the good of the Indians and not for gold." The captains were to see that the usual peaceful exhortations and "requirements" were made before force was used. No other opinions have been found and apparently the judges never rendered a collective decision.

What then was the real result and the real meaning of the great dispute at Valladolid? One not unsurprising result was that Sepúlveda became the hero of the conquistadores and other Spaniards who wished to wage war against the Indians. The Town Council of Mexico City, the richest and most important city in all the Indies, gratefully recognized what he had done on their behalf and as a token of their appreciation and "to encourage him in the future," voted on February 8, 1554, to present him with "some jewels and clothing from this land to the value of two hundred pesos." It is not known whether these gifts reached Sepúlveda, but it is significant that Spaniards across the seas recognized the importance of the issue sufficiently to be willing to reward the skill Sepúlveda had shown in defending their case. And he was so universally considered the outstanding leader of this point of view that the contemporary historian Francisco López de Gómara did not trouble to justify the conquest at all but recommended that his readers consult "Sepúlveda, the Emperor's Chronicler, who wrote most elegantly in Latin on this topic, and thus you will be completely satisfied on this matter."

Sepúlveda's doctrine, however, did not triumph. His books and various apologies were never allowed to be published in Spain in his lifetime; indeed not until the end of the eighteenth century did his *Opera* appear, and the book that was the immediate cause of the Valladolid dispute did not reach print until 1892. Moreover, his earlier books were suppressed and orders sent to the Indies that they be collected to prevent circulation. On the contrary Las Casas was able to publish at Seville in 1552, the year after the dispute ended, a whole galaxy of provocative treatises, including the *Confesionario* and the one giving his side of the controversy with Sepúlveda, and the notorious *Very Brief Account of the Destruction of the Indies*. Sepúlveda hastened to reply with a hot blast entitled *Rash, Scandalous, and Heretical Propositions Which Dr. Sepúlveda Noted in the Book on the Conquest of the Indies Which Friar Bartolomé de Las Casas Printed without a License*. But to no avail. These treatises were not suppressed. Las Casas continued to write and talk as he pleased as long as he lived, and even after his death in 1566 his books circulated everywhere, to the consternation and fury of conquistadores.

It may be worth pointing out that Sepúlveda never mentioned at Valladolid the name of Francisco de Vitoria, nor did he ever feel it necessary to reply to any of the important doctrines developed by that celebrated Dominican in his lectures at the University of Salamanca. And Las Casas referred to "el doctíssimo Maestro Vitoria" only once during the whole dispute. It is also curious that this dispute appeared to have no echo in the sessions of the Spanish Cortes of 1551 which met in Valladolid, although in previous years the affairs of the New World had often been discussed in the Cortes.

Did the dispute have any positive effect? Perhaps it would be prudent to begin the summing up by insisting that even now not all the facts are known. Certainly the conquests were not stopped, for at least by 1566 the King was again sending out orders permitting his viceroys in America to issue licenses for new discoveries, although strictly charging them to see that all necessary law and instructions be given to the leaders. Nor was the problem of just war in the Indies resolved, for Las Casas continued to present memorials to the King and Council of the Indies on the subject, and even tried to get the Pope to excommunicate and anathematize anyone who declared war against infidels just. It is doubtless true that the conquest of the Philippines from 1570 onward was carried on by relatively peaceful means because the Sepúlveda party had not triumphed,[18] and probably the standard law of 1573 on new discoveries was drawn up in such generous terms because of the battle of Las Casas fought at Valladolid. All regulations made for conquistadores since the Requirement was approved in 1513 were superseded by a general ordinance promulgated by Philip II on July 13, 1573, which was designed to regulate all future discoveries and pacifications by land or by sea. A detailed study of the provisions of this ordinance indicates how far the King had departed from the Requirement policy. The Spaniards were to explain the obligation resting upon the crown of Spain and the wonderful advantages bestowed upon those natives who had already submitted—a sort of justification by works. The Spaniards were charged, furthermore, with emphasizing particularly,

that the king has sent ecclesiastics who have taught the Indians the Christian doctrine and faith by which they could be saved. Moreover, the king has established justice in such a way that no one may aggravate another. The king has maintained the peace so that there are no killings or sacrifices, as was the custom in some parts. He has made it possible for the Indians to go safely by all roads and to peacefully carry on their civil pursuits. He has freed them from burdens and servitude; he has made known to them the use of bread, wine, oil and many other foods, woolen cloth, silk, linen, horses, cows, tools, arms and many other things from Spain; he has instructed them in crafts and trades by which they live excellently. All these advantages will those Indians enjoy, who embrace our Holy Faith and render obedience to our king.[19]

To avoid all possibility of misunderstanding, the law decreed particularly that the word "conquest" should no longer be used but the term "pacification." [20] The vices of the Indians were to be dealt with very gently at first "so as not to scandalize them or prejudice them against Christianity." If, after all the explanation, natives still opposed a Spanish settlement and the preaching of Christianity, the Spaniards might use force but must do as little harm as possible. No license was given to enslave the captives. This general order governed conquests as long as Spain ruled her American colonies, even though some Spaniards could always be found who thought that the Indians could be subjugated by force of arms, because of their infidelity.

The dispute had a further significance. At a time when many men doubted whether the Indians could be saved at all, Las Casas lifted his voice in their behalf and exerted all "his godly zeal of converting soules to Jesus Christ from the power of Ethnicke darkness" as the Elizabethans described it, and exclaimed, as did Montesinos forty years before on the island of Hispaniola: "Are these Indians not men? Do they not have rational minds? Are you not obliged to love them as you love yourselves?"

When considered in this way, the disputation at Valladolid in 1550 and 1551 stands forth clearly, not as a personal struggle between a friar and a scholar, not merely as a loud argument to approve or disapprove the printing of Sepúlveda's treatise, but as the passionate record of a crucial event in the history of humanity. Because Sepúlveda's ideas failed to triumph, Spain through the mouth of Las Casas made a substantial contribution toward the development of one of the most important hypotheses ever set forth—the idea that the Indians discovered in Spain's onward rush through the lands of the New World were not beasts, not slaves by nature, not childlike creatures with a limited or static understanding, but men capable of becoming

Christians, who had every right to enjoy their property, political liberty, and human dignity, who should be incorporated into the Spanish and Christian civilization rather than enslaved or destroyed. One more painful and faltering step was thus taken along the road of justice for all races in a world of many races, for when Las Casas spoke at Valladolid for the American Indians his argumentation had another usefulness: it strengthened the hands of all those who in his time and in the centuries to follow worked in the belief that all the peoples of the world are human beings with the potentialities and responsibilities of men.

Chapter IX

THE WAGING OF JUST WAR IN THE INDIES [1]

Just War in Mexico and in Nicaragua

It HAS been shown that the Requirement, although not universally practiced, was used in many parts of the Indies throughout the sixteenth century. Picturesque as were many of the incidents which attended the reading of the document to the plumed and painted natives, the fact must not be obscured that even Spaniards who did not use the Requirement felt the necessity to justify war against the Indians. Even during that tumultuous decade which followed the first proclamation of the Requirement in 1514, the idea was abroad that conquests ought to be made according to certain principles and that Indians could not be enslaved unless a just reason sanctioned this action. When Governor Diego Velázquez of Cuba offered about 1516 to help Bernal Díaz and other poor Spaniards to buy a barque on condition that they enslave the Indians of the Guanajes Islands to pay for it, the much needed financial assistance was rejected; for, wrote Bernal Díaz: "as we soldiers knew that what Diego Velázquez asked of us was not just, we answered that it was neither in accordance with the law of God nor of the king that we should make free men slaves." [2]

Cortés provided a convincing example of that remarkable mixture of "Gott und Gewinn" which a modern historian considers to have been the spirit of the Spanish people at the time America was discovered. On December 26, 1520, just before undertaking the siege of Mexico City, Cortés proclaimed in his Tlaxcala "Military and Civil Ordinances" that the primary motive of the war he was waging was the spiritual conquest of the natives of Mexico. War with any other intention would be unjust and all damage done would have to be repaired; moreover, the King would have no reason to reward those who had served in such a war.

A continuing concern to make sure that wars were just in Mexico may be seen in the royal orders of 1528 and in the instructions laid down for the first viceroy, Antonio de Mendoza. The justice of warring against the notorious Chichimeca Indians of Mexico was

133

a burning issue throughout the sixteenth century. The problem was to be found on the outer reaches of the viceroyalty in the frontier province of New Mexico. There in 1599 Governor Oñate was confronted by a rebellion of the Ácoma Indians. Oñate requested the friars to advise him. In this far-off region on the very periphery of the Spanish empire, the Commissary General Friar Alonso Martínez carefully worked out the opinion that war against the rebels was just, and that all captives might be enslaved. A whole page of specific citations was given including Augustine, Thomas Aquinas, Ostiensis, Aristotle, Soto, and many others. All the other friars having approved this opinion, Oñate explained the whole matter to his men one Sunday after Mass, and the Spaniards then proceeded to wipe out Ácoma. As the poet-historian Villagrá described this event:

Having received this learned and well-reasoned opinion from the churchmen, the governor was reassured by the fact that the reasons given concurred with the causes set forth. All doubt being removed from his mind, he therefore publicly proclaimed that war by blood and fire be declared against the Indians of Ácoma.[3]

All of this discussion of the justice of wars had its effect eventually on the common soldier, the backbone of all armies. Diego García de Palacio, judge of the Mexican Audiencia, wrote a treatise in 1583 on the art of war in which he found it necessary to discuss the question whether soldiers should make certain that a given war was just before embarking on it. The answer was clear. In general a soldier leaves such problems to the prince who has the responsibility for undertaking wars, unless the injustice of the war is so clear that even the soldiers see it. In this case, even though the prince commands war, the soldier need not obey, for he is subject to a greater prince, namely God.

An excellent example of the confusion and doubt of the justice of their conquests which friars could sow in the minds of the Spanish soldiers themselves may be found in the evidence given by the Governor of Nicaragua, Rodrigo de Contreras, in a legal deposition he presented to Bishop Diego Álvarez Osorio on March 23, 1536.[4] From the questions put to the witnesses, it appears that Governor Contreras had requested Bartolomé de Las Casas to accompany Captain Diego Machuca de Zuazo on an expedition. Las Casas refused to comply, alleging that Contreras was wrong in trying to make such conquests. But, continued Las Casas with a wealth of learned references from which his writings were by this time never free, he would gladly set out on condition that the Governor give him fifty men and leave the captain behind. Under these conditions he would indeed undertake to pacify the provinces. In making these startling proposals to the Governor, Las Casas may have been influenced by the success of Friar Jacobo Testera and other Francisans in Yucatan who were believed to have conquered the Indians in 1534 by peaceful means alone, without the aid of soldiers. It was shortly after this episode that Las Casas composed the treatise *The Only Method of Attracting All People to the True Faith,* and soon afterward that he first proposed the peaceful conquest of the wildest Indians in Guatemala which later became famous as the Vera Paz experiment.

When Governor Contreras refused to consider the friar's demands, Las Casas, in the words of one of his opponents, made public "many things in disservice to God which were sufficient to misguide the people." The Governor meanwhile proceeding to order the expedition, Las Casas preached against it in and out of the pulpit, declaring that soldiers who went were opposing God's will and endangering their souls. All who dared to go on this godless expedition would be refused confession on their return, would be excommunicated, and would certainly go to hell. These sermons were most successful from the viewpoint of Las Casas, for the common soldiers were much excited and alarmed. Some rebelled, refusing to go on the expedition altogether and the allegiance of many others to the Governor hung in the balance. Martín Mimbreño testified that in order to win back the soldiers he had to convince them that the conquest was in the king's interest and would lead to a spread of the faith. Although by no means all of the ecclesiastics of Nicaragua supported Las Casas, and the Vicar General himself flatly declared to certain distressed citizens that Las Casas lied when he said they would be excommunicated, yet the whole incident shows the great effect upon ordinary Spaniards when a great preacher made them feel a connection between the justice of their cause and their personal salvation. Governor Contreras was so angry that he is supposed to have ejected Las Casas forthwith from Nicaragua.

Just War Against the Chiriguanaes in Peru

Viceregal Peru with its magnificent court and capital in Lima was also torn by disputes over just war. During the earliest days of the conquest Bernardino de Minaya, the Dominican who influenced Pope Paul III to issue his momentous bulls on the nature of the American Indian, had opposed Pizarro's method of fighting the natives. Subsequent civil wars among the Spaniards themselves prevented much consideration of the ethics of warfare against the natives, but it is known that even during this period at least one group of ecclesiastics discussed just war. After royal power was reëstablished and the Viceroy Francisco de Toledo was ruling ably over the vast colonial empire, just war for the first time became a real problem in Peru. As early as December 19, 1568, the King had instructed Toledo to pacify the Chiriguanaes. These fierce Indians, particularly, had long been causing trouble by their frequent raids on Spanish settlements and attacks on Indians friendly to the Spaniards.

When Viceroy Toledo undertook to subjugate the Indians definitively and proceeded to have the Inca Tupac Amaru himself executed, the Chiriguanaes showed themselves as ingenious as they had been brave. They despatched thirty warrior chieftains to negotiate with the Viceroy at Chuquisaca, where they presented a statement to Toledo that a young man named St. James, sent by Jesus, had miraculously appeared among them and had converted their people to the Christian faith. The chieftains moreover assured the Viceroy that their people would no longer fight against the Indians friendly to Spaniards, would neither eat human flesh nor marry their sisters. They wished to serve God and the king of Spain and requested friars to instruct and baptize them. As a testimony of good will, the Indians presented some crosses.

This pious discourse profoundly moved the Viceroy, and his court "wept for joy and gave thanks to heaven." Friar Reginaldo de Lizárraga, however, suspected treachery and advised Toledo that the whole scheme was probably a clever ruse to gain time while the Indians back in their mountain fastnesses collected food and arms and occupied the strategic sites against an expected Spanish invasion. Strange to say, the Viceroy, by no means an idealist or soft-headed administrator, on this occasion waved aside the friar's misgivings which proved only too well founded. When within a few days a heavy rain fell, which the chieftains considered would stop any projected invasion, they straightway fled from Toledo's court. The Viceroy "prepared horses, arms, and all manner of cumbrous, ostentatious and useless paraphernalia in order to lend to his expedition that ponderous dignity which, so he judged, would most impress his barbarian foes." [5] He also took along his three wise men, the Jesuit José de Acosta and the lawyers Juan de Matienzo and Juan Polo de Ondegardo. The expedition met humiliating defeat and "after a thousand unfortunate incidents returned, having accomplished nothing except the expenditure of much money from the royal treasury." When Toledo held a meeting in April 1574 in Chuquisaca to pronounce upon the justice of war against these deceptive Indians, he was in no mood to tolerate theological hairsplitting. The 1530 order of Charles V against enslaving captives being cited, Toledo replied that he had never seen this law, and at the vote all but one member of the group asserted that the war would be just and all captives could be enslaved. Toledo advised the King in an official report dated

1580 that a general proclamation of just war against rebels and apostates ought to be issued, and this was done in 1584.

Just War in Chile

The Dominican Gil González took his duties in Chile just as seriously as did Las Casas in Nicaragua. His unsuccessful efforts to force Governor García Hurtado de Mendoza to read the Requirement and observe all due form in waging war kept this frontier province in an uproar during the early days of its conquest. When in 1561 young Mendoza was succeeded by Francisco de Villagrán, González at once bombarded the new Governor "with eloquence and good reasons" and was able to convince him that war against the Araucanian Indians on the Chilean frontier ought not to be made cruelly or barbarously but with humanity and justice, "bringing them to the dominion of the king by peaceful methods, by good treatment and by teaching them the principles of Christianity." [6] Villagrán succumbed to the friar's arguments and when he left Santiago in 1561 for a campaign in the south, the Dominican accompanied him as official counselor of the expedition, despite the stiff opposition of certain army captains who preferred a Franciscan with different opinions. When Friar González returned from the southern campaign, he found the Franciscans supporting his demand that future wars be more justly waged. Other troubles befell him, however, including difficulties with the Inquisition, and he returned discouraged to Peru in 1563.

The struggle continued, however. In 1571 Bishop San Miguel sent the first of his many representations to the King advocating justice for the Indians. In general, the Spaniards who had to deal with the stubborn and intelligent Araucanians were usually unmoved by the passionate declarations of the ecclesiastics, although doubt seems to have gnawed at the consciences of at least a few soldiers, as may be seen from the wills they left. Cristóbal Maldonado presented two memorials to the Council of the Indies advocating that war be declared on the Indians "by fire and by sword" but the Council on November 25, 1574, refused to adopt this policy, just as they had rejected the advice given by Juan de Herrera a few years earlier that "war in Chile should be gallant war, as they call it, either destroying their crops and so reducing them by hunger or using the mailed fist, and enslaving the older Indians." [7] And, added Herrera, "Whilst war is going on in Chile, the courts, the magistrates, and officials of the King are not wanted . . . and affairs ought to be carried on rather according as necessity required than by the letter of the law."

No one in authority adopted this advice and Herrera himself was careful to observe all the legal formalities in his war on the Indians. Mindful of the power of Friar Gil González, Herrera punctiliously drew up a legal proclamation which called upon the Indians to cease their rebellion and notified their Spanish protectors of the document, especially González. Governor Rodrigo de Quiroga was just as mindful of the juridical processes before he attacked the Indians in 1577.

Subsequent ecclesiastical battles over just war in Chile in the latter part of the century were complicated by the fact that the Indians had now to be considered rebellious apostates. When the Araucanians rose in 1598 in bloody revolt, even killing Governor Martín García Oñez de Loyola, the hard-pressed frontier colony demanded action. Before a crowded meeting of local notables in Santiago Cathedral, Melchor Calderón, church treasurer, presented a *Treatise on the Importance and Usefulness of Enslaving the Rebel Indians of Chile*.[8] Calderón had been a resident of Chile since 1555 and had a long record of fair dealing with the natives which gave added weight to his words. "With tears in his eyes and deep manifestations of sympathy for the victims of the recent revolt," he brought forward his treatise and delivered it to the Jesuit rector Luis de Valdivia who thereupon read it to assembled officials, captains, and friars. Calderón justified war against and enslavement of the Indians, citing David's war against the Amorites for their resistance to the royal dominion, and invoking the names of the theologians Francisco de Vitoria, Alfonso de Castro, and Diego de Covarrubias. He further maintained that when the Indians impeded traffic on royal roads, that alone was sufficient cause for enslaving them. Philip II had recently condemned the Moors in Granada for rebellion: he must now be asked to condemn the Araucanians for their crimes of rebellion, murder, and apostasy. When Valdivia finished reading the treatise, "one and all unanimously agreed to inform the Viceroy that in their opinion it was just to enslave natives captured in the wars in Chile."

In this case the course of Spanish justice proved almost incredibly tortuous. The Viceroy, having received Calderón's treatise, called upon the Archbishop of Lima and various other ecclesiastics to render him an opinion on the following questions:

1. May the king justly make war on his vassals who have rejected his authority without bloodshed, in order to put them again under his rule?
2. May the king justly make war on vassals to punish them for leaving the faith, if they have done so without rejecting his authority?
3. May the king justly make war on rebel, apostate vassals who wage war against his loyal subjects?
4. May the king justly make war on those who have never accepted Chris-

tianity or subjected themselves to his rule if they wage war against his subjects? [9]

The veteran Archbishop Reginaldo de Lizárraga in July 1599 gave an affirmative answer to all the above questions and supported his decision by referring to similar action taken concerning the Chiriguanaes Indians by a group of ecclesiastics in the time of the great Viceroy Francisco de Toledo.

Lizárraga felt even more strongly against the Chilean Indians than against those of Peru, for he considered them "more bellicose, and more dishonorable." [10] In fact, they were to him a people "without a king, without law, honor, or shame." Given this attitude toward the Chilean Indians, Lizárraga's opinion that Spaniards could justly war on them and enslave them is understandable. Jesuits, Franciscans, and Dominicans, for once agreeing with one another, supported the Archbishop. As a consequence the Governor of Chile, Alonso de Ribera, decided that until the King and Council of the Indies should determine otherwise he was safe in sanctioning the enslavement of the Indians.

Yet a still more secure legal basis was sought for the Chilean authorities and when the Augustinian Juan de Vascones was sent to represent Chile at court, he carried along a "Petition in law" to the King and Council of the Indies in which no less than nine reasons justifying war against the Araucanian rebels were set forth, each one supported by a wealth of scholastic authorities. The nine reasons Vascones elucidates contain no particularly new doctrine, and it is clear that the cruelty and rebellion of Chilean natives who had been exposed to Christian teachings were responsible for his firm opinion. A royal order dated August 16, 1604, informed the Governor of Chile that Vascones was returning to Chile with a thousand soldiers but no specific sanction to enslave the Indians was given at this time.

Despite continued protest from Chile, Philip III did not formally give this permission until May 26, 1608. Then he ordered that all male Indians aged ten and a half and all females nine and a half years or older captured in rebellion might be enslaved by their captors who could dispose of them as they saw fit. All natives under the assigned ages were to be taken from the war territory and entrusted to persons "who would teach them the faith as was done with the Moors in the Kingdom of Granada."

Just War in the Philippines

One of the best examples of the difficulties which arose when the Spaniards attempted to conduct their conquests according to Christian doctrine is to be seen in the history of the Spanish occupation of the Philippine Islands.

It has not been generally understood that the same laws, theoretical problems, and bitter disputes as were found in America likewise arose in the Philippines. Professor Albert G. Keller even went so far as to assert that:

Laws favoring the natives were promulgated, but there was no such occasion for reaffirmation, and no such disputes over enforcement, as in America. The representatives of the "practical," as against the "theoretical," were not in the field in the early times.[11]

Anyone who dips into the sea of documents presented by Emma H. Blair and James A. Robertson in their monumental collection, *The Philippine Islands, 1493–1898,* and the series now being published, the *Catálogo de los documentos relativos a las Islas Filipinas existentes en el Archivo de Indias,* will soon discover that here as elsewhere friars were obliged to carry on desperate battles for their theories. As Governor Tello wrote to Philip II: "When these islands were conquered, the natives were placed in obedience to Your Majesty with just as many Requirements as in the other parts of the Indies." [12] Friars became just as powerful in Manila as in Lima or Mexico City, and just as the Spaniards called the natives of the Philippine Islands "Indians" as in all other parts of the empire, so did they attempt to apply the same theories in Luzon as in Chile and Florida. "In each friar in the Philippines the king has the equivalent of a captain general and a whole army" [13] was the phrase used in those days to describe the influence wielded by ecclesiastics. Antonio de Morga complained once that friars wanted to have a hand in all governmental affairs "through the medium of conscience and theology, by means of which they interpret and pick flaws in His Majesty's ordinances," [14] and according to a modern church historian "there shone brilliantly in the Philippine Islands many worthy disciples of Bartolomé de Las Casas." [15] In the period 1570 to 1600 every type of theoretical problem raised in other parts of the Indies was found as well in the Philippines. Powerful voices were heard above the general tumult, and although Friar Martín de Rada has been called "the Las Casas of the Philippines," such ecclesiastics as Domingo de Salazar, Bishop of Manila, or Miguel de Benavides, Bishop of New Segovia, might as justly bear this title.

The usual disputes concerning just war arose during the earlier years of the conquest. Father Francisco Javier Montalbán has produced a study in which he undertook to show that the instructions given in 1559 to Miguel López de Legaspi, the founder of Spanish rule in the Philippine Islands, were drawn up as a direct result of teachings of Francisco de Vitoria. Certainly the main provisions followed the principles laid down by Vitoria in his lectures as *prima* professor at the University of Salamanca. If any natives refused to listen to Legaspi's demand for submission, or if they opposed the preaching of the faith, Legaspi was "to use all good means to overcome them and to proceed with all manner of discretion, kindness and moderation." If the natives tried to prevent the Spaniards from making settlements, "they must be told that the Spaniards are not trying to settle there in order to do others any harm or wrong or to seize their possessions but only to have friendship with them and teach them to live in a civilized manner and recognize God, and to explain to them the law of Jesus Christ by which they will be saved." After this message and warning had been given three times, Legaspi, after consulting the ecclesiastics attached to his expedition, might proceed with the settlement.[16] The Spaniards were to defend themselves from the natives without doing more injury than was necessary for their own defense and for making the settlement. No mention was made of just war or enslavement of the captives although some Spaniards such as Andrés de Mirandola advocated a military conquest of the islands "because the people are extremely vicious, treacherous, and possessed of many evil customs."

Legaspi carried out his instructions with a noteworthy zeal and intelligence. Though importuned by his men and menaced by the ever-present dangers of famine and mutiny, he permitted no raids or wars against the natives, for he hoped to convince them of his friendliness and to achieve a peaceful conquest. When war came, as it did at Manila in 1570, it was only after the natives "had been required many times, by means of an interpreter, to receive them in peace." [17] Legaspi was not the only man to "require" the natives; as late as 1599 Governor Tello complained that some chieftains had abused the law by requesting a year to think the matter over and he feared that "if the decree continues to be enforced, other delays will be demanded and the king will hold nothing securely." [18]

After the conquest, the friars and the colonists were soon divided on the issue of slavery. As early as 1573 the Augustinian Diego de Herrera hastened to Spain—a long and tedious journey requiring some six months—to report to the King certain excesses committed in unjust wars against the natives. He declared:

It is considered just cause for war in the War Council if the natives say that they do not care for the friendship of the Spaniards, or if they build any forts to defend themselves. Such natives are killed, captured, pillaged, and their houses burned. For that reason occurred the war of Bitis and Lubao in which forts were taken by Juan de Salcedo; and those of Cainta, where the night before, an Indian having climbed into a palm tree cried out:

"Spaniards, what did my ancestors do or owe to you that you should come to pillage?" . . . It is considered occasion for just war by the War Council and a village may be destroyed and all those captured may be enslaved if any Spaniard has been killed in the village; although the occasions that the dead man might have given or the wrongs that he might have committed are not considered, nor the fact that the natives do not understand and have no one whom they can ask to avenge them unless it be God and their justice.[19]

Another Augustinian, Martín de Rada, already referred to as "the Las Casas of the Philippines," supported Herrera in June 1574 with a memorial against unjust conquests. He asserted that when Captain Juan de Salcedo and Captain Pedro de Chávez went to pacify Luzon, "all the villages were summoned to submit peacefully and to pay tribute immediately unless they wished war." The natives failing to yield immediately, the Spaniards attacked and pillaged their villages. Rada submitted that this was not just war and specifically dissociated himself from such proceedings, insisting that he had never given his approval to these illegal expeditions. Governor Guido de Lavezaris and other prominent Spaniards at once despatched a counterstatement. Friar Andrés de Urdañeta had sanctioned their wars, they said, and had carried out punctiliously all the necessary legal formalities. They added that "though the friars may be moved by Christian zeal, their proposals are dangerous to the Spaniards and natives alike." [20] The royal decision of November 1574 ordered that the Spaniards in the Philippine Islands should not hold as slaves any natives for any reason whatsoever.

One of the basic problems, wrote Governor Sande in 1557, was the difficult nature of the natives.

They are not simple, or foolish, or frightened by anything whatever. They can be dealt with only by force, or by gifts of gold or silver. If they were like those of New Spain, Peru, Tierra Firme, or the other explored places where the ships of Castile may enter, sound reasoning might have some effect. But these natives first inquire if they must be Christians, must pay money, forsake their wives, and other similar things. They kill Spaniards so boldly, that without arquebuses we could do nothing.[21]

As in the other Spanish colonies, the issuance of a royal ordinance on behalf of the natives neither put a stop to the disputes nor wholly protected the natives. Another Augustinian, Francisco de Ortega, hastened to Spain with a memorial for the King. On April 24, 1580, Philip ordered Governor Ronquillo de Peñalosa to carry out rigorously the standard 1573 law governing explorations and conquests. In addition, all slaves were to be freed, the implication being that they had not been captured in just war. Governor Peñalosa at once hastened to the Bishop of Manila, Domingo de Salazar, to enquire whether the King's instruction to free all slaves "might be carried out with more mildness and less severity and hardship to the community." Bishop Salazar informed the Governor that the matter was a serious one requiring a discussion with the superiors and learned persons of the various orders. Salazar called these persons together in the Augustinian monastery on October 16, 1581, and presented them with the following set of propositions:

1. Will the hardship or any other reason be a sufficient reason for the Governor to neglect to proclaim and execute this decree?

2. Does the petition presented to the King on behalf of the masters of the slaves afford the Governor a reason for neglecting to enforce the law?

3. Must the Governor order immediate execution of the order or may he assign a time limit?

The theologians gave an emphatic negative to the first two questions and agreed on the third "that the freedom of Indians could not be deferred as it is a matter of natural and divine law and clear justice." In order, however, to prevent the great disturbance which would certainly follow if the masters lost all their slaves at one blow, the Governor ought to proclaim the law at once but at the same time order the Indians not to leave their masters for twenty or thirty days. Whoever dared detain his slaves longer "would commit mortal sin and would be obliged to make proper restitution." On June 23, 1587, a royal order was issued requiring conquistadores to make restitution for all harm unjustly done to natives, but Salazar never felt that sufficient payment was made by any Spaniard.

It is not difficult to see why some Spaniards disliked Bishop Salazar from the first. Governor Peñalosa reported that the islands had been thrown into great confusion by the decree and besought the King to modify it radically. Yet Philip repeated the order in 1589 and instructed the new Governor, Gómez Pérez Dasmariñas, to make war "only after consulting with the ecclesiastics and lawyers on matters of law, and on those of action with the captains and other experienced, conscientious men." This decree was followed by a papal proclamation of Gregory XIV to the same effect.

The decade 1590–1600 saw more struggles over just war. As Bishop Salazar truly reported to the King in 1591, "bringing justice into the land is like bringing firebrands." Governors were excommunicated and threatened with hell-fire from the pulpits of Manila, many of the inevitable theological conferences were called, and enough treatises were written concerning justice in the Philippines to fill a volume. The Jesuit Alonso Sánchez, the most prominent exponent of the fire and sword method, composed some forty-two treatises in all, and argued vociferously before King Philip and three different popes but never succeeded in seeing his ideas made law. Indeed, the instructions issued by Governor Juan de Cuéllar in 1590 concerning the pacification of the warlike Zambales Indians contained familiar provisions. The Spaniards were not to offend any natives on their journey whether the Indians were peaceful or at war. On arrival they were to explain to the Zambales "with the mildest and most appropriate words" the dangers of continuing to rob and murder Spaniards. The Zambales were to be exhorted with much love to submit peacefully to the king's jurisdiction and to accept the true God; if they did not, severe punishment was to follow and they were to be treated as common enemies.

The Zambales did not cease their robberies and murders, and in 1592 Governor Dasmariñas determined to make open war against them if it could be done conscientiously. Therefore, he collected a quantity of information on their treachery, the injuries they had committed, and their head-hunting proclivities. Dasmariñas then requested the Augustinians, Dominicans, Franciscans, and Jesuits to advise him whether war would be just. The friars presented an elaborate reply approving the projected war "by fire and sword" and fortifying their opinion by citations from doctors of law, theologians, and the Bible. Dasmariñas sent off the original opinions to Philip II and at once struck at the Zambales. Twenty-five hundred natives were killed or taken captive and four hundred of the survivors given to Dasmariñas who, as he reported to Philip, "utilized them for Your Majesty's service on the galleys, where they are learning to row."

Not all wars enjoyed such complete theological support. Many were undertaken, complained the Factor Francisco de las Missas to Philip in a letter in 1596, without complying with the King's regulations in more than the most superficial sense. Spaniards about to go on an expedition called together a few of their friends who constituted their committee to decide whether the war was just. If by chance one of the committee opposed the projected expedition, another member, "more susceptible to reason," replaced him. Missas therefore suggested a permanent committee be set up of prominent ecclesiastics and captains with authority to pronounce on the validity of all wars undertaken in the islands. The end of the century, then, was not a time when friars and colonists looked back with complacency upon a profitable and relatively bloodless conquest. As the Archbishop of Manila, Friar Ignacio Santibáñez, sorrowfully reported to the King on June 24, 1598, "Everything here is like a clock out of order."

Without going into further detail on the waging of just war in the Philippines, or into the interminable disputes between the ecclesiastics and governors between 1590 and 1600, it should be pointed out that one theoretical problem peculiar to the islands was the Moslem question. Plain unvarnished infidels were familiar to the Spaniards in the Indies, but what attitude ought they to take toward Moslems, notorious infidels and long-standing enemies of Spain, who were found in great numbers in the Philippines? Moriscos in Spain were shown little mercy. Even Vitoria believed that there must be perpetual warfare against Saracens.

Given this spirit in Spain, Philip II's instruction to Legaspi shows a remarkably benevolent attitude. He ordered that "under no consideration whatsoever shall you enslave those Indians who have adopted the worship of Mahomet; but you shall endeavor to convert them and to persuade them to accept our holy Catholic faith by good and legitimate means." Philippine Moslems, however, were to be enslaved if they tried to preach their faith or if they waged war on the Spaniards or the Christianized Indians. Philip, moreover, decreed on July 4, 1570, that the Mindanaos might justly be enslaved because they were semisavages and Moslems; but other Moslems were protected by royal ordinance, despite frequent appeals by colonists in the Philippines, from Spanish onslaughts in the name of religion.

The strength of the feeling against the Moslems in the Philippines may be judged perhaps by the attitude of Melchor Dávalos, a judge of the Audiencia in Manila. Soon after his arrival in 1584, he fell into dispute with various theologians who held that neither the audiencia nor the ecclesiastics had power to punish idolatrous natives. This opinion so offended his sense of justice that he composed two treatises as well as a set of laws against idolatry which he wanted the audiencia to proclaim. These essays, which Dávalos sent to Philip II, contained learned references and citations to many of the great jurists and theologians. The burden of both writings was "that all Moslems are enemies of the Church and of Spain" and that Spaniards were in duty bound to war against them, to punish them for their idolatrous habits. The authority of Pope Clement V was invoked because he had declared, with the approval of the Council of Vienna, that no Catholic prince ought to allow a Moslem to live under his jurisdiction. Dávalos warned Philip that some of the Turks vanquished at Lepanto had come to the East to preach their doctrine and to advise their fellow infidels in the wars waged against Spain in the Philippines. Spaniards must subjugate "these bestial Moslems that they may live according to reason," Dávalos continued and reminded Philip that the Romans had similarly justified their conquests. Writers who opposed Ostiensis' view of the plenitude of papal power "only created confusion" and might well be turned over to the Inquisition as heretics. Even without a papal bull, however, Spain had the right to conquer the Indies and to preach the faith. In none of the ordinances governing conquests, however, had he found regulations concerning Moslems. Therefore he had composed his treatises advocating war against the Moslems of the Philippines as a punishment for their idolatry and infidelity.

Philip II never adopted this harsh advice and dubious theory but continued his attempt to regulate Spanish action in the Philippines by milder means. By the end of the century the heroic period of the conquest of the islands had passed and the mighty Indian champions had either died or transferred their activities to the greener fields of China, where the issue of just war between Spaniards and natives had become a difficult one. That story cannot be told here, but enough has already been said to indicate that just war as waged in the Spanish Asiatic dominions in the sixteenth century followed much the same pattern as that in America.

Chapter X

THE JUST TITLES OF SPAIN TO THE INDIES [1]

Why the Dispute Arose

OF THE half dozen treatises ordered by the King as replies to the questions posed by Montesinos relating to the just title of Spain to the Indies, only two have been preserved. Only the work by Friar Matías de Paz has been published, while that of Dr. Juan López de Palacios Rubios is just now being prepared for the press in Mexico. Their basic doctrines were known, however, to some contemporary writers and thinkers on the problem. As the conquest spread from the Caribbean Islands to Mexico and Peru, to far-off Chile and the Philippines, there issued a flood of controversial books and treatises by missionaries and officials in the New World and by academic theorists and professional jurists in Spain, which remind one of the bitter and learned polemics produced during the medieval investiture controversy. As during other times of confusion and violence, a great literary outpouring accompanied the spread of empire.

All theorists whose opinions were sought by the crown in 1512 agreed, however, as had all Spaniards since the Indies were first discovered, that the papal concession and that alone justified sufficiently the Spanish title and that this concession was given for the conversion of the Indians. Hence the problem became one of working out specific ordinances to ensure their good treatment and the effective preaching of the faith. The Laws of Burgos, promulgated on December 27, 1512, together with a clarification of the laws six months later, were the logical result, therefore, of the deliberations on the just title of Spain. Most Spaniards of that time, if they gave the matter any thought at all, would probably have agreed with Charles V as he proudly announced on September 14, 1519, the incorporation of the New World into the territory under the royal crown of Castile: "By donation of the Holy Apostolic See and other just and legitimate titles we are lord of the West Indies, the islands and mainlands of the Ocean Sea already discovered and to be discovered." [2]

If Columbus, the Spanish monarchs, the friars, and the conquistadores all agreed that Spanish overlordship rested upon the papal

147

donation, where did doubt arise as to the justice of Spain's title? They arose, most naturally, outside Spain as a result of the jealousy of Spain's European rivals who wished to share the fruits of coloniza- tion and the prestige of empire. Samuel Johnson was to give classic utterance in the eighteenth century to the frustration felt by non- Spaniards when he cried:

> Has Heaven reserved, in pity to the poor,
> No pathless waste, or undiscovered shore?
> No secret island in the boundless main?
> No peaceful desert, yet unclaimed by Spain? [3]

The foreign questioning of Spain's title began, however, in the sixteenth century. Francis I of France declared in his well-known statement: "The sun shines on me as well as on others. I should be very happy to see the clause in Adam's will which excluded me from my share when the world was being divided."

This query echoed from court to court in Europe and evoked spirited rejoiners by conquistadores and other patriotic Spaniards, well represented by Gonzalo Jiménez de Quesada. Though not treated well at the Spanish court after his labors in the New World, and in- deed while traveling to escape persecution, this bold soldier who opened up the kingdom of New Granada brushed aside the question raised by Francis I as a trifling matter caused by jealousy of the Spaniards and declared:

The western Indies belong to Spain by the partition which touches the borders of our seas and by the concession of the popes, who are vicars of God throughout the universe. This conquest, with these and other very just titles, cost Spain great treasures, and infinite labor and blood. The barbaric peoples living there profited by their learning of God received with the Christian religion, as well as by the simultaneous arrival of letters and disciplines and all the arts and good breeding, whose value cannot be estimated. It would be sad to relate of Spain that she did not defend her rights, for God has given her the power, industry and ability to do so.[4]

Before the end of the sixteenth century the Spanish nation was extremely sensitive to attacks on the justice of her rule in America. We find Antonio de Herrera, first great official chronicler of Spain's work in the Indies, undertaking his study about 1600 "so that foreign nations might know that these Catholic kings and their councilors have complied with the provisions of the papal bull, and have not simply despoiled those lands, as some say." [5] The same at- titude may be seen underlying the boast of Juan de Mariana, per- haps the outstanding historian of his time, writing about 1600: "the most honorable and advantageous enterprise that Spain ever undertook was the discovery of the West Indies, properly called the New World." [6]

Besides the jealousy of foreign nations, the bitter disputes over the treatment of the Indians stimulated Spain's concern to justify her title. If this title depended upon the papal donation which was made for the purpose of bringing the Indians to Christianity, treatment of the Indians became a matter of first importance. It would have been a far easier matter if there had been no Indians! But there were uncounted thousands, and the papal donation made their good treatment and the justice of Spanish rule mutually dependent.

After Burgos

The basic questions on the just title of Spain to the New World were not, however, answered at Burgos in 1512 by the specialists called in to depose on the query made by Montesinos. Controversy broke out again at San Pablo convent in Valladolid in 1513. At this time Martín Fernández de Enciso had to meet the criticism of those who strongly believed in the second proposition of Matías de Paz that the Indians must be required to accept the faith and the sovereignty of Spain. Then was worked out the famous Requirement whose history has been related.

In the years immediately following the Requirement, no critical voice seems to have been lifted in Spain or America on the subject. The Pope had given the Spanish monarchy this vast New World territory for the conversion of the Indians, and Spain had carefully and most legally provided for their conversion and good treatment. Nonofficial opinion held to the same view.

Questions on the just title of Spain never wholly ceased, however. At one time a Scottish Franciscan enquired, in the presence of the eight preachers to the King, "With what justice are the Spaniards able to enter the Indies as they are now doing?" [7] Later on, meetings of "theologians, ecclesiastics, members of the royal council, and other learned and holy persons" were held to enquire into the matter.

The conquest of Peru by Pizarro and the consequent charges of cruelty caused another wave of doubts and questionings. Francisco de Vitoria engaged in a correspondence with his friend and brother Dominican Miguel de Arcos of Seville in 1534, which showed his deep concern over the treatment of the Indians by Spaniards in Peru. He realized the gravity and delicacy of the subject, but appears to have made no thorough or formal statement until the winter of 1537–38 when in the course of his university lecture on human sacrifices, he concluded, "Christian princes had no more authority over infidels with papal authorization than without it." Here we see a denial, probably the first by a Spanish writer, that the papal donation provided the fundamental basis for Spanish rule in the Indies.[8] In 1539 he was to develop the whole problem in classic fashion in *De Indis* and *De Jure Belli,* which will be described later.

At least one conquistador, Gonzalo Jiménez de Quesada, adopted a most unusual attitude for a fighting man to assume, and illustrates the danger of falling into easy generalizations on the ideas held by sixteenth-century Spanish soldiers. Jiménez de Quesada exhorted his men in 1538 to treat the Indians of Colombia well for "after all, even the ground we tread upon is theirs, by natural and divine right, and they allow us as a favor to be here and owe us nothing." [9] Nothing here about the papal donation at all although he invoked it at other times as has been pointed out. Many of the conquistadores did cite the papal donation, however, as the history of the Requirement has shown.

It was only natural, of course, that the principal treatises on this subject were written in Spain. Dominicans, above all, were discussing and disputing these questions in Salamanca, and many treatises and opinions were being drawn up. So exasperated and alarmed did the King become that on November 10, 1539, he ordered the Prior of San Esteban Monastery in Salamanca to keep his friars quiet on Spain's right to the Indies. The King informed the Prior that such discussion was extremely pernicious and scandalous, and ordered him to collect all sermons and other dissertations that the monks had prepared on this dangerous subject so that they might be duly studied. The Prior was to make sure that no further statements be made or printed without express royal permission.[10] The crown may have adopted such a stern attitude because it feared the encroachment of the church in the administration of New World affairs. Only the year before, Charles had found it necessary to revoke the famous bull of Pope Paul III "Sublimis Deus," not because he disagreed with its championship of the Indians but because it seemed to infringe on royal prerogative in America since it had been sent to the Indies without receiving prior approval of the Council of the Indies.

Many of the doubts and memorials which so angered Charles V had been stimulated by the lectures of Francisco de Vitoria, whose theories merit separate treatment.

The Contribution and Influence of
Francisco de Vitoria

It will not be necessary to describe here in detail the work of that great Dominican and great Spaniard, Vitoria. His theories and his life have been perceptively and lovingly set forth during the last quarter century by such experts as Friar Luis Getino of Madrid, Friar Vicente Beltrán de Heredia of Salamanca, Friar Honorio Muñoz of Manila, and in the English-speaking world by the late James Brown Scott of Washington. The relatively brief treatment here of Vitoria does not mean to suggest that he is not worthy of a much more extended discussion. For a thorough understanding of his views, the works of the above-mentioned authorities are available, indeed indispensable. For the purposes of this study, however, attention will be limited to selected aspects of Vitoria's thought.

What were the special contributions of Vitoria to the problem of the just title of Spain? First, he appears to have been the first Spaniard to assert that the papal grant had no temporal value. Secondly, he emphasized the fact that certain titles were illegitimate and these he specified in detail.[11] The emperor, he stated, was not the lord of the whole world and neither was the pope, who had no temporal power over the Indians or over other unbelievers. A refusal by the Indians to recognize any dominion of the pope is no reason for making war on them or for seizing their goods, nor are they bound to hearken to the faith. Even if the emperor were the lord of the whole world, that would not entitle him to seize the Indian provinces, erect new lords, or levy taxes.

The way having been cleared for the lawful titles, Vitoria declares that Spaniards have a right to travel to America and live there, providing they do no harm to the natives, and the Indians may not prevent them. If they do, the Spaniards may justly war against them, and this would be "the first title which the Spaniards might have for seizing the provinces and sovereignty of the natives."

Spaniards have the right "to preach and declare the gospel in barbarian lands." If war were necessary to achieve this just end, it should be waged in "moderation and proportion . . . and with an intent directed more to the welfare of the aborigines than to their own gain." Under such circumstances, this would be a second lawful title whereby the Indians might fall into the power of Spain. If the Indian princes attempt to force any of the converted aborigines to return to idolatry, this would constitute a third title.

Spaniards may intervene and dethrone rulers, to rescue innocent people "from an unjust death" such as cannibalism. "True and voluntary choice" of the Spaniards as rulers by the Indians also constituted a just title. Spaniards could justly take up the cause of allies and friends, as when the Tlaxcalans requested aid of the Spaniards against the other Mexican Indians.

Spaniards might assume the burden of a mandate to fit the natives for admission to the international community upon a basis of equality. Vitoria was not quite sure about this last title, but he considered that it might "be maintained that in the natives' own interests the sovereigns of Spain might undertake the administration of their country, providing them with prefects and governors for their towns, and might even give them new lords, so long as this was clearly for their benefit."

Much attention has been given to the question whether Vitoria did or did not exert influence upon his contemporaries and upon the actual course of events in the New World. He did not struggle in the market place as did Las Casas and the other defenders of the Indians. He did not participate in the numerous meetings convoked by the King, he never went to America, and his death in 1546 prevented his being appointed one of the judges at the great Valladolid dispute between Las Casas and Sepúlveda in 1550 and 1551. As Vitoria himself said in *De Indis,* "it is to be noted that I have seen nothing written on this question and have never been present at any discussion or council on this matter." [12] What then was his real influence?

The Argentine writer Roberto Levillier denied that Vitoria had any influence in the affairs of the Indies. It is now known, however, that Vitoria's pupils were to be found throughout the Indies and in important positions in Spain. These pupils and followers carried their master's doctrine to the New World and tried to put it into effect, particularly in the Philippines. Alonso de la Vera Cruz in Mexico, Bartolomé de Ledesma in Peru, Domingo de Salazar and Miguel de Benavides in the Philippines, Domingo de Soto and Melchor Cano in Spain—to mention only a few—were all "blossoms of the Vitorian tree," as one writer has termed them.[13]

Not only friars and respectful, admiring pupils invoked Vitoria but also such secular writers as the royal official Alonso de Zurita, the colonist of New Spain Juan Suárez de Peralta, and that doughty fighter Bernardo Vargas Machuca. This argument must not be pressed too far, however, for such theorists as Ayala and Covarrubias never seem to have looked upon Vitoria as an authority, and neither Las Casas nor Sepúlveda took him into account in their mighty Valladolid conflict over the justice of wars against the Indians. But it appears that his denial of the universal temporal jurisdiction of the pope, and hence that Spain's title depended upon the papal grant, came to be the accepted doctrine in Spain by about 1550, except by Las Casas, of course, who never accepted this and had a somewhat different set of political principles to which we now turn.

Las Casas: Political Theorist [14]

After 1550, Vitoria's authority increased steadily until he has come to be regarded as perhaps the greatest thinker Spain has contributed to the field of international law, while Las Casas has been largely forgotten as a theorist. Indeed, until recently few persons have considered Las Casas a political thinker at all but rather a noble humanitarian or a saintly fanatic, when harsher terms have not been applied. Few have realized that under the fire and brimstone of his sulphurous invective lay a closely reasoned structure of thought based upon the most fundamental political concepts of medieval Europe. Many of his writings discussed that central problem with which all political theorists must grapple—what makes political domination legitimate? More specifically, what made Spain's rule in America just? It was Las Casas' treatise on this subject, the *Treatise Concerning the Imperial Sovereignty and Universal Pre-Eminence Which the Kings of Castile and Leon Enjoy over the Indies,* which so angered Viceroy Francisco de Toledo that he spent much time and effort in attempting to prove that the Inca rule had been illegitimate and Spanish rule just. Before describing this attempt, it is necessary to have firmly in mind the political theories of Las Casas which so disturbed Viceroy Toledo that he organized in Cuzco, ancient Andean capital of the Incas, a formal enquiry into the justice of Indian rule prior to the Spaniards' arrival.

It will not be possible or necessary to plunge into a detailed exposition of Las Casas' theories on the origin of government, power of the pope, or theory of kingship. His thoughts on these subjects have been set forth elsewhere and do not directly relate to our present story of the struggle over the just titles of Spain to the New World. We only need to know for this purpose that for Las Casas the true title of Spain and the only possible justification lay in the donation by the pope, which was made in order to bring the Indians to a knowledge of Christ. The pope had, however, no coercive authority but only voluntary jurisdiction. Specifically, the pope had no authority to force infidels to accept Christianity and therefore could not bestow such power on the Spanish kings. Nor had he authority to punish the sins of non-Christians. God in His wisdom, but no man, might judge of these things. Furthermore, the pope had no authority to deprive non-Christians of their lands or property.

Though the pope might not use force, he had authority over all secular matters in the world insofar as that was necessary for spiritual ends. It followed, therefore, that the pope had the right and duty to divide among Christian kings the authority over the infidel world necessary for carrying out these grave responsibilities. He would naturally make different arrangements for the various classes of infidels. For example, the Turks and Moslems who impeded the faith and who harmed the faithful were obviously on a different plane from the New World natives who had their own political organization and had never harmed Christians. When absolutely necessary to advance the faith, the pope might depose an infidel king, deprive him of his jurisdiction and royal dignity, and substitute another rule. This would be an extraordinary step and would be taken not because the ruler was an infidel but because he was impeding the faith. Las Casas clearly stated that the infidels should retain all their estates, dignities, and jurisdictions in their realms, just as the Christians do in theirs. The proof of this was very evident, "for both infidels and Christians are rational beings. Natural law is common to all men everywhere, more or less." [15]

It was not difficult for Las Casas to show that the king of Spain and the Spaniards held their lands and mines in the New World against the will of native kings. The Spaniards had not entered those kingdoms in the way that natural and human law require. The king ought, therefore, to restore the property to the rightful owners even though the encomenderos rebel and he has to kill some of them. Furthermore, the Spaniards who have robbed Indian sepulchers and treasure houses must return what they have stolen "to the penny." These forthright and logical conclusions demonstrate that the political theories of Las Casas on the monarchy were not academic speculations but were designed to have an immediate and practical application in the New World.

In fact, it may be said that every one of Las Casas' erudite though bellicose treatises had a most practical and immediate purpose in view. The *Advice and Regulations for Confessors* was designed to withhold the sacraments of the church from all persons who held Indians or who did not properly compensate them for their labor. The hubbub raised in the Indies by these stringent rules was so great that Las Casas wrote another tract and presented it to the Council of the Indies to sustain his previous regulations. His enemies charged that in this treatise he denied the jurisdiction of the kings of Castile in the New World when he asserted that everything the Spaniards had done in the Indies had been illegal, without the authority of the prince, and against all justice. Las Casas therefore wrote another treatise, entitled *Thirty Very Juridical Propositions,* to justify his position.

Not having stilled his opponents with this treatise he composed the above-mentioned 160-page *Treatise Concerning the Imperial Sovereignty and Universal Pre-Eminence Which the Kings of Castile and Leon Enjoy over the Indies,* printed in Seville in 1553. Reading this tremendous accumulation of legal citations, explosive argument, and close reasoning, we come to understand what Las Casas meant when he once said, "For forty-eight years I have been engaged in studying and inquiring into the law. I believe, if I am not mistaken, I have penetrated into the heart of this subject until I have arrived at the fundamental principles involved." [16]

He disposes summarily, in this last treatise, of the illegal and unjust titles some persons have brought forward. To those who suggest that Spain's proximity to the Indies gave her a superior right, Las Casas points out that Portugal really lies closer to the New World. To those who urge the greater wisdom and understanding of Spaniards as justifying their lordship over the Indians, he replies that many other nations are wiser and of greater genius than Spain— witness the Greeks, the Africans, and the Asians. To those who cite the opinion of Ostiensis to the effect that all infidels are unworthy of exercising jurisdiction, he retorts that these persons do not really understand the true meaning of Ostiensis as he proved in detail in a Latin treatise. As for those who establish Spain's title because Indians are idolatrous or commit unnatural crimes, they do not seem to realize that the Indians live for the most part an orderly, political life in towns and in some respects are superior to Spaniards. And the worst reason of all is that advanced by those who justify Spain's title by her mere superiority in arms, which is an "absurd nefarious argument unworthy of being advanced by reasonable and Christian men." [17]

The question has been raised whether Las Casas or Vitoria struck the heavier blows on behalf of the Indians. This is a sterile argument and scarcely worthy of detailed consideration. They were both great figures who played significant, though very different, roles in the greatest drama of their time, the conquest of America. It is one of the surest indications of Spain's genius that she could produce simultaneously two such figures: one an apostle who burned with a fierce zeal on behalf of those newly discovered Indians and who defended them with all the weapons at his disposal, particularly theoretical arguments; the other an academic and cloistered thinker who treated the most fundamental problems and delivered such convincing decisions that within a quarter of a century of his death his opinions had come to be generally accepted in Spain, and who today is justly honored as one of the first and most important founders of international law.

Above all, the theories developed by both Vitoria and Las Casas had an influence, usually a disturbing one, in the New World as the following chapters will illustrate as they describe the struggle over the just title of Spain in Mexico, the Philippines, and Peru.

Chapter XI

JUST TITLE DISCUSSIONS IN MEXICO AND THE PHILIPPINES

The Town Fathers of Mexico City

Las Casas made his final departure from America in 1547 and never again was to visit the lands he had traversed for almost half a century or to see the Indian nations whose cause he had supported ever since his conversion while preparing the Whitsunday sermon in 1514 in Cuba. He returned to Spain, resigned his bishopric, and devoted the last twenty years of his life to serving as a sort of attorney-at-large for the natives of the Indies. These labors involved many appearances before royal tribunals and much polemical writing, at which he was an old and accomplished hand. His mighty conflict with Sepúlveda has been described, which was followed by the publication in Seville during 1552 and 1553 of eight powerfully written tracts for the times. These treatises, as we have seen, constitute a bitter indictment of the cruelty and avarice of the conquistadores, of their disregard for the rights of the Indians, and of their unjust conquest and wars. Las Casas' basic contention was that the consent of the original native population, or at least of the original native chiefs, was the indispensable basis for the establishment of any legitimate or justifiable government, and that this consent had not been obtained. Whatever right Spain enjoyed in the New World was based on the papal grant, Las Casas believed, and the Pope had given this right only that the natives might be converted to the faith.

By speaking and writing freely on these matters Las Casas became the most fiercely hated man in all the Spanish realms. To the many Spaniards who had crossed the seas in search of personal wealth and fame, his words were, or course, most unwelcome doctrine, amounting practically to treason. The royal officials and burghers of Mexico became alarmed because they were already disturbed by friars who in 1552 dared to assert publicly that the pope, not the king of Spain, owned the land. In the same year "certain Indians of the pueblo of Texcuco" presented a petition to the Town Council in which it was claimed that a large part of Mexico was still owned by the Indians, a point of view not congenial to the town fathers.[1]

156

Not only friars and Indians raised embarrassing questions. In 1554, a group of lawyers in Mexico, who were discussing the right of the king to levy ordinary tributes on Indians, stated their opinion that neither infidelity nor idolatry nor the Indians' offenses against natural law nor the duty of planting the faith was a sufficient title to justify Spain's rule. Only if all or a majority of the inhabitants freely chose the king could he rule over them justly.

The questioning did not abate, for on January 24, 1558, the Town Council of Mexico City again took cognizance of the problem by voting a salary to Dr. Francisco Cervantes de Salazar, one of the most learned men in the country, who had started to write a book "in which is established the just title of the king to New Spain, and a general history of this New World," and continued to pay this salary for at least five years.[2] In 1562, this same Town Council informed the King that Las Casas' writings had caused so much trouble and discontent in Mexico that it had arranged for the town attorneys and two theologians to prepare a formal statement to be sent to the Council of the Indies against "this audacious friar and his doctrine." [3] It appears from the records of the Town Council that many persons, in Mexico City had been busily writing on the subject in refutation of Las Casas ever since his printed works had arrived there, and the Town Council had requested several times that the King reprove Las Casas and prohibit the printing of his books.

On April 10, 1562, the council decided to aid the Franciscan Alonso de Santiago, who had already written on "the sound title that His Majesty holds to these parts of the Indies," for which opinions the friar had been badly treated by his Franciscan superiors so that he lacked the necessary funds to enable him to proceed to Spain. Because it was only just to aid the friar on account of his sufferings for "the common good," the Town Council decided to pay Santiago's travel expenses to Spain.

But a determined Franciscan provincial could, in more than one way, avoid complying with the wishes of the Town Council. On January 15, 1563, the council entered a long complaint on the subject, stating that the royal order to send Alonso de Santiago to Spain had been ignored by the Franciscan authorities. Instead the friar had been ordered away to New Galicia under the displeasure of his superiors. All this greatly angered the council, which ordered its representative in Spain to take measures to have the royal will complied with, and to see that the Franciscan authorities responsible for the flouting of the royal order were duly reprimanded. Another grant of money was made on behalf of the friar who wrote so well concerning the king's title to New Spain, and in addition regidor Juan Velázquez de Salazar was given three hundred pesos to spend on behalf of Fray Alonso who was "old and infirm." Special provision was made for a horse to carry him to the port of embarkation and for a considerable array of clothing, food, and wine to make the long journey to Spain more bearable.[4]

Notwithstanding all the efforts of the town fathers, the books of Las Casas continued to circulate in Mexico and to enjoy support, particularly among the friars. Licentiate Valderrama indignantly reported to the King on February 24, 1564, that the friars appeared to hope that soon there would be no Indians paying tribute to the crown, for they publicly stated and even preached that the Pope had conceded this land to the king only for the spiritual good of the Indians and that, once the Indians had become Christians, the king would be obliged to leave these kingdoms to the natives. The Town Council continued to protest to Spain against such doctrines, and its representatives in Spain continued to present treatises supporting the just title of the king to the Indies.

Trouble in Manila

Questions were asked in Mexico by Dominicans and other friars concerning the justice of the conquest of the Philippine Islands even before the Spaniards had established themselves firmly in the islands. One friar, the Augustinian Martín de Rada, on the other hand, directed a complete justification of the war against the Zambales and their subjection to Spain to his provincial on July 16, 1577, from Calompit.[5] The Jesuit Alonzo Sánchez likewise felt no qualms of conscience and penned a number of treatises, emphatically asserting the right of the king of Spain to wage just war against the Philippine natives and to rule over them. But the most important treatises on the just title of Spain in the Philippines were composed by the Dominicans Domingo de Salazar and Miguel de Benavides.

Salazar served as first bishop of Manila, and became known as a vigorous defender of the rights of the natives in that outpost of the Spanish empire.[6] He was born about 1513, in the village of La Bastida in Old Castile, of a distinguished and well-to-do family. After a period of study at the University of Salamanca, where he sat under the renowned Francisco de Vitoria, he entered the Order of Preachers in 1545 at the convent of San Esteban and pronounced his religious vows there on November 26, 1546. Shortly afterward he departed to preach the faith in New Spain.

Few missionaries have had so wide or so varied a career as Salazar. Being of a studious disposition, he was made a professor in the House of Dominican Studies on his arrival in Mexico City and so devoted himself to the study of Indian languages that he became a noted

DOMINGO DE SALAZAR, FIRST BISHOP OF MANILA

pulpit orator in the native tongues. In 1552–53 he accompanied the venerable Gregorio de Beteta to the northern parts of South America on mission affairs. This earlier part of his life is not well known but records have been found showing that he appeared in 1556 in Mexico City to present his opinion that Indians should not be made to pay tithes. In 1558, he was sent to Florida and took part in the hardships of the Tristán de Luna expedition, from which he returned in 1561. Back in Mexico City, he won the degree of Master of Sacred Theology and became prior of the Dominican convent there.

For more than a quarter of a century, Salazar labored toward the conversion and instruction of the Indians of New Spain and was described by a contemporary, Alonso de Zurita, as a "disciple of Friar Francisco de Vitoria who has lived many years in New Spain and in other parts of the Indies, converting the Indians with great zeal, diligence, and care, because he is a very good friar, exemplary in every virtue, a highly approved preacher whose doctrine is substantial and learned." [7]

The justice of Spanish rule in the New World was discussed in Mexico City in the very year that Salazar began his missionary work there, at the famous junta of 1546 at which Las Casas played such an important role. Zurita tells us that Salazar began to write while at the University of Mexico a treatise in Latin on the justice of Spain's rule in the Indies, which was inspired by the works of Las Casas. Though deeply versed in the doctrines of Las Casas and Vitoria—once Salazar wrote that he "had been brought up in the doctrine of the Bishop of Chiapa" [8]—he was no blind follower, according to Zurita to whom Salazar once loaned the manuscript work in Madrid in 1576. Zurita declared that Salazar demonstrated great ability in this treatise, which evidently was never completed or printed and whose present survival is doubtful. Salazar seems to have presented this Latin treatise to the Council of the Indies and to have discussed it there in 1592–93, at about the same time he presented a treatise in Spanish concerning tribute. Fortunately a copy of a portion of what may have been a summary in Spanish of this Latin treatise has been preserved in the Dominican archive in Manila. [9]

During a trip to Spain in 1576 on affairs of his order, Salazar seized the opportunity to present the Indian viewpoint on the repartimiento question and it is alleged that for this he was thrown into prison for a time. Once released, he delivered a series of lectures on the same subject in the church attached to the Atocha convent in Madrid where Las Casas had died. This stout support of an unpopular cause won Salazar the attention of Philip II who appointed him the first bishop of Manila in 1579. After journeying halfway round the world and losing all but one of his missionary companions by pestilence or other misfortune, he reached his new post in 1581. At Manila he found his bishopric "like sheep without a shepherd" and in the course of his attempts to protect the natives was warned by one soldier to his face that he had better moderate his enthusiasm; for if he did not, the speaker pointedly boasted of his ability to hit a mitre at fifty paces with his arquebus. During another dispute the Governor himself laid violent hands on Bishop Salazar.

These unseemly incidents occurred because the new Bishop found himself the center of a bitter controversy concerning the justice of Spanish rule. The stiff-necked attitude of the ecclesiastics helped to increase the chaos in this frontier province, and Salazar's own pertinacity in such matters as insisting that Chinese converts to Christianity cut off their pigtails, as a visible symbol of their acceptance of the new faith, alienated many persons. The Governor protested strongly and the dispute finally was settled by a royal order of June 23, 1587, which directed Salazar to withdraw from this intransigent position and to treat the newly converted Chinese with all kindness, as though they were "young and tender plants." [10] Salazar also became involved in a quarrel with the Augustinians over the administration of the sacraments which led to the exchange of many sharp letters bristling with citations of various papal bulls and the doctrines of church fathers. It is not difficult to understand the attitude of one of the early governors who reported that the energetic Salazar was disliked from the first "on account of the austerity of his disposition and his wish to dominate." [11]

The root of much of the discord was the need to determine under what conditions the natives were to pay tribute to their Spanish overlords. Encomenderos enjoyed by law the right to collect tribute from the natives and in return were supposed to provide religious instruction for them. Disputes having arisen over alleged neglect of religious instruction by the encomenderos, the elderly Bishop began in June 1591 the tedious and perilous journey to the royal court to lay the case for the Indians before the King, and arrived there early in 1593.

It was probably sometime during the early months of 1593 that Salazar presented the *Treatise Concerning the Tributes to Be Levied on the Infidels of the Philippine Islands* to the Council of the Indies and Philip II. Though tribute was the chief question at issue, Salazar took occasion to discuss the very foundations of Spanish authority in the Philippines. Reading through this lengthy and carefully organized presentation of the legal problems involved in the conquest and settlement of the Philippines, one finds the most complete exposition of theoretical problems in the Philippines that we have.[12]

Most of this treatise concerns the levying of tribute but in conclusion Salazar replies to those of his critics who contend that he fails clearly to recognize the rights of the kings of Spain to the Indies. He states: "The dominon which Your Highness enjoys in the Indies is better, sounder, and more excellent than the lordship of any other king in any part of the world." [13] The treatise in which Salazar explained the precise way in which he justified Spanish rule has unfortunately not come down to us.

It was while Salazar was arguing before the Council of the Indies on behalf of the natives of the Philippines that "death surprised him," on December 4, 1594. He was an obstinate and implacable fighter for what he conceived to be justice, whose presence in the Philippines was resented just as keenly by the officials there as had been Las Casas in America. As Governor Pérez Dasmariñas had reported to the King in a long letter which reveals the impasse that had been reached in Manila on all questions affecting the natives, "so firm is Salazar in his own opinion that he does not wish to call it opinion, but truth." Moreover, "he declares that if all the ecclesiastical orders in this bishopric and the universities of Salamanca and Alcalá in addition should say the contrary, he would not forsake his opinion; and he is very certain that Your Majesty will oblige me to follow his opinion." [14]

We now turn from the story of justice on Spain's far-flung Philippine frontier to the most interesting incident in the whole history of the controversy over Spain's title—the attempt Viceroy Francisco de Toledo made to demonstrate the injustice of Inca rule and thereby to establish the justice of Spain's title to Peru.

Chapter XII

FRANCISCO DE TOLEDO AND THE JUST TITLES TO THE INCA EMPIRE[1]

Defense of the Spanish Title to Peru

THE best example of the effect produced by Las Casas' theoretical writings concerning the just title Spain held to America occurred in the Andean regions of Peru during the rule of Viceroy Francisco de Toledo, wise lawgiver, energetic administrator, and greatest ruler Spain ever sent to Peru, who laid the basis for Spanish dominion there during the years 1569–82. Before his coming, Peru had had a most turbulent and bloody history, and Toledo arrived with one great aim—to establish without question in this territory the position of the king of Spain. Toledo reached Lima in 1569 while Ovando was inspecting the Council of the Indies in Spain and studying ways and means of improving the administration and, at the same time, of defending Spain from the attacks of foreigners who claimed that Spain held no just title to the New World and was oppressing and exploiting its natives.

One of Toledo's earliest acts was to execute the Inca, Lord Tupac Amaru, the Indian leader who refused to accept Spanish rule. Presently, with a view to establishing Spain's juridical title to Peru, he undertook an extensive historical investigation which attempted to demonstrate the unjust nature of the Inca regime and thus demolish the doctrines of Las Casas. We have here one more illustration of the concern throughout the Indies in the sixteenth century to have "truthful and precise" history written, to the end that Spain's labors in the New World might be fully and honestly recorded. During the course of this investigation, Toledo and his associates accumulated an immense amount of raw material on Inca history and customs, designed to prove once and for all that Spain's rule in Peru was just by contrasting it with the injustice of Inca rule.

Even before Toledo's arrival in Peru, in fact in the instructions given to him by the King on January 28, 1568, he had been warned against free-speaking friars. The King had understood that "the ecclesiastics who have resided and reside in those parts on the pretext of protecting the Indians have wished to busy themselves concerning the justice and the lordship of the Indies and in other matters which lead them into much scandal, particularly when they treat these subjects in pulpits and public places." Therefore, he warned Toledo to take care to prevent such occurrences by conferring with the provincials and superiors of these ecclesiastics, for in no wise should such scandals be permitted. So serious did Toledo consider this problem that early in his career as viceroy he conferred with the higher ecclesiastical authorities of Peru to determine whether the newly established Inquisition could be utilized, not to smoke out heretics but to impose silence "on the preachers and confessors in this realm who hold contrary opinions on jurisdictional matters and on security of conscience." [2]

Of all the ecclesiastics, the most troublesome was Las Casas and his doctrines which lived on after his death in 1566 to agitate some Spaniards as violently as during his long lifetime. As Viceroy Toledo expressed it, "the books of the fanatic and virulent Bishop of Chiapa served as the spearhead of the attack on Spanish rule in America." [3] Most of these attacks were launched by friars, and Toledo complained bitterly throughout his rule against the "perverse and high-handed procedure" of the ecclesiastics. They were quick to detect "tyrannical and unjust" aspects of everything Toledo tried to do, he complained, and even went so far as to hide Indians from the royal tax collectors when they considered tributes unjustly levied. It is understandable, therefore, why the Viceroy felt so keenly that the writings of Las Casas must be suppressed; to this end he collected as many copies as he could find, thus retiring them from circulation, and petitioned the King to allow no more to be shipped from Spain.

It is not clear which of the many treatises Las Casas wrote was most abhorrent to the Viceroy. If he had known of it, doubtless the *Solution to the Twelve Doubts* would have been the most obnoxious of all. This treatise, written in 1564 when Las Casas was ninety years old but only published in 1822, clearly and emphatically proclaimed the principle that all infidels, no matter what their sect or their sins against natural or divine law, justly hold jurisdiction over those things which they acquired without prejudicing anyone else. [4]

The Viceroy took three positive steps to combat Las Casas. First, he inspired the composition of a treatise against Las Casas' ideas; secondly, he embarked upon an investigation of the justice of Inca rule by collecting the so-called *Informaciones;* and finally, he arranged for the preparation of a "true history" of Peru's past by Pedro Sarmiento de Gamboa.

The treatise is in the form of an anonymous letter dated at the valley of Yucay on March 16, 1571, and is entitled *Defense of the Legitimacy of the Rule of the Kings of Spain in the Indies, in Opposi-*

tion to Friar Bartolomé de Las Casas.[5] The author, who appears to
be rendering a formal opinion to Viceroy Toledo, has been identified
by some as Polo de Ondegardo, one of Toledo's principal jurists, by
others as Pedro Sarmiento de Gamboa, another principal officer of
the Viceroy, but perhaps was neither. For at one point, after referring
to himself he mentions "many other friars" as though he were one
himself, and the impression that the author is a friar is strengthened
when in closing he states that he was happy to give an opinion "on a
matter so appropriate to my profession." If the author was an ecclesiastic, he may have been the Viceroy's chaplain, the Franciscan Pedro
Gutiérrez.

At any rate this treatise was a frontal attack on the theories of Las
Casas who, the author points out, although he was never in Peru and
therefore could know nothing firsthand of conditions there, has
stirred up all the trouble. The author states that the Indies were
given to Spain as a reward for her eight centuries of warfare against
the Moslems, and insists that the Incas were tyrants in Peru "which
fact, Your Excellency is now making abundantly clear with great
authority in the investigation you are making." [6] Las Casas has persuaded many in Spain of the justice of Inca rule by false information,
states the author. Such was his influence with the Emperor and even
with theologians that the Emperor desired to abandon these kingdoms to the tyrannical Incas until Friar Francisco de Vitoria told
him that he should not, that if he did Christianity would perish there.
The Emperor then promised to leave them when they were able to
maintain themselves in the Christian faith. Las Casas wielded such
power that very few persons questioned his views, and the author of
the treatise confesses that he himself had followed Las Casas' doctrine until in Peru he saw its falseness.

Much harm will come if the just title of the king of Spain is not
clarified, continues the author. Christian government and justice
will be hindered, conversion will lag, and other Christian princes
will use the excuse of ill-treatment of the Indians to try to take over
part or all of the Indies. Moreover, and this is a curious sidelight on
the times, some Spaniards have married Indian women of the Inca
family in order to be in line to rule by hereditary right if the Incas
should return to power, as will happen, warns the author, if this indiscreet and mistaken Bishop has his way. Finally, Lutheran, English,
and French heretics will use the beclouded title of Spain as an excuse
to rob Spaniards in the Indies, to harry the land, to ascend rivers and
disseminate their heresies in all the empire.

The author then proceeds to state certain basic propositions, such
as, that the Incas were modern tyrants, that before Topa Inga conquered the land there was no general overlord, that the Pope made

the king of Spain lord over them and that, since they had no natural or legitimate lord, the king of Spain became their ruler. The author combats the idea put forward by Las Casas that the Incas were received voluntarily as lords, and the charge that, whereas the Spaniards levy taxes and send the money abroad, the Incas levied none and spent what money they had in Peru.

In a final burst, the author expresses amazement at those who

under the guise of zeal try to give these Indians titles and things unappropriate for them which do not belong to them and which God did not choose to give them . . . for they are minors who must be governed. . . . It has been a most delicate subtlety of the Devil to select as his instrument an ecclesiastic and apparently a person of zeal, but deceived and ill-speaking and of little discretion, as may be seen by the publication of his books, and by the disturbances he created in Peru when Blasco Núñez came.[7]

This was the formal opinion given to Toledo on the doctrine of Las Casas.

The "Informaciones" of Viceroy Francisco de Toledo

The *Informaciones* consisted of a formal enquiry, made by order of the Viceroy, into the ancient history of the Incas; the conquests of Tupac Yupanqui, next to the last ruler before the conquest; the institution of the Curacas; Inca religious beliefs and practices; and their sacrifices, nature, and customs. Information was taken down, by means of interpreters, from two hundred Indians at eleven different points in Peru during the period November 1570—March 1572, while Viceroy Toledo was making a general inspection of Peru at the beginning of his rule there, much in the same way the Inca rulers began their administration by first formally surveying their realms. The complete record of this enquiry has only recently been made available by the Argentine historian Roberto Levillier.[8]

Few episodes in the colonial history of Peru have been interpreted so variously by modern historians as this enquiry. Clements Markham, José de la Riva-Agüero, Horacio Urteaga, and Philip A. Means believed that Toledo organized this as a public spectacle to present the Incas as monsters of cruelty, to falsify their history and customs in order to make certain of Spain's title. They state that senile and servile "yes-men" were chosen as witnesses, and that if a witness happened to tell an unpalatable truth his answer was changed by the interpreter from no to yes, or yes to no as the occasion required. In short, they believe that it was intended to blacken the Incas.

Levillier rejects this conclusion vehemently. He points out that not one of these writers had available all the *Informaciones,* and insists that the enquiry was an honest and important investigation which constitutes one of the most trustworthy sources available for a reconstruction of the events and the spirit of the prodigious Inca history and civilization.[9]

These enquiries make curious and interesting reading. The records tell us, for example, that in the period January 4—February 27, 1572, there were examined at Cuzco these witnesses: Martín Sauasiray, aged sixty-five; Juan Chalcomayta, aged thirty; Juan Pizarro Yupangui, aged seventy-nine, of Ayacucho; Don Francisco Quispi, aged eighty; Balthasar Guambo, aged sixty; Gaspar Pacra of the Pueblo of Pisa, aged thirty-four; and a number of others. Among the questions put to them were these:

1. Is it true that the first Inca, he who was called Manco Capac, tyrannically subjugated the Indians living around Cuzco by force of arms and despoiled them of their lands, killing them, warring against them, and otherwise maltreating them? And did all the rest of the Incas do likewise, until the fourth, called Maita Capac, completed the conquest?
2. Is it true that the Indians never recognized voluntarily these Incas as their lords, and only obeyed them through fear of the great cruelties inflicted against them?
3. Is it true that neither you nor your ancestors ever elected the Incas as your lords, but that they supported their tyrannical position by force of arms and the inculcation of fear? [10]

Practically all the questions were of this yes or no character, and there were evidently more yes-men than no-men in the group interrogated, for the answers all tended to establish that the whole history of the Incas, from 565 A. D. when Manco Capac was alleged to have founded the dynasty until 1533 when Francisco Pizarro won Peru for Spain, was but a succession of tyrannical and brutal overlords who ruled despotically. It was thereupon an easy transition for the interrogators to elicit that the Spanish invasion was thus a deliverance and greatly to the advantage of the Indians, who were now to be Christianized by the ecclesiastics and protected by the crown. Another set of questions put to a different set of witnesses drew information that the Incas sacrificed to their gods and idols the most beautiful children to be found, that the Incas realized the laziness of their subjects and kept them at work, even if it had no real value, and that some of the Indians were cannibals.

Althouth Levillier has published all these *Informaciones* in a bulky volume,[11] and vigorously attacked the interpretation that they were part of a denigration campaign instigated by Toledo, we can probably never be quite certain that the last word has been said on this controversy. It is clear, however, that Toledo had a definite end in view when he instituted the enquiries, and that his great desire was to combat the theories of Las Casas. As the Viceroy declared when transmitting the *Informaciones* to the King, he "had seen how badly the rights of the king of Spain to the Indies were treated in Spain and in the Indies and how unreasonable and dangerous it was to attribute to these Incas the true lordship of these kingdoms." [12]

The enquiry had proven, Toledo informed the King, that "Your Majesty is the legitimate ruler of this kingdom and the Incas are tyrannical usurpers," and he may therefore bestow the lands of Peru upon Spaniards and ignore the scruples raised against Spanish dominion. Moreover, as legitimate ruler "Your Majesty rightfully exercises jurisdiction over the Indians and, given their weak reason and rude understanding, Your Majesty must devise laws for their conservation and require them to obey these ordinances." [13] Toledo closed the letter with the earnest hope that "such a variety of opinion on matters of great importance will cease" and that the King, his ministers, and the inhabitants of Peru will no longer have their consciences so disturbed and confused as in the past "whenever some ignorant person dares to open his mouth and cry to high heaven."

The Viceroy was not, however, able to convince all Spaniards even in Peru. The Jesuit José de Acosta, perhaps the outstanding ecclesiastic of the time, without mentioning Toledo by name rejected the theory that Indians could be deprived of dominion if they persisted in error. Acosta affirmed:

We must reject those false titles of dominion which some persons are trying to propagate, unnecessary defenders of the royal authority in my opinion, not to say deceivers, who would prove their assertions by the tyranny of the Incas . . . which we do not understand and do not admit. For it is not lawful to rob a thief, nor does the crime committed by some one else add to our own justice.[14]

Another prominent figure of the time, Juan de Matienzo, jurist and adviser of Toledo, was just as certain that the Viceroy was absolutely right. In the *Gobierno del Perú*, not published until over three centuries after it was written, Matienzo first described the cruelty and tyranny of the Incas, how they killed five thousand persons at one time in one place and tore out their hearts, how they sacrificed boys to their idols, how they burned alive the women and children of their chief men, and how the Incas governed in their own interest and not for the welfare of their people. Then Matienzo made a rousing justification of Spanish rule, declaring:

The Indies were justly won. By the concession of the pope, or because those kingdoms were found deserted by the Spaniards. Or because of their abominable sins against nature. Or because of their infidelity. Although this last reason alone would be sufficient, as would each of the others, the tyranny of the Indians is enough to establish the fact that the kingdom of

Peru was justly gained and that His Majesty has a very just title to it. . . .
Moreover, the Indians have learned to trade and thereby win profits, and
to use mechanical and agricultural instruments, which is no less a just
title than the others.[15]

Curiously enough, just as certain historians today accuse the
Spaniards of hypocritically seeking to justify their rule, so Juan Polo
de Ondegardo, another important adviser to Toledo, stated that the
Incas, once they had determined upon a particular conquest, "looked
for some title and pretext to accomplish what they wanted to do,
which is only natural." [16]

The "Indian History" of Pedro Sarmiento de Gamboa

The enquiry into Inca history and Indian customs was not enough.
Neither did the treatise Defense of the Legitimacy of the Rule of the
King of Spain in the Indies wholly satisfy the Viceroy or the conquistadores and their descendants. What the situation really required, they felt, was a history—a true history, which would supplant
the false histories then current. In the very year, 1571, when Toledo
was proceeding in leisurely fashion through Peru on his viceregal
visit, having called in the "most ancient and most reliable" Indians to
provide information for his enquiry, a Historia del Perú by Diego
Fernández was published in Seville. This was like a red flag to Toledo,
who promptly assailed it because Fernández stated that the Incas
were natural lords of their realms, having been elected by their
chieftains. Later, when the enquiry was completed, Toledo protested
again, citing the Informaciones as proof that Fernández was wrong,
and urged that this history, and other printed works such as the
writings of Las Casas, should not be given credence by the King or
Council of the Indies. Probably as a result of the Viceroy's first protest, the Council forbade the circulation of Fernández's history among
the general public, and referred the work for examination to the
first Historian-in-Chief of the Council of the Indies, the recently
appointed Juan López de Velasco. On May 16, 1572, he rendered
his opinion, the principal point of which was that copies of the
book should be sent to the Peruvian Audiencia for private reading
by persons who had knowledge of the events treated by Fernández.
Once their report was in, the question of suppressing the book could
be considered. The Licentiate Santillán was apparently deputed by
the audiencia to write this report and he listed sixty-eight specific
objections, to which Fernández replied.

The widespread and intense dissatisfaction among the Spanish
rulers of Peru with the historical accounts of Spanish deeds in the
New World and with the justification of Spanish rule in Peru is well

illustrated by the expressive memorial drawn up by the Town Council of Cuzco and forwarded to the Council of the Indies on October 24, 1572. These worthies wrote in an injured tone, pointing out that even barbarians with no knowledge of writing, such as the Incas, had a high opinion of the importance of recording history, whereas Spaniards, "having performed great feats and having labored more greatly and with more determination than any other nation in the world," had permitted these great deeds to be forgotten. Or even worse, the story had been twisted. The Town Council complained: "When we read the histories written about us, we think they must be describing another kind of people." Some writers had even doubted the justice of Spanish rule in Peru. Yet this rule was based upon the papal concession, and the kings of Spain had faithfully observed the conditions of the trust by expending large sums on monasteries, hospitals, priests, judges and other royal officials. Indeed, these Cuzco citizens questioned whether there existed in the world a dominion based upon such just and such reasonable titles. Certainly dominions in France, Germany, and other places "have their rights to possession written in the bones of men." The Spaniards in Cuzco then cast an envious glance at those happy peoples in other realms, for "they do not have to reply to scruples because nobody raises them. We, the inhabitants of this land, have been less fortunate." [17]

Then they proceeded to describe the tyranny of the Incas, to deplore their bad customs—in much the same vein as the *Informaciones* —and to approve heartily Viceroy Toledo's enquiry. They concluded with the statement that of the one thousand encomenderos appointed by the King in Peru, eight hundred had been killed in putting down rebellions and in defense of the realm, and those who remained required assistance and favors.

It was to satisfy the demand for an honest history, and to meet the threat to Spanish rule in America which Toledo found in the doctrines of Las Casas and Fernández, that he commissioned Pedro Sarmiento de Gamboa to write a history to set at rest forever these doubts concerning justice.

Sarmiento was one of that group of able officials with whom the Viceroy had surrounded himself, and upon whom he leaned heavily in the administration of his far-flung realm. As a soldier, astronomer, and later explorer of the Solomon Islands and the Straits of Magellan, Sarmiento was typical of the principal Spanish administrative officers who kept the large and complicated machinery of empire in motion. For two years he had been traversing Peru, drawing out from the oldest inhabitants their recollection of the events of the past. To a considerable extent Sarmiento depended upon the *Informaciones* brought forth by Toledo's enquiry, but he had also carried on other investigations in the valley of the Jauja, in Guamanga, but principally in Cuzco where the Incas had made their capital and where the best informants still lived.

Sarmiento officially presented his history to the Viceroy on February 29, 1572, for examination and correction.[18] Toledo thereupon ordered the "principal and most able descendants" of the Incas to be brought together to listen to a reading of the history. Each Indian swore by the cross to tell the truth and to indicate, by means of an interpreter, whatever corrections he considered necessary. Day after day the history was read, chapter by chapter. Now and then some name was corrected, or other minor change made, as when Doña María Cusi Guarcai objected to the prominent place accorded to certain Incas not of her own family, but all the listeners declared that they found the history good and true and according to the tales handed down by their fathers. The four living conquistadores who had entered Peru with Pizarro almost half a century before also testified that the history coincided with what they had been told by other Indians.

The corrected version was then legally certified and despatched to the King, with a covering letter from the Viceroy, a genealogical tree, and four painted cloths illustrating certain events of Inca history. These paintings had also been examined by various competent Indians and pronounced good. The Viceroy suggested in his letter that such an accurate history, which would serve as the best possible justification of Spain's title to America, should be published, "in order to refute the other false and lying books that have circulated in these parts, and to explain the truth, not only to our own people but to foreign nations as well." [19]

The *Indian History* of Sarmiento described in detail the history of the Incas, their cruelty, their revolting customs, and their tyranny, in a tone and in a spirit reminiscent of that in which Las Casas had denounced the conquistadores in his *Very Brief Account of the Destruction of the Indies*. Sarmiento concluded that because of the sins of the Incas against the law of nature they should be forced to obey it,

as had been taught by the Archbishop of Florence and confirmed by Friar Francisco de Vitoria in the discussion he made concerning the title of the Indies. Therefore Your Majesty by this title alone holds just as sufficient and legitimate title to the Indies as any prince in the world holds to any realm whatsoever, because in all the lands thus far discovered in the two seas to the North and to the South there has been found this general violation of the law of nature.[20]

But the King never published the history so laboriously compiled by Pedro Sarmiento de Gamboa. It was allowed to remain in obscurity and never permitted to be circulated through Europe to counteract the writings of Bishop Bartolomé de Las Casas; indeed, it has never been published in Spain and only saw the light of day in 1906, because of the interest of a German scholar.[21]

We have found no documents to explain the royal indifference to a history which so stoutly defended the king's title to Peru. Perhaps ecclesiastical pressure was strong enough to prevent the publication of this history so opposed to the doctrines of Las Casas. Toledo never abandoned his official interest in the history of the Incas, an interest maintained by later viceroys. Spaniards continued to question the right of their king to the Indies, and Licenciado Francisco Falcón introduced a modern idea, comparable to the mandate system under the League of Nations, when he maintained that if the Incas "came to such a state as to be able to rule themselves, as they will with the aid of God, their independence should be restored by the crown." [22]

Modern historians show the same two well-defined attitudes toward the history compiled by Sarmiento, as they do on the reliability of the *Informaciones*. Markham attempted to discredit Sarmiento's work, and Means considers it "an abominably unjust and inaccurate account of a great but fallen dynasty" and the author a pliant tool who was willing to aid in the Viceroy's "nefarious literary attack." [23] Levillier, on the other hand, defends the essential truthfulness of Sarmiento's history, lashes out at Markham for what appears to be his plain mendacity, and supports Viceroy Toledo at every point.[24] Today, just as almost four hundred years ago, the differences of opinion on the justice of Spanish rule in Peru are deep, bitter, and apparently irreconcilable.

Epilogue

Two incidents occurred after the Viceroy Toledo's historical investigations which show that scruples concerning the justice of Spanish rule were raised not merely by theologians, jurists, historians, and other erudite persons, but by ordinary folk as well. When Sarmiento de Gamboa went on his ill-fated expedition to the Straits of Magellan in 1581–82, one of his sea captains, Diego Flores, exclaimed petulantly "that he didn't see what title the king had to the Indies anyway." [25] Sarmiento was greatly distressed and proceeded to inform Flores of all the titles the king held, described by Friar Francisco de Vitoria in his treatises, and in his own history prepared ten years previously for Viceroy Toledo. But none of these reasons persuaded the captain until Sarmiento showed him the bull of Alexander VI and sternly warned him that anyone who contradicted this title contradicted the power of the pope and soiled the royal conscience. Only then did Flores fall silent.

The second incident involved the last will and testament of that gallant conquistador Mancio Serra, who had been present at the verification exercises held in Cuzco in 1572 in connection with Sarmiento's history. Serra was famous throughout Peru for having been awarded the celebrated golden image of the sun which had been the chief ornament of the Temple of the Sun in Cuzco, and was even more famous for having promptly lost it in a card game. In 1589 Serra, now the oldest living conquistador, was on his deathbed, and, wishing to ease his conscience, solemnly swore to the following deposition before a notary public:

That the Incas had ruled so wisely that in all their realms there was not a single thief, vicious or lazy man, or adulterous woman; that immoral persons were not countenanced; that every man had an honest and profitable occupation; that the mountains, mines, and lands were all so administered that everyone had enough; that the Incas were obeyed and respected by their subjects and considered very capable rulers.[26]

Ironically enough, the Viceroy Toledo seems to have agreed with Serra to some extent, in spite of the history composed by Sarmiento, for the many laws and administrative regulations he worked out for the Indians—which won for him the name of "Solon of Peru"—were based on the system developed centuries before by the Incas.

For those of us reared in the English tradition, the great attention paid by Spaniards to the legal basis of their rule may seem curious and bizarre. Certainly, few instances may be discovered in our own colonial history of English preoccupation with such matters. Roger Williams, in Rhode Island, did compose a manuscript in which he questioned the right of Plymouth to Indian lands unless by direct purchase in a voluntary sale, but after the chief men and ministers of Boston condemned these "errors and presumptions in which treason might lurk" he wrote "very submissively" to Governor Winthrop offering to burn part or all of the manuscript.[27] To Spaniards, however, the basis for the just title by which their king ruled the Indies was a palpitating question throughout most of the sixteenth century.

CONCLUSION

THE story and the meaning of Spanish efforts to work out just methods of treating the Indians and Indian problems cannot be summed up in a few paragraphs, as those who have followed this account of the struggle for justice as it unfolded itself in all the far corners of Spain's vast overseas empire will readily comprehend Nor can the struggle be easily and confidently "explained." Certain traits of Spanish character, however—its individualism, religiosity, legalism, and passion for extremes—can help us to understand the panorama of curious fact and contradictory action spread before the reader in this volume. Once the friars had questioned the right by which Spaniards held Indians, thus precipitating the struggle for justice, their champions never resigned themselves to what they considered the injustice of the world about them any more than Don Quixote did. It was not a simple or easy struggle, and there was no decisive victory. Even late in the sixteenth century the Jesuit missionary José de Acosta found not only a diversity of opinion on Indian affairs but also that "not a few people doubted whether the Indians could be saved." [1]

The historian who is confronted by the mass of printed and manuscript material available on the struggle, or views the colonial monuments in Spanish America which remain to testify to the imperial grandeur that was Spain, can easily see today that the crown and the nation were attempting to achieve the impossible in the sixteenth century. As Spanish rulers the kings sought imperial dominion, prestige, and revenue—in short, conquest and the fruits of conquest which involve war. As heads of the church in America they were urgently committed to the great enterprise of winning the Indians to the faith—which requires peace. The pursuit of this double purpose made inevitable both a vacillating royal policy and a mighty conflict of ideas and of men. It was the tragedy of the Indians that the accomplishment of either of the two Spanish purposes necessitated the overthrow of established Indian values and the disruption of the Indian cultures.

The sermons of Montesinos constituted the opening act in this tragedy. Every one of the solutions worked out in those early years—the Laws of Burgos, the Requirement, and the establishment of the title of Spain to America upon the papal donation—were later amended or found wanting. Nor did the four experiments carried on during the hurly-burly of the first half-century of the conquest help much in the clarification of these problems. Their failures were due to various reasons, of course. The attempt to discover whether Indians could live like Christian Spaniards rested on the fundamental misconception that one culture may be imposed on another almost overnight. The plans to colonize Venezuela with farmers and to win the Indians to Christianity by peaceful means alone were thwarted by human nature, both Indian and Spanish, and more particularly by human greed and the implacable hostility of worldly minded Spaniards. The encomienda system could not be abolished in 1542 because it was too firmly entrenched and had too many beneficiaries—lay, ecclesiastical, and administrative.

Yet the crown continued to listen to those idealists who had been responsible for the experiments and even for a time suspended conquest in America while its justice was being debated at Valladolid. Impatient conquistadores champed at the bit while intricate discussions were held concerning the applicability to the Indians of the Aristotelian doctrine of slavery. Though the conquests were continued, the regulations governing them and those who waged just war in Mexico, Peru, and even on the periphery of the empire in New Mexico, Chile, and the Philippines never escaped the scrutiny of those who insisted that the Christianization of the Indians and their welfare were the principal aims of the conquest.

Closely allied to this concern for the justice of the wars was the desire to establish the just title of Spain to the Indies on solid foundations. Ferdinand and his councilors were most astonished when Montesinos first questioned Spain's title. The King indignantly cited an earlier discussion in 1503, at which it was unanimously agreed that the papal donation provided ample justification, a point of view that generally prevailed during the first half-century of the conquest. Francisco de Vitoria's lectures at Salamanca changed all this when he denied the universal temporal authority of the pope, hence denied his right to bestow temporal power, and established the title upon other grounds. Las Casas, a more sulphurous and polemical theorist, felt that the pope could grant Spain sufficient temporal power to achieve her spiritual obligations in the Indies, but strenuously argued in favor of the political and economic rights of the Indian rulers.

The struggle did not remain an academic exercise carried on by cloistered philosophers in Spain with learned footnotes as their most deadly weapons. The battle came to be fought by men of action, ecclesiastics as well as conquistadores, who carried their fundamental disagreements to all the distant corners of the empire. The most extensive ventilation of the dispute in America was ordered by the Viceroy Francisco de Toledo, who sought to establish the justice of

Spain's rule to Peru partly by proving the injustice of the Inca overlords.

The thesis of this book is that the clash of arms was not the only
struggle during the conquest. The clash of ideas that accompanied
the discovery of America and the establishment of Spanish rule there
is a story that must be told as an integral part of the conquest, and
endows it with a unique character worthy of note. Of course, many
nations have had a "habit of acting under an odd mixture of selfish
and altruistic motives," as Woodrow Wilson expressed it when describing the history of the United States.[2] No European nation however, with the possible exception of Portugal, took her Christian duty
toward native peoples so seriously as did Spain. Certainly England
did not, for as one New England preacher said, "the Puritan hoped
to meet the Pequod Indians in heaven, but wished to keep apart
from them on earth, nay, to exterminate them from the land." [3]

The Spaniards, or at least many of them, had an entirely different
attitude toward the Indians and the desirability of incorporating
them into a Christian and European civilization, as the disputes on
their character have shown. Those loud and dogmatic voices quarrel-
ing over the Indians have a peculiarly human ring, representing as
they do opposed theories of human values as well as philosophical
and theological differences.

A homely illustration of this may be seen in the encounter between
the saintly Bishop Juan de Zumárraga and certain secular Spaniards
in Mexico who urged him to have less to do with the evil-smelling
and poorly clad Indians. "Your Reverend Lordship is no longer young
or robust, but old and infirm," they warned him, "and your constant
mingling with the Indians may bring you great harm." Whereupon
the Bishop indignantly replied:

You are the ones who give out an evil smell according to my way of thinking,
and you are the ones who are repulsive and disgusting to me, because you
seek only vain frivolities and because you lead soft lives just as though you
were not Christians. These poor Indians have a heavenly smell to me;
they comfort me and give me health, for they exemplify for me that harshness of life and penitence which I must espouse if I am to be saved.[4]

This revealing incident demonstrates the human and therefore en-
during quality of the struggle. Concern over the glaring inequalities
in the conditions of men, and the duty of Christians to mitigate them
and to emphasize the common burdens all men must bear, is deep-
seated in Spanish-American literature of all centuries. The spirit
shown by Zumárraga was shared by many other ecclesiastics, whether
or not they agreed with the theories of Las Casas. As Frank Tannenbaum has well said, in summing up the action of Spain in Mexico:

The Indian was robbed, abused, enslaved, branded, worked against his will on plantations and in mines. Everything evil that one human being can do to another was done to him. This need not be denied—it cannot be. But the cruelty, the brutality, the harshness are not the whole story. The Indian woman was taken as a wife by the conquerors; her children given a place in the household. . . . A community, a church, a law, a body of rights —all these were given to him largely because he was considered a human being possessed of a soul and capable of redemption . . . men like Las Casas, Quiroga, Zumárraga, and Fuenleal labored, fought, and defended the Indian against the rapacity of the white man, and in that defense initiated a series of currents, ideals, ideas, laws, and practices, within which the Indian has the more easily saved his race from extermination, and, by saving his race, has saved his genius for the world.[5]

The echoes of this sixteenth-century conflict are heard today in every Spanish-speaking land. Mexicans, for example, have refused to permit even a picture of Cortés the conquistador to be hung in a public place, while they long ago erected an imposing monument to Las Casas the Apostle to the Indians near the cathedral in Mexico, as well as placing his bust in a prominent place in the Ministry of Education building along with Quetzalcoatl, Plato, and Buddha.[6] And the concept of race, the idea that any group of people might be inferior as a group, against which Las Casas fought at Valladolid in 1550, today seems so erroneous to some that the First Interamerican Demographic Congress, held in Mexico in 1943, attempted to suppress the use of the word or the concept. In Cuba the feeling is so strong against it that there is no "Day of the Race" celebration on October 12, but a "Fiesta in Commemoration of the Discovery of America."[7] In Guatemala, Rafael Arévalo Martínez recently stirred up an extensive and violent controversy in the newspapers by publishing an article entitled "De Aristóteles a Hitler,"[8] in which he strongly supported the declaration of Las Casas against Aristotle's theory of natural slavery as being applicable to the Indians.

The struggle has also had a profound influence on the writing of the history of Spain in America. No other aspect of Spain's colonial history has evoked so continuously such bitter differences of interpretation. One might almost classify historians in this field—as did William Burghardt Dubois in preparing a bibliography on the Negro —according to their attitude toward Indians and their champions. The friars and others who spoke freely of Spanish abuses and clamored vigorously for their own concept of justice for the Indians were looked upon at the time as noble apostles or impractical troublemakers. Later on they were charged with being rebels and fanatics, careless of the truth and their nation's honor, or soft, muddleheaded humanitarians.[9]

This divergence persists today and may be best seen in reactions to Las Casas. One writer, in a prominent Madrid newspaper, declared in 1927 that Las Casas was not really in his right mind,[10] and was answered at once by another Spaniard who declared:

Far from considering Las Casas crazy, we believe that he was a genuinely Spanish figure, exhibiting all the virtues and defects of our race. We must not accuse him of insanity in order to combat his exaggerations. He was a Spaniard through and through. To maintain otherwise is to perpetuate in a certain sense the black legend.[11]

The tendency to regard Las Casas and the reformers as true Spaniards has been growing, particularly in Spanish America. The Cuban José María Chacón y Calvo has advocated the view that the widespread criticism permitted, and even stimulated, by the crown really constitutes one of the glories of Spanish civilization.[12] The pendulum is swinging so far in this direction that the twenty-sixth Congress of Americanists, which met in Seville in 1935, approved unanimously, although after acrimonious debate, the proposition put forward by various Spanish-American delegates, that the men who criticized Spain's colonial practices—Montesinos, Las Casas, and Vitoria— should be considered "as authentic representatives in the New World of the Spanish conscience." [13] A striking example of this new attitude was exhibited in 1944 by the Cuban Enrique Gay Calbó on the occasion of the unveiling in Havana of a picture of Las Casas. Gay Calbó declared:

We, the American descendants of Spaniards . . . believe that the true Spain is not that of Sepúlveda and Charles V, but that of Las Casas and Vitoria. . . . It appears appropriate to Cubans that in a public building there should be placed the picture of Friar Bartolomé de Las Casas, a true and exemplary Spaniard.[14]

This new spirit has not swept all before it, however, for in Mexico one prominent jurist has publicly labeled Las Casas as being very closely related to the Communists, a sort of "pre-Marxian who, preached the class struggle." [15] In present-day Spain, too, publications supporting Sepúlveda have appeared and one of Spain's greatest living scholars, Ramón Menéndez Pidal, recently attacked Las Casas.[16]

But in judging these attitudes we must not struggle out of one pit of prejudices to fall into another. Not Las Casas, not Sepúlveda, nor any other single individual exclusively represents the complete Spanish genius.[17] Even remembering the extraordinary and marvelous variety of men who made up the company of Spaniards in the New World, we come closer to the truth when we say: Spanish character was so fashioned that it can be likened to a medal stamped on each of its two sides with a strong and resolute face. One face is that of an imperialistic conquistador and the other is a friar devoted to God. Both these faces are undeniably and typically Spanish. Both friar and conquistador were imprisoned within the thinking of their own kind and their own time; neither, when he was most himself, could understand or forgive the other. Yet they were inseparably yoked, sent together into a new world, and together were responsible for the action and achievement of Spain in America. To appreciate the full power and depth of Spanish character, one must turn the medal and see both of these bold and purposeful Spanish faces. More, one must recognize as equally significant the attitude of the crown in permitting experiments and disputes of a most fundamental nature in those tumultuous years during which its policies and practices were evolving. It is to Spain's everlasting credit that she allowed men to insist that all her actions in America be just, and that at times she listened to these voices.

The struggle which Montesinos started is not yet over, in America or in the world. Thus the dust which covers the writings upon which this study is based cannot obscure the quality of life in the ideas and episodes set forth here. The cry of Montesinos denouncing the enslavement of the Indians, the loud voice of Bartolomé de Las Casas proclaiming that all the peoples of the world are men—these have not lost their validity today and they will still have it tomorrow. For in a sense they are timeless.

In the years since the ideals of justice for the American Indians were first enunciated and fought for, Spain has lost her empire, and the tread of Spanish soldiers no longer shakes the world, as it did in the sixteenth century. The horses of Cortés, which so amazed and frightened the hosts of Montezuma, have been superseded by steel tanks, and these in turn have been robbed of most of their significance by the atomic bomb. Just around the corner, we are told, are even greater atomic bombs and various instruments of bacterial warfare which will doubtless be as terrible a shock to our present puny atomic age as was the first roar of the cannons of Cortés to the Aztecs armed only with arrows and spears.

Whatever means men develop, however, to destroy their fellow men, the real problems between nations do not lie in the realm of mechanics. They lie in the more difficult field of human relationships. Some Spaniards long ago discerned this truth, which the whole world must understand today if it is to survive. The specific methods used to apply the theories worked out by sixteenth-century Spaniards are now as outmoded as the blowguns with which Indians shot poisoned arrows at the conquistadores, but the ideals which some Spaniards sought to put into practice as they opened up the New World will never lose their shining brightness as long as men believe that other peoples have a right to live, that just methods may be found for the conduct of relations between peoples, and that essentially all the peoples of the world are men.

NOTES

INTRODUCTION

[1] *History of America*, II, 353.

[2] A critical essay on previous contributions and on the materials available for this study will be found in the bibliographical appendix.

[3] *New Viewpoints* was published in Philadelphia in 1943, and *Filosofía* in Mexico City in 1947.

[4] Wesley Mitchell (ed.), *What Veblen Taught*, p. 370. As an indication of the persistence today of this view, Buell G. Gallagher has this to say in his serious study entitled *Color and Conscience: The Irrepressible Conflict* (p. 54): "The magnificent splendor of the Incas and the Aztecs was fit plunder for men who felt no inhibitions in carrying out their mission of conquest and freebootery."

[5] London, 1947.

[6] *Hakluytus Posthumus, or Purchas His Pilgrimes*, XVIII (MacLehose ed.), 81–82.

[7] "The Religious Character of Colonial Law in Sixteenth Century Spain," *Proceedings of the Sixth International Congress of Philosophy, 1926* (1927), p. 483.

[8] For a more complete treatment of the climate of opinion, with citations to a variety of illustrations, see the writer's *Lucha por justicia en América*, Part II. For a useful bibliographical survey, see Otis H. Green's "A Critical Survey of Scholarship in the Field of Spanish Renaissance Literature, 1914–1944," *Studies in Philology*, XLIV (1947), 228–64.

[9] The statement comes from the famous Dominican theologian Francisco de Vitoria. James Brown Scott, *The Spanish Origin of International Law. Francisco de Vitoria and his Law of Nations*, pp. lxxxi–lxxxii.

[10] Jeannette M. Connor (ed.), *Colonial Records of Spanish Florida*, II, 86–87.

[11] *Documentos inéditos de Ultramar*, XXI, 103; *Documentos inéditos de América*, XXVI, 16–18. Pedro de Aguado, *Historia de Santa Marta y Nuevo Reino de Granada*, I, 619. Ed. by Jerónimo Becker.

[12] Roger B. Merriman, *Rise of the Spanish Empire*, IV, 26.

[13] Canto 34.

[14] Bernal Díaz del Castillo, *Historia verdadera de la conquista de la Nueva España*, I, 228–29. Edited by Ramón Iglesia.

[15] Emiliano Jos, *La expedición de Ursúa al Dorado*, pp. 76–79.

[16] Miguel de Unamuno, *Del sentimiento trágico de la vida*, p. 316; Ludwig Pfandl, *Cultura y costumbres del pueblo español de los siglos XVI y XVII*, pp. 311–13; John A. Mackay, *The Other Spanish Christ*, p. 164. For some wise observations on the quixotic aspects of the conquest see *ibid.*, pp. 16–18.

[17] This statement appears in an undated memorial sent to the King by Bernardino de Minaya and found in the Archivo General de Simancas, Sección ·de Estado, Legajo 892, fol. 197 ff. A transcription of pertinent parts of the document is given by the writer in *Lucha por justicia en América*, Part II, chap. 3.

[18] *Bartolomé de Las Casas o Casaus, Colección de tratados*, pp. 561, 617.

[19] Bernal Díaz, *Verdadera historia*, II, 394.

[20] Américo de Castro, *Antonio de Guevara. El Villano del Danubio y otros fragmentos*, p. xvi,

21 This subject has been given fuller treatment by the writer in "Free Speech in Sixteenth-Century Spanish America," *Hispanic American Historical Review,* XXVI (1946), 135–49.

22 Archivo de Indias, Filipinas 339, Book DDI, Part II, p. 155 verso.

23 José María Chacón y Calvo (ed.), *Cedulario Cubano,* p. 203.

24 This prohibition was invoked against Francisco Pizarro on behalf of Diego de Almagro in a royal order dated August 9, 1538, in which the previous order of December 15, 1521, was reaffirmed. Jorge A. Garcés (ed.), *Colección de cédulas reales dirigidas a la audiencia de Quito,* p. 5.

25 The powerful attack on the motives and accomplishments of Las Casas is found in Motolinía's letter to Charles V dated January 2, 1555. The original Spanish version is printed in *Documentos inéditos de América,* XX, 175–213 and an excellent English translation of most of it was made by Lesley B. Simpson in *The Encomienda in New Spain,* pp. 249–72.

26 James Brown Scott, *Francisco de Vitoria,* pp. 84–85.

27 For a more thorough description of this subject, see the writer's *First Social Experiments in America,* Appendix 2, and *Lucha por justicia en América,* Part II, chap. 3.

28 Las Casas, *Colección de tratados,* pp. 7–8.

29 This estimate has been compiled from Oviedo's remarks in his *Historia general y natural de las Indians,* Primera Parte, Lib. 2, cap. 6; Lib. 4, cap. 2; Lib. 5, Prohemio, caps. 2–3; Lib. 6, cap. 9.

30 The manuscript is in the Convento de San Felipe, in Sucre, Bolivia. A transcription was published by the writer in *Lucha por justicia en América,* Part II, chap. 3.

31 *Documentos inéditos de América,* VI: 499.

PART I

CHAPTER I

1 *Literary Currents in Hispanic America,* p. 15.

2 *Ibid.,* pp. 15–16. The report of the sermon is given by Las Casas, *Historia de las Indias,* Lib. 3, cap. 4. Other information on this episode is given in Lib. 3, caps. 3–12, 17–19, 33–35, 81–87, 94–95. Much information on the early Dominicans in America is given by Antonio Figueras, "Principios de la expansión dominicana en Indias," *Missionalia hispánica,* Año 1 (1944), Nos. 1 and 2, pp. 303–40, and Benno M. Biermann, "Die erster Dominikaner in Amerika," *Missionswissenschaft und Religionswissenschaft* (Münster i W., 1947), pp. 56–65.

3 Las Casas, *Historia de las Indias,* Lib. 3, cap. 5.

4 Chacón y Calvo, *Cedulario cubano,* p. 431.

5 *Ibid.,* pp. 445–47.

6 Helps, *Spanish Conquest in America,* I, 105.

7 Las Casas, *Historia de las Indias,* Lib. 1, caps. 112–16; Cecil Jane, "The Administration of the Colons in Española, 1493–1500," *Proceedings of the Twenty-First International Congress of Americanists* (1924), Part I.

8 The best general treatment in English on the encomienda remains Lesley B. Simpson's *The Encomienda in New Spain.* Silvio Zavala has made many important contributions, as may be seen from his works listed in the bibliography. For definitions and usages see Antonio de León Pinelo, *Tratado de confirmaciones reales,* pp. 13–14, and Daniel Granada, "Terminología indiana. Apuntamientos sobre la encomienda," *Boletín de la real academia española,* VIII (1921), 727–40; IX (1922).

9 The difference between the encomienda in the islands and on the mainland is

set forth by Erich Zurkalowski, "El establecimiento de las encomiendas en el Perú y sus antecedentes," *Revista histórica*, VI (Lima, 1919), 254–69.

[10] *Documentos inéditos de América*, XXXI, 209–12.

[11] *Ibid.*, XXXI, 436–39.

[12] Zavala, *La encomienda indiana*, p. 7 ff.

[13] The story of Las Casas' early life is based on his *Historia de las Indias*, Lib. III, caps. 28–32; 79–80.

[14] Luis G. Alonso Getino, *Los dominicos y las leyes nuevas*, p. 46.

CHAPTER II

[1] Our principal source for this early battle is Las Casas, *Historia de las Indias*, Lib. 3, caps. 6–7.

[2] *Ibid.*, Lib. 3, cap. 12. For other references on the Burgos meetings see Robert Streit, "Zur Vorgeschichte der 1. Junta von Burgos 1512," *Zeitschrift für Missonswissenschaft* (1922), pp. 165–75, and "Die erste Junta von Burgos in Jahre 1512," *ibid.* (1923), pp. 65–78.

[3] The best edition of these laws is provided by Rafael Altamira, "El texto de las leyes de Burgos de 1512," *Revista de historia de América* (1938), No. 4, pp. 5–79. See also the writer's "Las leyes de Burgos en 1512 y 1513," in *Anuario de historia argentina, 1942* (1943), 33–56.

[4] Alamán, *Obras*, I, 41.

[5] Benzoni, *History of the New World*, p. 32.

[6] Chacón y Calvo, *Cedulario cubano*, p. 429–31.

[7] Simpson, *Encomienda in New Spain*, p. 32.

[8] Chacón y Calvo, *Cedulario cubano*, p. 103.

[9] *Ibid.*, pp. 318–19.

[10] For a résumé of past and present interpretations, see Zavala, *New Viewpoints*, pp. 17–28. The lastest study is by Manuel Giménez Fernández, *Las bulas alejandrinas de 1493 referentes a las Indias*.

[11] Chacón y Calvo, *Cedulario cubano*, pp. 430–31.

[12] Las Casas, *Historia de las Indias*, Lib. 3, caps. 7–9.

[13] *Documentos inéditos de América*, VII, 24–25.

[14] "Un precursor del maestro Vitoria. El P. Matías de Paz, O.P., y su tratado De Dominio Regum Hispaniae super Indos," *La ciencia tomista*, XL (1929), 173–90, and "El tratado del Padre Matías de Paz, O.P., acerca del dominio de los reyes sobre los indios de América," *Archivum fratrum praedicatorum*, III (1933), 133–81.

[15] Las Casas, *Historia de las Indias*, Lib. 3, cap. 8, gives a summary of the treatise.

[16] Manuel María Hoyos, *Historia del Colegio de San Gregorio de Valladolid por el . . . Fr. Gonzalo de Arriaga*, I: 174–77.

[17] Corollary 2 in Conclusion I of the treatise, Beltrán de Heredia, *Un precursor del maestro Vitoria*, p. 181.

[18] *Ibid.*, p. 180.

[19] *Documentos inéditos de América*, VII: 24–25.

[20] *Ibid.*, I: 442.

[21] Some persons will doubtless wonder why John Major was not included among the pre-Vitorian theorists. His remarks on the conquest, which are imbedded in his *Commentaries on the Second Book of Sentences* of 1510, constitute probably the first extended theoretical treatment of Spain in America. Major conceded complete temporal power to neither the pope nor the emperor, and declared that mere infidelity did not deprive infidels of dominion, though armed opposition to preaching of the faith did. He also supported Aristotle's theory of natural slavery.

Major is not included here because he seems to have had no great influence on the course of events in the New World. Vitoria cited him in his manuscript works but not in his printed volumes (Alonso Getino, *Francisco de Vitoria*, p. 274). For an excellent account of Major and the text of his remarks, see Pedro Leturia, "Maior y Vitoria ante la conquista de América," *Estudios eclesiásticos*, II (1932), 44–82. Alonso Getino found many references to Major in Vitoria's manuscript works, but none of his published books (*Anuario de la Asociación Francisco de Vitoria*, III (1932), p. 274). The final truth on Major's influence among contemporary Spaniards is not yet known. Silvio Zavala has the impression that he had a greater influence than is indicated in this note, but we must await Zavala's monograph on this point.

CHAPTER III

1 Kirkpatrick, *Spanish Conquistadores*, p. 55; Winsor, *Narrative and Critical History*, II, 196–97, 211; Helps, *Spanish Conquest in America*, I, 261. A full-length biography of Pedrarias has recently appeared by Pablo Álvarez Rubiano (Madrid, 1944).

2 *Suma de Geografía* (Sevilla, 1519).

3 The essential details concerning the formulation of the Requirement all come from the memorial written by Enciso and published in *Documentos inéditos de América*, I, 441–50. After defending the King's rights at another meeting, held in the Alhambra in 1526, he petitioned for compensation (Archivo de Indias, Patronato 170, ramo 33, No. 2). The Council of the Indies rewarded Enciso by granting him the right to take fifty slaves to America free of duty and to embark on an expedition (*ibid.*, Contratación 5090).

4 Enciso memorial, *loc. cit.*, I, 442.

5 Llorente, *Colección de obras de Las Casas*, I, 452.

6 La Briére, *La conception du droit international chez les théologiens catholiques*, Première leçon, p. 5; Vanderpol, *Le droit de guerre d'après les théologiens et les canonistes du Moyen-Age*, pp. 207–22, and *La doctrine scolastique du droit de guerre*, pp. 161–70.

Enciso's interpretation appears dubious because the Canaanites were not to be required, or even allowed, to accept "the true faith." According to the Old Testament, the Lord deliberately raised a series of ramparts designed to protect his people from contamination, intellectual or religious, by the Gentiles.

7 Enciso memorial, *loc. cit.*, I, 448–49. The idea that Indian idolatry justified war did not die. Las Casas petitioned Pope Pius V about 1560 to excommunicate anyone holding this view (*Documentos inéditos de México*, II, 599–600) and the contrary argument may be seen in the 1612 treatise against Las Casas written by Bernardo de Vargas Machuca, which is printed by Fabié, *Vida y escritos de Las Casas*, II, 411–517.

The Bible was used occasionally in the English colonies to justify wars against Indians, according to Manypenny, *Our Indian Wards*, p. 13.

8 The document has been printed many times and may easily be consulted in *Documentos inéditos de Ultramar*, XX, 311–14. An English translation is given in Helps, *Spanish Conquest in America*, I, 264–67. The copy from which Pedrarias' Requirement document was made still exists in Archivo de Indias, Panamá, 233, Lib. 1, pp. 49–50 verso.

9 Oviedo, *Historia general y natural de las Indias*, Primera Parte, Lib. 29, cap. 7.

10 The writer has collected a number of instances in an article on this subject, "A aplicação do requerimento na America Espanhola," *Revista do Brasil* (Rio de Janeiro, Sept. 1938), 231–48.

[11] Oviedo, *op. cit.*, Primera Parte, Lib. XXIX, cap. 7.

[12] Charles Petrie and Louis Bertrand, *History of Spain*, p. 265.

[13] Las Casas, *Historia de las Indias*, Lib. 3, cap. 58. See also caps. 7–8, 57, 63, 67, 69, 166, 167.

[14] Oviedo, *op. cit.*, Primera Parte, Lib. 29, cap. 7.

[15] Bayle, *España en Indias*, p. 74. A more detailed statement on the interpretations placed upon the Requirement from 1514 to the present time is given in the writer's article "The Requerimiento and its Interpreters," *Revista de historia de américa* (1938), No. 1, pp. 25–34.

PART II

INTRODUCTION

[1] The introduction and first chapter are based upon an earlier work by the writer, *The First Social Experiments in America*.

[2] Robert Blakey, *History of Political Literature*, II, 365–70.

[3] Constantino Bayle has published a solid study of a somewhat similar problem, communion for Indians, in his documented article "La comunión entre los indios americanos," *Missionalia hispánica* (1944), Nos. 1 and 2, pp. 13–72.

CHAPTER IV

[1] The experiencia in Cuba may have influenced the crown to oppose other radical proposals for governing the Indians. It was in the years 1532–35 that Vasco de Quiroga presented various utopian plans which did not find favor in Spain. For a description of these plans, see Zavala's *The American Utopia of the Sixteenth Century*.

CHAPTER V

[1] Luis Rubio y Moreno (ed.), *Pasajeros a Indias*, I: 291–97.

[2] *Documentos inéditos de Ultramar*, XIV: 97.

[3] Rubio y Moreno, *op. cit.*, I: 304–7.

[4] Zavala, *New Viewpoints*, p. 110.

[5] *Documentos inéditos de América*, VII: 14–65.

[6] Zavala, *La "Utopía" de Tomás Moro en la Nueva España*.

[7] *Documentos inéditos de América*, VII: 24–25.

[8] *Ibid.*, VI: 37 ff.

[9] Las Casas, *Historia de las Indias*, Lib. 3, cap. 104. This proposal and the principle behind it had been previously suggested by Córdoba. The general royal instruction of June 13, 1513, advocated by this pioneer missionary, prohibited Spaniards from even talking to Indians, except by authorization of the Dominicans. Archivo de Indias, Indiferente General 419, Lib. 4: 144–144 verso.

[10] *Ibid.*, Indiferente General 419, Lib. 6: 25 verso–28.

[11] Las Casas, *Historia de las Indias*, Lib. 3, caps. 99–105.

[12] Fabié, *Vida y escritos de Las Casas*, II: 49–55.

[13] Las Casas, *Historia de las Indias*, Lib. 3, caps. 102, 129. See also Zavala, "¿Las Casas esclavista?" *Cuadernos americanos* (1944), No. 2, Año 3, pp. 149–54.

[14] *Documentos inéditos de América*, XXXIV: 200–201. The Dominican memorial is printed ibid., XII: 107–8.

[15] *Ibid.*, XXXIV: 214–15. The citizens' plans are printed, *ibid.*, XXXIV: 544–57, and Zuazo's remarks in *Documentos inéditos de España*, II: 371.

[16] Manuel Serrano y Sanz, *Orígenes de dominación española*, pp. 580–82.

[17] *Ibid.*, pp. 582–83.

[18] *Ibid.*, p. 428.

[19] *Ibid.*, p. 583.

[20] Archivo de Indias, Indiferente General 419, Lib. 7: 97; Serrano y Sanz, *op. cit.*, pp. 428–32; Las Casas, *Historia de las Indias*, Lib. 3, cap. 105; *Documentos inéditos de Ultramar*, IX: 94–95, 109–14. Other orders still in manuscript are to be found in the Archivo de Indias, Indiferente General 419, Lib. 7: 95–96, 97, 108, 110–12, 120. Other documentation on this episode may be found in Alejandro Tapia y Rivera, *Biblioteca Histórica de Puerto Rico*, 162–63; Archivo de Indias, Contratación 4675, cuaderno 1: 93, 96–97, 115–20, 128–29 and Indiferente General 420, Lib. 8: 81, 148–52, 232–33.

[21] Archivo de Indias, Indiferente General 420, Lib. 8: 152–53.

[22] Las Casas, *Historia de las Indias*, Lib. 3, cap. 105.

[23] Serrano y Sanz gives a highly colored version of this recruiting campaign, which he considers harebrained and quixotic, *op. cit.*, p. 435.

[24] Tapia y Rivera, *op. cit.*, p. 163.

[25] Figueroa reported to the King concerning the pitiful condition of these settlers on July 6, September 16, and November 13, 1520. *Documentos inéditos de América*, I: 416, 420–21.

[26] Archivo de Indias, Contratación 4675, fol. 132.

[27] Las Casas, *Historia de las Indias*, Lib. 3, cap. 132. Another colonization plan of the time has been described by Pablo Álvarez Rubiano in "Importancia político-social de las mercedes de 1519 concedidas a los labradores de Tierra Firme," *Revista de Indias,* Año 2 (1941), No. 5, pp. 133–48.

[28] For a full account of Oviedo's plans and his contempt for Las Casas' project, see his *Historia general y natural de las Indias,* Primera Parte, Lib. 19, cap. 5, and Segunda Parte, Lib. 7, cap. 1. Francisco López de Gómara also attacked the colonization scheme in another history of the time, Ramón Iglesia, *Cronistas e historiadores de la conquista de México,* pp. 130–33.

[29] Las Casas, *Historia de las Indias*, Lib. 3, cap. 136.

[30] *Ibid.*, Lib. 3, cap. 138.

[31] Iglesia, *op. cit.*, pp. 130–131.

[32] Las Casas, *Historia de las Indias,* Lib. 3, cap. 138.

[33] *Ibid.*, Lib. 3, caps. 139–41.

[34] Archivo de Indias, Patronato 252.

[35] Las Casas, *Historia de las Indias,* Lib. 3, cap. 155.

[36] The agreement of May 19, 1520, is to be found in manuscript in Archivo de Indias, Contratación 5090, Lib. 3, fol. 1 ff. and in Patronato 252, No. 3. It is printed in *Documentos inéditos de América,* VII: 65–89. For the joke, see Las Casas, *Historia de las Indias,* Lib. 3, cap. 155.

[37] Archivo de Indias, Contratación 5090, Lib. 3. Many royal orders of this nature are to be found here, dated July 30, 1520.

[38] Prudencio de Sandoval, *Historia de la vida y hechos del emperador Carlos V,* I: 219.

[39] Archivo de Indias, Contratación 5090, Lib. 3.

[40] Las Casas, *Historia de las Indias,* Lib. 3, cap. 156.

[41] Pedro Gutiérrez de Santa Clara, *Historia de las guerras civiles del Perú,* I: 36–40. This chronicler has some details not found elsewhere, such as the names of some of the persons who went with Las Casas.

[42] Archivo de Indias, Contratación 4675, cuaderno 1, fol. 143. Las Casas certified only 70 of the 98 who wanted to go.

[43] The deaths occurred on September 3, 1520, according to a report made on November 14 by royal officials of Hispaniola. *Documentos inéditos de América,* I: 422–27.

[44] Las Casas, *Historia de las Indias,* Lib. 3, cap. 157.

[45] *Ibid.*, Lib. 3, cap. 158.

46 Much information on the way wine and guns got to Indians is given in Archivo de Indias, Justicia 47.

47 Las Casas, *Historia de las Indias*, Lib. 3, cap. 159.

48 *Documentos inéditos de América*, VII: 109–16.

49 Las Casas, *Historia de las Indias*, Lib. 3, cap. 100.

50 According to one ecclesiastical authority, it was Pedro de Córdoba who persuaded Las Casas to join the Dominican Order. Justo Cuervo, *Historiadores del convento de San Esteban de Salamanca*, II: 42. A manuscript "Historia eclesiástica de la isla española de Santo Domingo hasta el año 1650," by Luis Gerónimo de Alcozer has a description of Las Casas' entrance into the order. *Biblioteca Nacional* (Madrid), Ms. 3000, p. 63 ff. See also Antonio de Remesal, *Historia de Chiapa*, Lib. 2, cap. 23, and Lib. 3, cap. 1.

51 *Ibid.*, Lib. 3, caps. 1–3. Some writers have questioned the importance of this episode but the German Dominican Benno M. Biermann has published a letter written by Las Casas in 1534 describing the whole affair, "Zwei Briefe von Fray Bartolomé de Las Casas," *Archivum fratrum praedicatorum* (1934), IV, 187–220.

52 Mariano Cuevas, *Historia de la iglesia en México*, I: 456.

53 Fabié, *Vida y escritos de Las Casas*, II: 59–60.

54 *Ibid.*, II: 79.

55 Archivo de Indias, Patronato 18, No. 1, ramo 3.

56 *Ibid.*, Indiferente General 420, Lib. 420, fol. 213–15.

57 Vargas Machuca, writing about 1612, attacked the plan. Fabié, *Vida y escritos de Las Casas*, II: 430–32.

58 *Documentos inéditos de América*, IV: 146. It is interesting to observe, however, that such a hardheaded Spaniard as Gregorio López approved Las Casas' ideas on this point. Ramón Riaza, "El primer impugnador de Vitoria: Gregorio López," *Anuario de la Asociación Francisco de Vitoria* (1932), III: 120.

59 Francisco López de Gómara, *Historia de las Indias*, p. 297.

60 John A. Mackay makes this parallel in his valuable work *The Other Spanish Christ*, p. 46.

CHAPTER VI

1 This chapter is based upon the writer's introduction to this publication, which was entitled *Del único modo de atraer a todas las gentes a la religión verdadera* (México, 1941). The Latin text was prepared by Agustín Millares Carlo and the Spanish translation by Atenógenes Santamaría.

2 On this fundamental bull and its background the writer has given considerable detail in "Pope Paul III and the American Indians," *Harvard Theological Review*, XXX (1937), 65–102.

3 *Ibid.*, pp. 71–72.

4 *Del único modo*, p. 95.

5 *Ibid.*, p. 397.

6 *Ibid.*, pp. 167, 169.

7 *Ibid.*, pp. 411, 413, 415.

8 *Ibid.*, p. 421.

9 *Ibid.*, p. 499.

Edmundo O'Gorman has developed an entirely different interpretation on Las Casas' attitude toward war in his brilliant, but unconvincing at least to this writer, *Fundamentos de la historia de América*. He asserts: "For Las Casas, war is not evil, but good, inasmuch as it is a way to bring about justice. What happens is that there are unjust wars and he considers those made for the purpose of preaching the faith unjust, not because the intention is not praiseworthy *but because the method is not effective*." (*Op. cit.*, pp. 56–57. Italics are O'Gorman's.)

In the light of Las Casas' statements on war given above, this interpretation seems to me a strained one, impossible of proof. Las Casas, in common with practically all Spaniards of his time (Vives was an exception who condemned all war), believed that war could be just under certain conditions. In the *Del único modo* treatise (p. 515) he refers once, almost casually, to the fact that "no war is just unless there is a just cause for declaring it," and he clearly followed Augustine on what constituted just war. What distinguished Las Casas, however, was not that he agreed with most of his contemporaries on the theory of just war but that he declared the wars against the New World natives to be unjust. He condemned the use of force, not merely because the clamor and horror of armed conflict did not provide a suitable background for Indians to listen to and consider the new doctrine of love and salvation, but also—and here is a point O'Gorman does not mention—because warlike methods had been condemned by Christ, by the apostles, and by the fathers of the church and other authorities. The practice of using force and war to advance Christianity was directly contrary to the faith that was being preached, Las Casas held, and therefore he advocated peaceful preaching. If I understand O'Gorman correctly he would make Las Casas practically a pragmatist whereas he was, or so it seems to me, a Christian thinker.

¹⁰ O'Gorman in *Fundamentos de la historia de América* (pp. 58–59) has elaborated a distinctly different interpretation. For him, the "central idea of Las Casas is not *evangelization by peaceful means*, as has been traditionally asserted; it is *evangelization by means of reason*, which is not the same thing" (italics by O'Gorman). This exegesis seems to me a shaky one, dependent upon a questionable emphasis for whatever appearance of truth it presents. The idea that infidels should be persuaded by reason to accept the faith was indeed put forward by Las Casas, as safely grounded in the works of Augustine and Thomas Aquinas. Las Casas takes this idea for granted and never argues the point. The second idea, that the faith should be preached peacefully, was much more important in Las Casas' mind and his contemporaries required much more instruction and persuasion on this point, if we are to judge from the amount of space in the treatise *Del único modo* devoted to expounding and defending it. The infidels must be taught the faith by a method both "pacífica y razonable" Las Casas says (*op. cit.*, p. 199). O'Gorman has been much struck by the evidences he finds in Las Casas' thought of Cartesian rationalism. To this writer, however, O'Gorman deceives himself inasmuch as the treatise as a whole clearly shows that Las Casas' stress was laid upon peaceful as opposed to warlike methods. Anyone who is doubtful on this essential point should read the treatise. (See particularly pp. 13, 21, 27, 35, 39, 41, 43–51, 55, 57, 95, 137, 149, 163, 177–89, 215, 227–29, 339, 395, 399, 411, 435, 475.)

¹¹ Here again O'Gorman reaches an original and dissenting opinion for he believes "that when Las Casas . . . embarks on the Vera Paz experiment his attitude is in no essential respect different from that of the physical scientist who, armed with a hypothesis, interrogates nature" (*Fundamentos de la historia de América*, pp. 77–81). But surely this is to misunderstand either the spirit of Las Casas or the nature of an experiment. The physical scientist develops a hypothesis which may or may not be proved correct when put to the test of experiment. He may or may not believe that the hypothesis is correct, and he certainly does not consider whether the hypothesis is in accordance with Christian justice or precepts. And whatever the result of the experiment may be, the physical scientist accepts the decision rendered by nature. The hypothesis for him is an instrument to be used to explore or verify nature and not a religious truth to be defended or demonstrated.

How different was the approach of Las Casas! He was convinced, profoundly and passionately, that the peaceful method of preaching the faith was the only true and just method for a Christian to practice. He was eager for an opportunity to demonstrate this truth he held so strongly by putting the idea into practice in Guatemala, but his spirit in so doing seems to me to have nothing in common with that of a physical scientist in conducting his experiments.

12 *Del único modo,* p. 273.

13 For these later attempts, see the writer's description given in *Del único modo,* pp. xxxix–xliii. Another attempt at peaceful preaching has just been brought to light by a newly discovered letter by Domingo de Betanzos dated December 3, 1540, in which the labors of Domingo de Santa María in Misteca, New Spain, are movingly described. Alonso Getino, *Los dominicos y las leyes nuevas,* pp. 57–61.

14 E. G. R. Taylor, *The Original Writings and Correspondence of the Two Richard Hakluyts,* II. 503.

CHAPTER VII

1 Las Casas, *Historia de las Indias,* Lib. 3, cap. 136.

2 Zavala has made substantial contributions in *La encomienda indiana* and other works cited in the bibliography, as has Lesley B. Simpson in *The Encomienda in New Spain,* of which a new and revised edition is under way. These works are based primarily on printed documents which exist in large quantities, although even larger quantities of manuscripts await the investigator. Much raw material on various aspects of the history of Indian labor has been dug out and published by Vicente Dávila, *Encomiendas;* Domingo Amunátegui y Solar, *Las encomiendas de indígenas de Chile;* Simpson, *Studies in the Administration of the Indians in New Spain;* and by Zavala and his wife, María Castelo, *Fuentes para la historia del trabajo en Nueva España.*

The basic Spanish works, from the legal viewpoint are by Diego de Encinas, *Provisiones, cédulas, instrucciones y cartas;* Juan de Solórzano, *Política indiana;* and Antonio de León Pinelo, *Tratado de confirmaciones reales.* Many treatises on encomienda problems were written during the sixteenth century and later, but most of them did not survive and are now known only by their citation in León Pinelo's great bibliography, *Epitome de la biblioteca oriental y occidental.*

3 Jiménez de la Espada, *Relaciones geográficas,* IV: 15.

4 Scholes has given his opinion on this subject in an extensive note to the writer.

5 *Historia del mondo nuovo* (Venice, 1565).

6 *A Documentary History of American Industrial Society* and *Florida Plantation Records from the Papers of George Noble Jones.*

7 Simpson, *Encomienda in New Spain,* p. 125.

8 Referred to in the 1922 edition of the *Tratado* on pp. 355, 380.

9 Chamberlain, *Castilian backgrounds of the repartimiento—encomienda* (Contributions to American Anthropology and History, Carnegie Institution of Washington, Publ. No. 509, V, 19–66).

10 Las Casas, *Historia de las Indias,* Lib. 3, caps. 135–36.

11 *Documentos inéditos de Ultramar,* IX: 268 ff.

12 *Ibid.,* XX: 261–62.

13 Zavala, *New Viewpoints,* p. 75. The decision to abolish encomiendas is in Archivo de Indias, Indiferente General 737. The Count of Osorno opposed the abolition (*Ibid.,* Indiferente General 1530, pp. 871–76).

14 *Documentos escogidos del archivo de la Casa de Alba,* p. 208.

15 *Documentos inéditos de América,* XLI: 198–204.

16 Remesal, *Historia de Chiapa,* Lib. 3, cap. 10.

17 Gutiérrez de Santa Clara, *Historia de las guerras civiles del Perú,* I: 39–40.

18 *Documentos inéditos de América,* III: 543–53.

19 Las Casas, *Colección de tratados,* pp. 325–432. The quotation is based on propositions 5, 9, and 16.

20 *Ibid.,* pp. 1–100.

21 One of the best and most recent examples of this is Rómulo Carbia's *Historia de la leyenda negra hispanoamericana* (1943).

22 Some bibliographical assistance for such a study will be found in the writer's "Dos Palabras on Antonio de Ulloa and the *Noticias Secretas,*" *Hispanic American Historical Review,* III (1936), 479–514.

23 Agustín Rivera, *Principios críticos,* I: 262–75.

24 Arthur S. Aiton, "The Secret Visita Against Viceroy Mendoza," *New Spain and the Anglo-American West,* I, 20.

25 Motolinía, *Historia de los indios de la Nueva España,* pp. 17–19.

26 *Documentos inéditos de América,* II: 113, 117, 118–19.

27 León Fernández, *Colección de documentos para la historia de Costa Rica,* VI: 206–207.

28 Pedro Cieza de León, *The Civil Wars of Peru . . . The War of Chupas,* pp. 338–40.

29 Archivo General de Simancas, Estado 2660. *Consulta* of March 12, 1638.

30 The Colombian Baldomero Sanín Cano has written an amusing essay on this subject, "El descubrimiento de América y la higiene," *Cuba contemporánea,* VII (1915), 28–37.

31 Hunnewell, *Illustrated Americana,* pp. 7–11.

32 Box made this statement in a review appearing in *History,* XX (London, 1935), p. 66.

33 *The New Laws.* The original ordinances are in Archivo de Indias, Indiferente General 423, Lib. 20: 106 verso–115. The additions dated June 4, 1543, are to be found in *ibid.,* Lib. 20: 130–34. The order regulating the printing of the laws appeared May 1, 1543 (*ibid.,* Lib. 20: 139 verso–140). The first edition of the printed laws was issued at Alcalá de Henares in 1543 and is now extremely rare. The facsimile of this edition and an English translation, which Henry Stevens brought out in 1893, is also quite rare today. The Instituto de Investigaciones Históricas of Buenos Aires published a facsimile reproduction in 1922, edited by Diego Luis Molinari, entitled *Leyes y ordenanzas nuevamente hechas por Su Magestad, para la gobernación de las Indias, en Valladolid M.D.C.III.* For further bibliographical details see J. F. V. Silva's "Elogio de Vaca de Castro por Antonio de Herrera," which also contains the text of the laws. The most recent republication of the laws appeared in Spain, *Las leyes nuevas, 1542–1543,* edited by Antonio Muro Orejón. A recent monograph on one aspect of the controversy is Luis Alonso Getino's *Influencia de los dominicos en las leyes nuevas.*

34 Stevens, *op. cit.,* p. 16.

35 Archivo de Indias, Indiferente General 1530 and 1624.

36 *Ibid.,* Patronato 231 and Patronato 185, ramo 24.

37 *Cortes de los antiguos reinos de León y de Castilla,* V: 255.

38 *El consejo real y supremo de las Indias,* pp. 60–70.

39 Archivo de Indias, Patronato 185, ramo 38; *Documentos inéditos de España,* XIII: 427–28.

40 Alonso de Santa Cruz, *Crónica del emperador Carlos V,* IV: 317–19.

41 Miguélez, *Catálogo de los códices españoles de la biblioteca del Escorial,* p. 246.

42 *Documentos inéditos de Ultramar,* XIV: 115.

43 Archivo de Indias, Guatemala 393, Lib. 20: 117 verso.

44 *Documentos inéditos de España,* XIII: 427–28. For detailed information on this treatise, see the writer's remarks on pp. 163–65 of this book.

45 P. A. Means, *The Fall of the Inca Empire,* p. 296.

46 *The Ottoman and the Spanish Empires,* p. 28.

47 Ignacio Bejarano (ed.), *Actas de cabildo de la ciudad de México,* IV: 349.

48 Georg Friederici, *Der Character der Entdeckung in Amerika,* I: 467.

49 Pedro Cieza de León, *The War of Quito* (Clements R. Markham, ed.), p. xi.

50 Archivo de Indias, Indiferente General 1530 and 1624. A useful volume of basic documents on sixteenth-century attitudes and opinions on the encomienda could be made of selections from these two *legajos.*

51 *Ibid.,* Indiferente General 1530, pp. 770–82. The representatives sent earlier by Mexico, with instructions dated November 28, 1542, had been ordered to warn the Council of the Indies against Las Casas, *Documentos inéditos de América,* VII: 396.

52 Archivo de Indias, Indiferente General 1530, pp. 783–85.

53 *Ibid.,* pp. 755–69.

54 *Ibid.,* Indiferente General 1624, pp. 140–42.

55 *Ibid.,* Indiferente General 1530, p. 828.

56 *Ibid.,* pp. 795–802.

57 *Ibid.,* pp. 803–8.

58 *Ibid.,* p. 809.

59 *Ibid.,* p. 811.

60 *Ibid.,* p. 814.

61 *Ibid.,* p. 817.

62 *Ibid.,* pp. 819–22 contains the Comendador de León's opinion and pp. 823–27 gives the Cardinal's.

63 Archivo de Simancas, Estado 69, pp. 13–14, 49–50.

64 Bibliothèque Nationale (Paris). Ms. Espagnols 325, p. 261.

65 The offer was referred to by Laurencio Surio in his *Comentarius Brevis,* according to Solórzano who cited it in his *Política indiana,* Lib. VI, cap. 1, No. 7. Later in the century, encomenderos and those who opposed making encomiendas perpetual vied with each other in offering the crown large sums.

66 Archivo de Indias, Indiferente General 427, Lib. 30, pp. 32–33. Printed in Vasco de Puga, *Provisiones instrucciones cédulas,* I: 472–78.

67 Archivo de Indias, Indiferente General 427, Lib. 30, pp. 35 verso–36.

68 Puga, *op. cit.,* I: 479–80; Encinas, *op. cit.,* II: 189–90.

69 Bejarano, *op. cit.,* V: 162.

70 *Documentos inéditos de América,* VII: 436–37.

71 Simpson, *Encomienda in New Spain,* p. 171.

72 Archivo de Indias, Guatemala 9.

73 Zavala, *New Viewpoints,* p. 71.

74 José María Chacón y Calvo, *Cedulario cubano,* p. 467.

75 *Documentos inéditos de América,* XXIV: 352–81.

76 Amunátegui, *Las encomiendas de indígenas en Chile,* I: 250–53.

77 Juan López de Velasco, *Geografía y descripción de las Indias,* p. 463.

78 Archivo de Indias, Indiferente General 427, Lib. 21: 83 verso–84; Lib. 30: 46–48 verso.

79 Levillier, *Don Francisco de Toledo, supremo organizador del Perú,* I: 183–84.

PART III

INTRODUCTION

1 The writer has collected and published a record of all treatises on this subject and on other questions of justice of America in *Cuerpo de documentos del siglo XVI,* pp. 515–36.

CHAPTER VIII

[1] This chapter is based on a previously published study by the writer, "The Development of Regulations for Conquistadores," *Contribuciones para el estudio de la historia de América,* pp. 71–87.

[2] *Documentos inéditos de América,* IX: 268–80.

[3] Medina, *Colección de documentos de historiadores de Chile,* I: 45.

[4] The rest of this chapter is based on studies by the writer, "La Controversia entre Las Casas y Sepúlveda en Valladolid, 1550–1551," *Revista de la universidad católica bolivariana,* VIII (1942), 125–37 and *Lucha para justicia en América,* Part IV, chap. 5.

A defense of Sepúlveda has appeared in Spain by Juan Beneyto Pérez, *Ginés de Sepúlveda, humanista y soldado* (1944).

[5] Archivo de Indias, Patronato 170, ramo 52.

[6] *Ibid.,* Lima 556, Lib. 6: 24–24 verso.

[7] A more detailed treatment of the *Apologetic History* will be found in the writer's *Las teorías políticas de Bartolomé de Las Casas.*

[8] Schlaifer, *Greek Theories of Slavery from Homer to Aristotle,* pp. 188–99. See also Sikes, *Anthropology of the Greeks,* p. 73.

[8a] The best and most recent study on the subject is by Zavala, "Las Casas ante la doctrina de la servidumbre natural," *Revista de la universidad de Buenos Aires,* Año II (1944), 45–58. See also his *Servidumbre natural y libertad cristiana, según los tratadistas de los siglos XVI y XVII.*

[9] O'Gorman, "Sobre la naturaleza bestial del indio americano," *Revista de la facultad de filosofía y letras* (México, 1941), No. 1: 141–58; No. 2: 305–15. It is important to realize that the full story of Las Casas' position cannot be understood until the disquisition he gave before the Valladolid meeting is available. Agustín Millares Carlo and I expect to edit this *Apologia,* in a Spanish translation, for the series Biblioteca Americana of the Fondo de Cultura Económica in Mexico City. The original manuscript, in Latin, is in the Bibliothèque Nationale (Paris).

[10] Las Casas, *Historia de las Indias,* Lib. 3, cap. 102. See also Zavala, *¿Las Casas esclavista?*

[11] Las Casas, *Historia de las Indias,* Lib. 3, cap. 149; Las Casas, *Colección de tratados,* p. 541.

[12] Las Casas, *Apologética historia,* pp. 127–29.

[13] Simón Bolívar. *Discursos y proclamas* (Rufino Blanco-Fombona, ed.), p. 47.

[14] Fernando Vázquez Menchaca, *Controversiarum Illustrium,* I: 8–10.

[15] *Ibid.,* I, cap. 10.

[16] Roberto Levillier, *Don Francisco de Toledo,* I: 178.

[17] Juan Ginés de Sepúlveda, *Democrates Alter,* p. 363.

[18] This conquest is described in the writer's *Cuerpo de documentos del siglo XVI,* pp. xxix–lvi.

[19] The law is printed in *Documentos inéditos de América,* XVI: 142–87. The quotation appears on pp. 182–83.

[20] *Ibid.,* p. 152.

CHAPTER IX

[1] This chapter is largely based on the writer's *Lucha para Justicia en América,* Part IV, chap. 4.

[2] Bernal Díaz, *Verdadera historia,* I: 7–8.

[3] Gaspar Pérez de Villagrá, *History of New Mexico,* p. 209.

[4] *Documentos inéditos de América,* VII: 116–46.

⁵ P. A. Means, *Biblioteca Andina*, p. 488. Many documents on this episode are in Ricardo Mujía, *Bolivia-Paraguay*, Anexos, II: 109–30, and Roberto Levillier, *Audiencia de Charcas*, I: 280–94. Some unpublished material, which however does not alter the description given in the printed documents, may be found in Archivo de Indias, Patronato 235, ramo 3.

⁶ Raimundo Ghigliazza, *Historia de la provincia dominicana de Chile*, I: 285. An interesting chapter on "Frai González de San Nicolás i la libertad de los indios" is in Crescente Errázuriz, *Los oríjenes de la iglesia chilena*. This section on Chile is based on a more detailed statement by the writer in *Cuerpo de documentos del siglo XVI*, pp. lvii–lxvi.

⁷ Medina, *Colección de historiadores de Chile*, II: 250–54.

⁸ Medina, *Biblioteca hispano-chilena*, II: 5–20.

⁹ Biblioteca Nacional (Madrid), Ms. 3044, No. 25, pp. 243–45

¹⁰ *Ibid.*, Ms. 2010, pp. 186–94.

¹¹ Albert G. Keller, *Colonization*, p. 350.

¹² Blair and Robertson, *The Philippine Islands*, X: 253–55.

¹³ *Ibid.*, I: 42.

¹⁴ *Ibid.*, X: 75–80.

¹⁵ Evaristo Fernández Arias, *Paralelo Entre la conquista y dominación de América y el descubrimiento y pacificación de Filipinas*, p. 34. A recent biography of one of the outstanding friars is by Manuel Merino, "Semblanzas misioneras: Fr. Martín de Rada, agustino," *Missionalia hispánica*, Año 1 (1944), Nos. 1 and 2, pp. 167–212.

¹⁶ Blair and Robertson, *op. cit.*, XXXIV: 249–54.

¹⁷ *Ibid.*, III: 295–97.

¹⁸ *Ibid.*, X: 253–55.

¹⁹ *Ibid.*, XXXIV: 275–76.

²⁰ Archivo de Indias, Filipinas 34.

²¹ The remainder of this chapter is based on a previous study by the author, *Cuerpo de documentos del siglo XVI*, pp. xxix–l.

CHAPTER X

¹ Based upon a fuller treatment in the writer's *Lucha para justicia en América*, Part V, chaps. 1–3.

² Ricardo Levene, *Introducción a la historia del derecho indiano* (Buenos Aires, 1924), pp. 56–57.

³ Samuel Johnson, *London: a Poem*.

⁴ Marcos Jiménez de la Espada, *Juan de Castellanos y su historia del Nuevo Reino de Granada*, p. 64.

⁵ Quoted in Medina, *El descubrimiento del Océano Pacifico*, II: 516.

⁶ Juan de Mariana, *Historia de España*, XXXI: 243.

⁷ Las Casas, *Historia de las Indias*, Lib. III, cap. 133.

⁸ Honorio Muñoz, *Vitoria and the Conquest of America*, p. 25.

⁹ Pedro Simón, *Noticias historiales de las conquistas de Tierra Firme en las Indias Occidentales*, II: 120.

¹⁰ James Brown Scott, *Francisco de Vitoria*, pp. 84–85.

¹¹ *Ibid.*, pp. 117 ff.

¹² *Ibid.*, p. xxiv.

¹³ *Ibid.*, p. 90.

¹⁴ Based on a fuller treatment in the writer's *Teorías políticas de Bartolomé de Las Casas*.

¹⁵ Las Casas, *Colección de tratados*, pp. 541–42.

¹⁶ Fabié, *Vida y escritos de Las Casas*, II, 577–78.

¹⁷ Las Casas, *Colección de tratados*, pp. 595–98.

CHAPTER XI

1 Ignacio Bejarano, *Actas de cabildo de la ciudad de México,* VI: 44. A more detailed treatment of these matters is in the writer's *Cuerpo de documentos del siglo XVI,* pp. xxii–xxix.

2 Bejarano, *op. cit.,* VI: 316–17; 353, 358, 383, 442; VII: 30, 74.

3 *Ibid.,* VI: 496–97.

4 *Ibid.,* VII: 30, 49, 100–101.

5 Bibliothèque Nationale (Paris). Fonds Espagnols, Ms. No. 325, fol. 42–44.

6 This section is based on a more detailed treatment by the writer in *Cuerpo de documentos del siglo XVI,* pp. xxxi–li.

7 Joaquín García Icazbalceta, *Nueva colección de documentos para la historia de México,* III: xxxiii–xxxiv.

8 Pedro Torres Lanzas (ed.), *Catálogo de documentos relativos a las Islas Filipinas,* III: cxcvi.

9 Printed in the writer's *Cuerpo de documentos del siglo XVI,* pp. l–li.

10 Blair and Robertson, *The Philippine Islands,* VII: 91–92.

11 *Ibid.,* VII: 92–93.

12 Printed in the writer's *Cuerpo de documentos del siglo XVI,* pp. 117–84.

13 Blair and Robertson, *op. cit.,* III: 149–68.

14 *Cuerpo de documentos del siglo XVI,* p. 181.

CHAPTER XII

1 Based on an article of the same title by the author which appeared in *The Americas,* in July 1946.

2 Roberto Levillier, *Francisco de Toledo,* I: 126–27.

3 Archivo de Indias, Lima 29, Lib. 5. Report of Toledo to the King, from Potosí, on March 20, 1573.

4 Juan de Llorente, *Colección de obras de Las Casas,* II: 175–327.

5 The treatise is printed in the *Documentos inéditos de España,* XIII: 425–69.

6 *Ibid.,* XIII: 431.

7 *Ibid.,* XIII: 455.

8 Levillier, *op. cit.,* II: 1–204.

9 *Ibid.,* I: 201–3; II: xxvi–c. The best and most up-to-date statement on Inca culture is by Rowe, *Inca Culture at the Time of the Spanish Conquest.*

10 Levillier, *op. cit.,* II: 182–95.

11 *Ibid.,* III.

12 *Ibid.,* II: 11.

13 *Ibid.,* II: 11–13.

14 León Lopetegui, *El Padre José de Acosta y las misiones,* pp. 251, 356.

15 José de Matienzo, *Gobierno del Perú,* cap. 2.

16 Juan Polo de Ondegardo, *Informaciones acerca de la religión y gobierno de los Incas,* I: 48.

17 Levillier, *Gobernantes del Perú,* VII: 115–30.

18 Levillier, *Francisco de Toledo,* III: 155–59.

19 Hans Steffen, "Anotaciones a la Historia Indica del Capitán Pedro Sarmiento de Gamboa," *Anales de la universidad de Santiago de Chile,* tomo 129 (1911), p. iiii.

20 Levillier, *Francisco de Toledo,* III: 10.

21 Richard Pietschmann, *Geschichte des Inkareiches von Pedro Sarmiento de Gamboa.*

22 *Documentos inéditos de América,* VII: 453.

23 P. A. Means, *Biblioteca Andina,* pp. 443, 462, 468–70.

24 Levillier, *Francisco de Toledo*, I: 297.

25 *Documentos inéditos de América*, V: 301–2.

26 Manuel de Mediburu, *Diccionario histórico biográfico del Perú*, X: 378; Means, *op. cit.*, p. 492. Raúl Porras Barrenechea, the Peruvian historian, considers the whole episode due to the pressure of friars and has written an amusing account, sans evidence, which tends to depreciate the honesty of the old conquistador's deathbed statement. "El testamento de Mancio Serra," *Mercurio peruano*, XXIII (1941), 55–62. Similar wills were made by other Spaniards, as recorded by José de la Riva-Agüero, *Nicolás de Ribera el viejo*, pp. 28–29. The late Bertram Lee, a North American engineer who had worked long and hard in Peruvian archives, stated to the writer in 1935 that he had seen many similar wills. Another illustration of this Spanish preoccupation with questions of justice is to be found in a manuscript in the Library of Congress relating to a little-known conquistador, Diego de Carvajal, who had fought for fifteen months against the natives of Chile in 1565 and 1566. On August 3, 1568, he appeared in Lima before a notary public and witnesses and stated that, inasmuch as it was then undecided whether the war was just or not, he felt obliged to pledge himself to make restitution to the Indians, as ordered by Archbishop Gerónimo de Loaysa on the advice of certain Franciscans and Dominicans. Stella R. Clemence, *The Harkness Collection in the Library of Congress*, p. 237.

27 James Ernst, *Roger Williams*, pp. 80, 101–3, 130.

CONCLUSION

1 Lopetegiu, *El padre José de Acosta y las misiones*, p. 101.

2 *Public Papers of Woodrow Wilson*, I: 404.

3 Theodore Parker, *Collected Works*, X: 121. Relatively little seems to have been written on the problems of justice in Portugal and Portuguese America. Madureira contributed a monograph on Brazil entitled *A liberdade dos indos e a companhia de Jesus*, and Costa Brochado has given a brief treatment of one aspect of the problem in Portugal in "O problema da guerra justa em Portugal," *Rumo* (Lisbon, 1946), No. 1.

4 Mendieta, *Historia eclesiástica indiana*, pp. 631–32.

5 Tannenbaum, *Peace by Revolution*, pp. 36–37.

6 Northrop, *The Meeting of East and West*, p. 6. Some interesting reflections on the relation of these four figures to Mexican civilization are given by Northrop, who has been influenced in his approach by Edmundo O'Gorman.

Humboldt remarked about 1800 that "we may traverse Spanish America from Buenos Aires to Monterey, and in no quarter shall we meet with a national monument which the public gratitude has raised to Christopher Columbus or Hernando Cortés," *Essai politique*, II, 60.

The first authorization obtained in Mexico to erect a statue of Cortés was arranged with Porfirio Díaz by Gabino Barreda and the other Positivist leaders of the time. Their plan to place the statue in the Paseo de la Reforma, though approved, was never consummated, according to Carleton Beals, *Porfirio Díaz*, p. 326. Further information on this topic is in Rafael Ramos Pedrueza, *Estudios históricos, sociales y literarios*, pp. 241–43, and Toribio Esquivel Obregón's *Hernán Cortés y el derecho internacional en el siglo XVI*, pp. 7–55.

7 Ortiz, *El engaño de las razas*, cap. 12.

8 *Boletín de la biblioteca nacional*, Año 1 (Guatemala, 1945), tercera época, No. 1, pp. 3–4.

9 Serrano y Sanz, *Orígenes de la dominación española en América*, p. 351.

10 "El Padre de Las Casas no estaba en sus cabales," was the statement signed by Dr. G. García Arista y Rivera, which appeared in the Madrid newspaper *A. B. C.*

for October 20, 1927. A large, curious work has recently appeared in Mexico entitled *Conquista y colonización de América por la calumniada España* by Pedro González-Blanco, who considers Las Casas an enemy of Spain.

[11] In an anonymous article "La locura de Fray Bartolomé de Las Casas, *Revista hispanoamericana de ciencias, letras y artes,* VI (Madrid, 1927), 284–90. A summary of the earlier criticism by Menéndez y Pelayo of Las Casas and an attack on this criticism is given by Manuel María Martínez, "El P. Las Casas ante la nueva crítica," *La ciencia tomista,* L (1934), 289–302.

[12] *Criticismo y colonización,* p. 17.

[13] Chacón y Calvo, *Cartas censorias de la conquista,* pp. 3–4.

[14] Gay Calbó, "Discurso sobre Fray Bartolomé de Las Casas," *Boletín del archivo nacional,* XLI (Habana, 1942), p. 106.

[15] Esquivel Obregón, *Apuntes para la historia del derecho en México,* II: 61.

[16] Menéndez Pidal delivered his attack in an article "¿Codicia insaciable? ¿Ilustres hazañas?" which appeared in the review *Escorial* in Spain and was in turn attacked by Armando Bazán for it in the *Repertorio americano* of Costa Rica.

It is interesting to note that an anthology *Juan Ginés Sepúlveda* (Madrid, 1940) was included in the series "Breviarios del Pensamiento Español," edited by Carlos Alonso del Real and published by Ediciones Fe. Although the editor did not praise Sepúlveda uncritically, he did consider him an important Spanish figure worthy of being included in a series devoted to Spanish thinkers from Seneca to José Antonio Primo de Rivera. Vitoria, but not Las Casas, was also included. A monograph on Sepúlveda, which unfortunately I have not been able to consult, has recently been published by the Instituto de Estudios Políticos in Madrid, entitled *Los imperialismos de Juan Ginés de Sepúlveda en su Demócrates Alter* (1947) by Teodoro Andrés Marcos.

[17] No two persons agree wholly concerning Spanish character. A recent and stimulating interpretation is by Edmundo O'Gorman, *Crisis y porvenir de la ciencia histórica,* pp. 340–46.

BIBLIOGRAPHICAL APPENDICES

1. BIBLIOGRAPHICAL WORKS

Of the many bibliographies consulted, the only ones which need to be mentioned individually are B. Sánchez Alonso's *Fuentes de la Historia Española Hispanoamericana*, the first two volumes of the *Bibliotheca Missionum* of Robert Streit, and the annual *Handbook of Latin American Studies*. The writer brought together in an appendix of his *Cuerpo de Documentos del Siglo XVI* a list, with bibliographical information whenever available, of all the sixteenth-century treatises published or known to have been written on subjects related to the struggle for justice in America. This list was published in 1943 and is not wholly complete or accurate now, but anyone interested in the subject will find useful information there.

2. COLLECTIONS OF PRINTED MATERIAL

The great collections of documents published on Spanish American history have been invaluable and are so frequently cited that abbreviations for their lengthy titles have been used, as indicated in the list of abbreviations. No specific collection devoted to treatises on the struggle for justice has appeared, except the writer's *Cuerpo de Documentos del Siglo XVI*, which brought together a number of hitherto unpublished treatises from various Spanish archives. References to many other individual treatises, published and unpublished, are given in the bibliographical appendix to this volume, referred to above.

3. PREVIOUS STUDIES

As stated in the Introduction, many writers in Spain and elsewhere have been interested in the struggle for justice. Of the colonial writers, no one can dispense with the great works by the seventeenth-century jurist and royal official Juan de Solórzano Pereira entitled *Disputationes de Indiarum Iure* and *Política Indiana*. Two nineteenth-century studies which helped to open up modern consideration of the problems of justice in America were articles by Edwardo Hinojosa, "La Influencia que Tuvieron en el Derecho Público . . . los filósofos y teólogos españoles," and Ernest Nys, "Les Publicistes Espagnols du XVIe Siècle et les Droits des Indiens." These brief analyses pointed the way, as did the later short but revealing studies by Fernando de los Ríos, "The Religious Character of Colonial Law in Sixteenth-Century Spain" and "Religión y Estado en la España del Siglo XVI."

The struggle for justice was a large problem, however, and each historian has selected that part which most interested him or for which materials were at hand. Thus, some students of international law devoted themselves to the theories of individual figures. Luis G. Alonso Getino, Vicente Beltrán de Heredia, James Brown Scott, and Honorio Muñoz produced studies on Francisco de Vitoria, and the bibliography on this Dominican thinker grows steadily, as may be seen from the list in Antonio Truyol Serra's *Los Principios del Derecho Publico en Francisco de Vitoria"* (Madrid, 1946). That these works are often highly controversial is well illustrated by two of the most recent treatments, by José Miranda, *Vitoria y los Intereses de la Conquista de América* (Mexico, 1947) and Teodoro Aṅdres Marcos, *Vitoria y Carlos V en la Soberania de Hispano América* (Salamanca, 1946).

Other individual thinkers have been studied, though no such extensive bibliography has developed as for Vitoria. Manuel García-Pelayo has provided an extensive introduction to Sepúlveda's *Tratado Sobre las Justas Causas de la Guerra Contra los Indios,* Pedro Leturia has done likewise for John Major in his article "Maior y Vitoria ante la Conquista de América," and the writer entered this interesting field of contention in giving the first treatment of Las Casas as a political theorist in *Las Teorías Políticas de Bartolomé de las Casas.* Two other fundamental treatises will be available through the Fondo de Cultura Económica in Mexico when Silvio Zavala completes his study for the first edition of the Palacios Rubios treatise *De Insulis,* and the writer brings out, in collaboration with Agustín Millares Carlo, the first edition of the work Las Casas read to the judges at Valladolid entitled *Argumentum Apologiae.*

A number of modern writers have concerned themselves with particular incidents in the struggle or certain aspects of it. The Dominicans have naturally emphasized the work of their order, as is illustrated by Luis G. Alonso Getino's *La Influencia de los Dominicos en las Nuevas Leyes* and Venancio Carro's two volumes *La Teología y los Teólogos—Juristas Españoles en la Conquista de América.* These volumes illustrate the dangers and difficulties inherent in writing the history of the conquest, even today. Carro's work, the most considerable in recent years on this topic, has been widely praised in Spain but has also been attacked in Mexico as a "Catholic, Hispanophile, clerical, and Dominican" interpretation.*

Perhaps the most prolific writers on various individual events of the struggle have been the Spanish Dominican Vicente Beltrán de Heredia, the Mexican historian Silvio Zavala, the Cuban diplomat José María Chacón y Calvo, and the writer. Their numerous articles and studies will be found listed in the bibliography and need not be repeated here. The present interpretation could not have been written without these careful studies on particular incidents.

General works are few in number. The most important ones, by Zavala,

---

* José Miranda, *Vitoria y los Intereses de la Conquista de América*, p. 7. Miranda goes on to say: "Obsérvese la saña con que combate el autor al insigne americanista Serrano Sanz, ardiente defensor del poder temporal, el menosprecio con que trata a Scoto y la baja estimación que da a la labor de los franciscanos en América."

have been referred to in the Introduction. Another publication which does not limit itself to a small part of the field is J. H. Parry's brief, well-written study on *The Spanish Theory of Empire in the Sixteenth Century*. Edmundo O'Gorman had made an unusual and valuable contribution by challenging the traditional interpretations. His volume *Fundamentos de la Historia de América* and articles entitled "Sobre la Naturaleza Bestial del Indio Americano" are particularly noteworthy, though it is clear that he has not yet brought out a well-rounded and complete interpretation of the conquest. Since completion of this volume, my attention has been called to a monograph by the German theologian Joseph Höffner entitled *Christentum und Menschenwürde—das Anliegen der spanischen Kolonialethik im Goldenen Zeitalter* (Trier, 1947), which is a valuable contribution based on the standard printed material.

The present work attempts to portray the historical development of the struggle for justice as the theories elaborated in Spain were tried out in America. For this reason the available manuscript material on Spain in America, to be described next, was an essential source.

4. MANUSCRIPT SOURCES

No attempt is made here to list all the manuscript items used for this study but the chief manuscript sources are listed below.

Archivo General de Indias (Seville, Spain)
  a. *Patronato*

All pertinent material in the 285 *legajos* of this rich section was examined. The most important items are: *No. 170,* "Papeles tocantes al buen gobierno de las Indias en general, 1480–1556"; *No. 171,* "Papeles sobre el buen gobierno de las Indias en general, 1562–1616"; *No. 172,* "Papeles tocantes al buen gobierno de la Isla Española, 1503–1531"; *No. 173,* "Papeles sobre el buen gobierno de la Isla Española, 1532–1586"; *No. 174,* "Cartas antiguas sobre buen gobierno de la Española, 1513–1586"; *No. 175,* "Papeles tocantes al buen gobierno de la Isla de San Juan de Puerto Rico, 1510–1599"; *No. 176,* "Cartas originales escritas a S.M. sobre puntos de buen gobierno de la isla de San Juan de Puerto Rico, 1518–1591"; *No. 178,* "Cartas sobre buen gobierno de Cuba, 1514–1572"; *Nos. 179,* "Papeles pertenecientes al buen gobierno de varias islas en América, 1515–1594"; *Nos. 180–182,* "Papeles sobre el buen gobierno de Nueva España, 1519–1580"; *Nos. 185, 188, 191, 192,* "Papeles sobre el buen gobierno del Perú, 1522–1624"; *No. 193,* "Papeles sobre el buen gobierno de Tierra Firme, 1512–1595"; *Nos. 195–197,* "Papeles sobre el buen gobierno del Nuevo Reino de Granada, 1520–1586"; *Nos. 228–229,* "Papeles pertenecientes a la guerra, socorro, y pacificación del Reino de Chile, 1570–1616"; *No. 231,* "Papeles pertenecientes a la libertad de los indios, su doctrina, buen tratamiento y modo de encomendarlos, 1512–1679"; *No. 252,* "Historia de las Indias, Papeles escritos por Fr. Bartolomé de Las Casas acerca de la historia de las Indias."

b. *Indiferente General*

Legajos Nos. 418–427, "Registros, Libros generalísimos de Reales Ordenes, Nombramientos, Gracias etc, 1492–1607"; *Nos. 737–738,* "Consultos del Consejo y Cámara, 1529–1576"; *Nos. 854–858,* "Papeles y borradores del Consejo"; *Nos. 1092–1105,* "Cartas remitidas al consejo, 1519–1594"; *Nos. 1202–1208,* "Expedientes, Informaciones y Probanzas, 1508–1549"; *Nos. 1373–1386,* "Peticiones y memoriales, 1560–1588"; *Nos. 1530,* Labeled "Descripción, poblaciones y derroteros de viajes, 1521–1818" but really consists of a mass of important opinions on Indian questions. The Library of Congress has microfilm copies and enlargements of this *legajo* and the next one listed. Their pages were arbitrarily numbered when microfilmed, and these are the page numbers cited in this volume. *No. 1624,* "Expedientes respectivos a la perpetuidad de las encomiendas de indios, 1517–1621"; *No. 2976,* "Documentos sobre si deben diezmos ó no los indios, 1531–1612"; *Nos. 2985–2986,* "Reales resoluciones sobre consultas, breves y expedientes, 1560–1589"; *No. 2987,* "Expediente sobre servicio personal por Juan Ramírez."

c. Miscellaneous

In the other sections of the *Archivo de Indias* such as "Chile," "Filipinas," "Quito," "Lima," "México," "Panamá," "Santo Domingo," "Guatemala," and "Santa Fe," all letters sent by ecclesiastics and laymen to the crown during the sixteenth century were examined. Whenever necessary, the "Justicia" section was searched for *residencia* material.

Academia de la Historia (Madrid, Spain)

All pertinent material in the ninety-two volume Juan Bautista Muñoz collection was consulted, as well as scattered items in other collections on theoretical matters.

Biblioteca del Palacio Nacional (Madrid, Spain)

Manuscript No. 175, Volume of important Indian papers labeled "División del obispado de las Charcas"; *Ms. No. 938,* Bartolomé de las Casas, "Quaestiones utrum Thesauri de Peru."

Minor Archives

For the purposes of this study, other archives such as the *Biblioteca Nacional* (Madrid), *Archivo General de Simancas* (Simancas, Spain), Archivo *Histórico Nacional* (Madrid), the New York Public Library, the John Carter Brown Library, the British Museum, the Bibliothèque Nationale (Paris) and the Monasterio de San Felipe, Sucre, Bolivia, were all of relatively minor importance. Whenever documents have been cited from these depositories, they have been described in the footnotes.

5. LIST OF WORKS CITED

Aguado, Pedro. *Historia de Santa Marta y Nuevo Reyno de Granada.* Ed. by Jerónimo Bécker. 2 vols. Madrid, 1916–17.

Aiton, Arthur S. "The Secret Visita Against Viceroy Mendoza," *New Spain and the Anglo-American West,* I (Los Angeles, 1932), 1–22.

Alamán, Lucas. *Obras.* 5 vols. México, 1899–1911.

Alonso del Real, Carlos, ed. and tr. *Juan Ginés de Sepúlveda.* (*Antología*). Madrid, 1940.

Alonso Getino, Luis G. *El maestro Fr. Francisco de Vitoria.* Rev. ed. Madrid, 1930.

————. *Influencia de los dominicos en las leyes nuevas.* Sevilla, 1945 (Publicaciones de la Escuela de Estudios Hispano-Americanos de la Universidad de Sevilla.)

Altamira, Rafael. "El texto de las leyes de Burgos de 1512," *Revista de historia de América* (México, 1938), No. 4, pp. 5–79.

Álvarez Rubiano, Pablo. "Importancia político-social de las mercedes de 1519 concedidas a los labradores de Tierra Firme," *Revista de Indias,* Año 2, No. 5 (Madrid, 1941), 133–48.

————. *Pedrarias Dávila. Contribución al estudio de la figura del gran justador, gobernador de Castilla del Oro y Nicaragua.* Madrid, 1944.

Amunátegui Solar, Domingo. *Las encomiendas indígenas de Chile.* 2 vols. Santiago, 1909–10.

Andrés Marcos, Teodoro. *Los imperialismos de Juan Ginés de Sepúlveda en su Democrates Alter.* Madrid, 1947. (Instituto de Estudios Políticos.)

————. *Vitoria y Carlos V en la soberanía de Hispano América.* Salamanca, 1946.

Arévalo Martínez, Rafael. "De Aristóteles a Hitler," *Boletín de la biblioteca nacional* (Guatemala, 1945), tercera época, No. 1, pp. 3–4.

Beals, Carleton. *Porfirio Diaz, Dictator of Mexico.* Philadelphia, 1932.

Bejarano, Ignacio, ed. *Actas de cabildo de la ciudad de México.* 12 vols. México, 1889–1900.

Beltrán de Heredia, Vicente. "El maestro Domingo de Soto en la controversia de Las Casas con Sepúlveda," *La ciencia tomista,* XLV (Salamanca, 1932), 35–49; 177–93.

————. "El tratado De Dominio Regum del Fr. Matías de Paz," *Archivum fratrum praedicatorum,* III (Rome, 1933), 131–81.

————. "Ideas del maestro Fray Francisco de Vitoria anteriores a las relecciones 'De Indis' acerca de la colonización de América según documentos inéditos," *Anuario de la asociación Francisco de Vitoria,* II (Madrid, 1930), 23–68.

————. "Un precursor del maestro Vitoria. El P. Matías de Paz, O.P., y su tratado *De Dominio Regum Hispaniae Super Indos,*" *La ciencia tomista,* XL (1929), 173–90.

Beneyto Pérez, Juan. *Ginés de Sepúlveda, humanista y soldado.* Madrid, 1944.

Benzoni, Girolamo. *Historia del mondo nuovo.* Venice, 1565.

————. *History of the New World, by Girolamo Benzoni.* Ed. by W. H. Smyth. London, 1857.

Biermann, Benno M. "Die erster Dominikaner in Amerika," *Missionswissenschaft und Religionswissenschaft* (Münster i W., 1947), pp. 56–65.

————. "Zwei Briefe von Fray Bartolomé de Las Casas," *Archivum fratrum praedicatorum*, IV (Rome, 1934), 187–220.

Blair, Emma H., and James A. Robertson. *The Philippine Islands, 1493–1898*. 55 vols. Cleveland, 1903–09.

Blakey, Robert. *History of Political Literature*. 2 vols. London, 1855.

Bolívar, Simón. *Discursos y proclamas*. Ed. by Rufino Blanco-Fombona. Paris, 1913.

Brochado, Costa. "O problema da guerra justa em Portugal," *Rumo* (Lisbon, 1946), No. 1.

Burgin, Miron, ed. *Handbook of Latin American Studies*. 11 vols. Cambridge, 1936–48.

Carbia, Rómulo D. *Historia de la leyenda negra hispano-americana*. Buenos Aires, 1943.

Carro, Venancio D. *La teologia y los teólogos-juristas españoles ante la conquista de América*. 2 vols. Madrid, 1944. (Escuela de Estudios Hispano-Americanos de la Universidad de Sevilla.)

Casas, Bartolomé de Las. *Apologética historia de las Indias*. Ed. by Manuel Serrano y Sanz. Madrid, 1909. (Nueva biblioteca de autores españoles, Vol. 13.)

————. *Colección de tratados, 1552–1553*. Buenos Aires, 1924. (Instituto de investigaciones históricas.)

————. *Del único modo de atraer a todas las gentes a la religión verdadera*. México, 1941. Transcription by Agustín Millares Carlo and Spanish translation by Atenógenes Santamaría. Introduction by Lewis Hanke.

————. *Historia de las Indias*. Ed. by Gonzalo de Reparaz. 3 vols. Barcelona, n.d. (1929?).

Castro, Américo de. *Antonio de Guevara. El villano del Danubio y otros fragmentos*. Princeton, 1945. (Princeton texts in literature and history.)

Chacón y Calvo, José María. *Cartas censorias de la conquista*. La Habana, 1938.

————. *Cedulario cubano. Los orígenes de la colonización (1493–1512)*. Madrid, n.d. (1930?). (Colección de documentos inéditos para la historia de Hispano-América, Vol. 6.)

————. *Criticismo y colonización*. La Habana, 1935.

————. *La experiencia del indio ¿un antecedente a las doctrinas de Vitoria?* Madrid, 1934. (Asociación Francisco de Vitoria.)

Chamberlain, Robert S. *Castilian Backgrounds of the Repartimiento-Encomienda*. Washington, 1939. (Contributions to American Anthropology and History, Carnegie Institution of Washington, Publ. 509, V, 19–66.)

Cieza de León, Pedro. *Civil Wars of Peru. The War of Chupas*. Trans. and ed. by Sir Clements R. Markham. London, 1918. (Hakluyt Society, Second series, No. 42.)

————. *The War of Quito and Inca Documents*. Trans. and ed. by Sir Clements R. Markham. London, 1913. (Hakluyt Society, Second series, No. 31.)

Clemence, Stella R., ed. *The Harkness Collection in the Library of Con-

gress. Calendar of Spanish Manuscripts Concerning Peru, 1531–1651. Washington, 1932.

Connor, Jeannette M., ed. *Colonial Records of Spanish Florida.* 2 vols. Deland, 1925–30.

Cortes de los antiguos reinos de León y de Castilla. 5 vols. Madrid, 1882–1903. (Real Academia de la Historia.)

Cuervo, Justo. *Historiadores del convento de San Esteban de Salamanca.* 3 vols. Salamanca, 1914–16.

Cuevas, Mariano. *Historia de la iglesia en México.* 5 vols. El Paso, Texas, 1921–28.

Dávila, Vicente. *Encomiendas.* 3 vols. Caracas, 1927–45.

Díaz del Castillo, Bernal. *Historia verdadera de la conquista de la Nueva Espana.* Ed. by Ramón Iglesia. 2 vols. México, 1943.

Documentos escogidos del archivo de la casa de Alba. Madrid, 1891.

Encinas, Diego de. *Provisiones, cédulas, capítulos de ordenanças, instrucciones y cartas . . . tocantes al buen govierno de las Indias, y administración de la justicia en ellas.* 4 vols. Madrid, 1596.

Ercilla y Zúñiga, Alonso de. *La araucana.* Salamanca, 1574.

Ernst, James. *Roger Williams.* New York, 1932.

Errázuriz, Crescente. *Los orígenes de la iglesia chilena.* Santiago, 1873.

Esquivel Obregón, Toribio. *Apuntes para la historia del derecho en México.* 3 vols. Mexico, 1937–43. (Trabajos jurídicos de homenaje a la escuela libre de derecho en su XXV aniversario, Vols. 1, 5, 7.)

————. *Hernán Cortés y el derecho internacional en el siglo XVI.* México, 1939.

Fabié, Antonio María. *Vida y escritos de Don Fray Bartolomé de Las Casas.* 2 vols. Madrid, 1879.

Fernández, León. *Colección de documentos para la historia de Costa Rica.* 10 vols. San José, 1881–1907.

Fernández Arias, Evaristo. *Paralelo entre la conquista y dominación de América y el descubrimiento y pacificación de Filipinas.* Madrid, 1893.

Fernández de Enciso, Martín. *Suma de geografía.* Sevilla, 1519.

Figueras, Antonio. "Principios de la expansión dominicana en Indias," *Missionalia hispánica,* Año 1 (Madrid, 1944), 303–40.

Friederici, Georg. *Der Character der Entdeckung in Amerika, seine Eroberung und Durchdringung charackterisiert.* Stuttgart, 1925.

Gallagher, Buell C. *Color and Conscience: The Irrepressible Conflict.* New York, 1946.

Garcés, Jorge A., ed. *Colección de cédulas reales dirigidas a la audiencia de Quito.* Quito, 1935. (Publicaciones del archivo municipal, tomo 9.)

García Icazbalceta, Joaquín, ed. *Nueva colección de documentos para la historia de México.* 6 vols. México, 1886–92.

Gay Calbó, Enrique. "Discurso sobre Fray Bartolomé de Las Casas," *Boletín del archivo nacional, XLII* (La Habana, 1942), 100–106.

Ghigliazza, Raimundo. *Historia de la provinciana dominicana de Chile.* Concepción, 1898.

Giménez Fernández, Manuel. *Nuevas consideraciones sobre la historia, sentido y valor de las bulas alejandrinas de 1493 referentes a las Indias.* Sevilla, 1944. (Escuela de Estudios Hispano-Americanos de la Universidad de Sevilla.)

González-Blanco, Pedro. *Conquista y colonización de América por la calumniada España.* México, 1945.

Granada, Daniel. "Terminología indiana. Apuntamientos sobre la encomienda," *Boletín de la real academia española,* VIII (1921), 727–40; IX (1922), 359–65.

Green, Otis H. "A Critical Survey of Scholarship in the Field of Spanish Renaissance Literature, 1914–1944," *Studies in Philology,* XLIV (April 1947), 228–64.

Gutiérrez de Santa Clara, Pedro. *Historia de las guerras civiles del Perú (1544–1588) y de otros sucesos de las Indias.* Ed. by Manuel Serrano y Sanz. 6 vols. Madrid, 1904–29.

Hanke, Lewis. "A aplicação do requerimiento na America Espanhola," *Revista do Brasil* (Rio de Janeiro, Sept. 1938), 231–48.

———. "Dos palabras on Antonio de Ulloa and the Noticias Secretas," *Hispanic American Historical Review,* XVI (1936), 479–514.

———. "El papa Paulo III y los indios de América," *Universidad católica bolivariana,* IV (Medellín, Colombia, 1940), 355–84.

———. "Free Speech in Sixteenth-Century Spanish America," *Hispanic American Historical Review,* XXVI (1946), 135–49.

———. "La controversia entre Las Casas y Sepúlveda en Valladolid," *Universidad católica bolivariana,* VIII (Medellín, Colombia, 1942), 65–97.

———. "La libertad de palabra en Hispanoamerica durante el siglo XVI," *Cuadernos americanos,* Año 5 (1946), No. 2, pp. 185–201.

———. *"La lucha por justicia en la conquista española de América.* Buenos Aires, 1949.

———. "Las leyes de Burgos en 1512 y 1513," *Anuario de historia argentina 1942* (Buenos Aires, 1943), 33–56.

———. *Las teorías políticas de Bartolomé de Las Casas.* Buenos Aires, 1935. (Publicaciones del instituto de investigaciones históricas, No. 67.)

———. "Pope Paul III and the American Indians," *Harvard Theological Review,* XXX (Cambridge, 1937), 65–102.

———. *The Development of Regulations for Conquistadores.* Buenos Aires, 1941. (Contribuciones para el estudio de la historia de América. Homenaje al Doctor Emilio Ravignani, pp. 71–87.)

———. *The First Social Experiments in America.* Cambridge, 1935.

———. "The Requerimiento and its Interpreters," *Revista de historia de América,* I (México, 1938), No. 1, pp. 25–34.

———. "Un festón de documentos lascasasianos," *Revista cubana,* XVI (La Habana, 1941), 150–211.

———. "Viceroy Francisco de Toledo and the Just Titles of Spain to the Inca Empire," *The Americas,* III (Washington, 1946), 3–19.

———, and Agustín Millares Carlo, eds. *Cuerpo de documentos del siglo XVI sobre los derechos de España en las Indias y las Filipinas.* México, 1943.

Helps, Arthur. *The Spanish Conquest in America and Its Relation to the History of Slavery and to the Government of the Colonies.* Ed. by M. Oppenheimer. 4 vols. London, 1900–1904.

Henríquez-Ureña, Pedro. *Literary Currents in Hispanic America.* Cambridge, 1945.

Hinojosa y Naveros, Eduardo de. *Influencia que tuvieron en el derecho público de su patria y singularmente en el derecho penal los filósofos y teólogos españoles, anteriores á nuestro siglo.* Madrid, 1890.

Höffner, Joseph. *Cristentum und Menschenwürde—das Anliegen der spanischen Kolonialethik im Goldenen Zeitalter.* Trier, 1947.

Hoyos, Manuel María, ed. *Historia del colegio de San Gregorio de Valladolid por el . . . Fr. Gonzalo de Arriaga.* 2 vols. Valladolid, 1928–30.

Humboldt, Alexander von. *Essai politique sur le royaume de la Nouvelle-Espagne.* 2 vols. Paris, 1811–12.

Hunnewell, James Frothingham. *Illustrated Americana, 1493–1889.* Worcester, 1890.

Iglesia, Ramón. *Cronistas e historiadores de la conquista de México.* México, 1942.

Jane, Cecil. "The Administration of the Colons in Española, 1493–1500," *Proceedings of the Twenty-first International Congress of Americanists,* Part I (The Hague, 1924), 381–402.

Jiménez de la Espada, Marcos. *Juan de Castellanos y su historia del Nuevo Reino de Granada.* Madrid, 1889.

———. *Relaciones geográficas de Indias.* 4 vols. Madrid, 1881.

Johnson, Samuel. *London: a Poem.* London, 1738.

Jos, Emiliano. *La expedición de Ursúa al Dorado, la rebelión de Lope de Aguirre y el itinerario de los "Marañones."* Huesca, 1927.

Keller, Albert G. *Colonization.* New York, 1908.

Kirkpatrick, F. A. *The Spanish Conquistadores.* London, 1934.

La Briére, Yves de. *La conception du droit international chez les théologiens catholiques.* Paris, 1930.

Landin Carrasco, Amancio. *Vida y viajes de Pedro Sarmiento de Gamboa.* Madrid, 1947. (Instituto histórico de la Marina.)

León Pinelo, Antonio de. *Epítome de la biblioteca oriental y occidental náutica y geografía.* 3 vols. Madrid, 1737–38.

———. *Tratado de confirmaciones reales, 1630.* Introduction by Diego Luis Molinari. Buenos Aires, 1922. (Biblioteca argentina de libros raros americanos, Vol. I.)

Leturia, Pedro. "Las grandes bulas misionales de Alejandro VI," *Bibliotheca hispana missionum,* I (Madrid, 1930), 211–51.

———. "Maior y Vitoria ante la conquista de América," *Estudios eclesiásticos,* II (Madrid, 1932), 44–82.

Levillier, Roberto. *Don Francisco de Toledo, supremo organizador del Perú; su vida, su obra (1515–1582).* 3 vols. Buenos Aires, 1935–42.

———, ed. *Gobernantes del Perú, cartas y papeles, siglo XVI.* 14 vols. Madrid, 1921–26.

———, ed. *La audiencia de Charcas. Correspondencia de presidentes y oidores, documentos del Archivo de Indias.* 3 vols. Madrid, 1918–22.

Llorente, Juan A. *Colección de las obras del obispo de Chiapa, Don Bartolomé de Las Casas.* 2 vols. Paris, 1822.

Lopetegui, León. *El padre José de Acosta y las misiones.* Madrid, 1942.

López de Gómara, Francisco. *Hispania victorix. Primera y segunda parte de la historia general de Indias.* Madrid, 1852. (Biblioteca de autores españoles, XXII: 155–355.)

López de Velasco, Juan. *Geografía y descripción de las Indias.* Ed. by Justo Zaragoza. Madrid, 1894.

Mackay, John A. *The Other Spanish Christ.* New York, 1933.

Madariaga, Salvador de. *The Rise of the Spanish American Empire.* London, 1947.

Madureira, J. M. de. "A liberdade dos indios e a companhia de Jesus," *Revista do instituto historico e geographico brasileiro. Tomo Especial. Congresso internacional de historia de America,* IV (Rio de Janeiro, 1927), 1–160.

Manypenny, George W. *Our Indian Wards.* Cincinnati, 1880.

Mariana, Juan de. *Historia de España.* Madrid, 1854. (Biblioteca de autores españoles, XXX–XXXI.)

Martínez, Manuel María. "El P. Las Casas ante la nueva crítica," *La ciencia tomista,* L (Salamanca, 1934), 289–302.

Matienzo, José de. *Gobierno del Perú. Buenos Aires,* 1910.

Means, Philip A. *Biblioteca Andina,* Part I. New Haven, 1928. (Transactions of the Connecticut Academy of Arts and Sciences, No. 29.)

———. *The Fall of the Inca Empire.* New York, 1932.

Medina, José Toribio. *Biblioteca hispano-chilena.* 3 vols. Santiago, 1897–99.

———, ed. *Colección de documentos inéditos para la historia de Chile desde el viaje de Magallanes hasta la batalla de Maipú.* 29 vols. Santiago, 1888–1901.

———, ed. *Colección de historiadores de Chile y otros documentos relativos a la historia nacional.* 45 vols. Santiago, 1861–1923.

———. *El descubrimiento del Océano Pacífico.* 3 vols. Santiago, 1913–20.

Mendiburu, Manuel de. *Diccionario histórico-biográfico del Perú.* Segunda edición. 11 vols. Lima, 1931–35.

Mendieta, Jerónimo de. *Historia eclesiástica indiana.* Ed. by Joaquín García Icazbalceta. México, 1870.

Merino, Manuel. "Semblanzas misioneras: Fr. Martín de Rada agustino," *Missionalia hispánica,* Año 1 (Madrid, 1944), Nos. 1 and 2, pp. 167–212.

Merriman, Roger B. *The Rise of the Spanish Empire in the Old World and in the New.* 4 vols. New York, 1918–34.

Miguélez, P. *Catálogo de los códices españoles de la biblioteca del Escorial.* Madrid, 1917.

Miranda, José. *Vitoria y los intereses de la conquista de América.* México, 1947.

Mitchell, Wesley, ed. *What Veblen Taught.* New York, 1936.

Molinari, Diego Luis, ed. *Leyes y ordenanzas nuevamente hechas por su Magestad, para la gobernación de las Indias, en Valladolid M.D.C. III.* Buenos Aires, 1922. (Instituto de Investigaciones Históricas.)

Motolinía, Fr. Toribio de Benavente o. *Historia de los indios de la Nueva España.* Ed. by Daniel Sánchez García. Barcelona, 1914.

Mujía, Ricardo, ed. *Bolivia-Paraguay; exposición de los títulos que consagran el derecho territorial de Bolivia, sobre la zona comprendida entre los ríos Pilcomayo y Paraguay. Anexos . . . Epoca colonial.* 5 vols. La Paz, 1914 (?).

Muñoz, Honorio. *Vitoria and the Conquest of America. A study on the first reading on the Indians "De Indis Prior,"* Manila, 1935. (Santo Tomás University Press.)

Muro Orejón, Antonio, ed. *Las leyes nuevas, 1542–1543.* Sevilla, 1946. (Escuela de Estudios Hispano-Americanos de la Universidad de Sevilla.)

Northrop, F. S. C. *The Meeting of East and West.* New York, 1946.

Nys, Ernest. "Les publicistes espagnols du XVIe siècle et les droits de Indiens," *Revue de droit international et de législation comparée,* XXI (1889), 532–60.

O'Gorman, Edmundo. *Crisis y porvenir de la ciencia histórica.* México, 1947.

———. *Fundamentos de la historia de América.* México, 1942.

———. "Sobre la naturaleza bestial del indio americano," *Filosofía y letras* (México, 1941), No. 1: 141–58; No. 2: 305–15. (Revista de la facultad de filosofía y letras, Universidad nacional autónoma de México.)

Ortiz Fernández, Fernando. *El engaño de las razas.* La Habana, 1945.

Oviedo y Valdés, Gonzalo Fernández de. *Historia general y natural de las Indias, islas y Tierra Firme del Mar Océano.* Ed. by José Amador de los Ríos. 4 vols. Madrid, 1851–55.

Parker, Theodore. *Collected Works.* 12 vols. London, 1863–65.

Parry, J. H. *The Spanish Theory of Empire in the Sixteenth Century.* Cambridge, England, 1940.

Pérez de Villagrá, Gaspar. *History of New Mexico.* Trans. by Gilberto Espinosa. Introduction and notes by F. W. Hodge. Los Angeles, 1933. (Quivira Society Publications, IV.)

Petrie, Charles A., and Louis Bertrand. *The History of Spain.* New York, 1934.

Pfandl, Ludwig. *Cultura y costumbres del pueblo español de los siglos XVI y XVII.* Barcelona, 1929.

Phillips, Ulrich B., ed. *A Documentary History of American Industrial Society.* 11 vols. Cleveland, 1910.

———. *Florida Plantation Records from the Papers of George Noble Jones.* St. Louis, 1927.

Pietschmann, Richard, ed. *Geschichte des Inkareiches, von Pedro Sarmiento de Gamboa.* Berlin, 1906. (Abhandlungen der Königlichen Gesellschaft der wissenschaften zu Göttingen. Philologisch-historisch klasse. Neue folge, Bd. VI, No. 4.)

Polo de Ondegardo, Juan. *Informaciones acerca de la religión y gobierno de los Incas.* Ed. by Horacio H. Urteaga. 2 vols. Lima, 1916–17. (Colección de libros y documentos referentes a la historia del Perú, III–IV.)

Porras Barrenechea, Raúl. "El testamento de Mancio Serra," *Mercurio peruano,* XXIII (1941), 55–62.

Puga, Vasco de. *Provisiones, cédulas, instrucciones de su Majestad.* 2 vols. México, 1878.

Purchas, Samuel. *Hakluytus Posthumus, or Purchas his Pilgrimes.* 20 vols. Glasgow, 1905–7. (Hakluyt Society. Extra series.)

Ramos Pedrueza, Rafael. *Estudios históricos, sociales y literarios.* México, 1923.

Ranke, Leopold von. *The Ottoman and the Spanish Empires in the Sixteenth and Seventeenth Centuries.* London, 1843.

Remesal, Antonio de. *Historia general de las Indias occidentales, y particular de la gobernación de Chiapas y Guatemala.* Madrid, 1619.

Riaza, Ramón. "El primer impugnador de Vitoria: Gregorio López, *Anuario de la asociación Francisco de Vitoria,* III (1932), 105–23.

Ricard, Robert. *La "Conquête Spirituelle" du Mexique. Essai sur l'apostolat et les méthodes missionaires des ordres mendiants en Nouvelle-Espagne de 1523–24 à 1572.* Paris, 1933. (Institut d'ethnologie.)

Ríos, Fernando de los. *Religión y estado en la España del siglo XVI.* New York, 1927.

———. "The Religious Character of Colonial Law in Sixteenth Century Spain," *Proceedings of the Sixth International Congress of Philosophy, 1926* (1927), 481–85.

Riva Agüero y Osma, José de la. *El primer alcalde de Lima, Nicolás de Ribera el Viejo y su posteridad. Lima,* 1935.

Rivera y Sanromán, Agustín. *Principios críticos sobre el virreinato de la Nueva España i sobre la revolución de independencia.* 3 vols. Lagos, 1884–88.

Robertson, William. *History of America.* 2 vols. London, 1777.

Rowe, John Howland. *Inca Culture at the Time of the Spanish Conquest.* Washington, 1946. (Handbook of South American Indians, ed. by Julian Steward, II, 183–330.)

Rubio Moreno, Luis, ed. *Pasajeros a Indias.* 2 vols. Madrid, 1930 (?). (Colección de documentos inéditos para la historia de Hispano-América, Vols. 8, 13.)

Sánchez Alonso, B. *Fuentes de la historia española e hispano-americana.* Second ed. Madrid, 1927.

Sandoval, Prudencio de. *Historia de la vida y hechos del emperador Carlos V . . . desde el año 1500 hasta el de 1557.* 2 vols. Pamplona, 1614–18.

Sanín Cano, Baldomero. "El descubrimiento de América y la higiene," *Cuba contemporánea,* VII (La Habana, 1915), 28–37.

Santa Cruz, Alonso de. *Crónica del emperador Carlos V.* 5 vols. Madrid, 1920–25.

Schäfer, Ernst. *El consejo real y supremo de las Indias; su historia, organización y labor administrativa hasta la terminación de la Casa de Austria.* Sevilla, 1935. (Publicaciones del Centro de estudios de historia de América, Universidad de Sevilla.)

Schlaifer, Robert O. *Greek Theories of Slavery from Homer to Aristotle.* Cambridge, 1936. (Harvard Studies in Classical Philology, No. 47.)

Scott, James Brown. *The Spanish Origin of International Law. Francisco de Vitoria and his Law of Nations.* Oxford, 1934.

Sepúlveda, Juan Ginés de. "Democrates alter," *Boletín de la real academia de historia*, XXI (Madrid, 1892), 257–369. Ed. by M. Menéndez y Pelayo.

———. *Opera*. 4 vols. Madrid, 1780.

———. *Tratado sobre las justas causas de la guerra contra los indios; con una advertencia de Marcelino Menéndez y Pelayo y un estudio por Manuel García-Pelayo*. México, 1941.

Serrano y Sanz, Manuel. *Orígenes de la dominación española en América*. Tomo primero. Madrid, 1918. (Nueva biblioteca de autores españoles, Vol. 25.)

Sikes, E. E. *Anthropology of the Greeks*. London, 1914.

Simón, Pedro. *Noticias historiales de las conquistas de Tierra Firme en las Indias occidentales*. 5 vols. Bogotá, 1882–92.

Silva, J. F. V. "Elogio de Vaca de Castro por Antonio de Herrera," *Revista de archivos, bibliotecas y museos*, Tercera época, Año 21 (Madrid, 1917), XXXVI: 13–42, 249–59, 407–18; XXXVII: 85–110, 360–82; Año 22 (1918), XXXVIII: 96–122.

Simpson, Lesley Byrd. *Studies in the Administration of the Indians in New Spain*. 4 parts. Berkeley, 1934–40.

———. *The Encomienda in New Spain*. Berkeley, 1929.

Solórzano Pereira, Juan de. *Disputationes de Indiarum iure: sive, de iusta Indiarum Occidentalium inquisitione, acquisitione et retentione*. 2 vols. Madrid, 1629–39.

———. *Política indiana*. Madrid, 1648.

Steffen, Hans. "Anotaciones a la *Historia índica* del Capitán Pedro Sarmiento de Gamboa," *Anales de la universidad de Santiago de Chile*, tomo 129 (Santiago, 1911), 1107–1214.

Stevens, Henry, ed. *The New Laws of the Indies*. London, 1893.

Streit, Robert. "Die erste Junta von Burgos in Jahre 1512," *Zeitschrift für Missionswissenschaft* (Münster i W., 1923), pp. 65–78.

———. "Zur Vorgeschichte der 1. Junta von Burgos 1512," *ibid.* (1922), pp. 166–75.

———, and Johannes Dindinger. *Bibliotheca Missionum*. 11 vols. Münster, 1916–39.

Tannenbaum, Frank. *Peace by Revolution, an Interpretation of Mexico*. New York, 1933.

Tapia y Rivera, Alejandro. *Biblioteca histórica de Puerto Rico*. Puerto Rico, 1854.

Taylor, E. G. R., ed. *The Original Writings and Correspondence of the two Richard Hakluyts*. 2 vols. London, 1935.

Torres Lanzas, Pedro, ed. *Catálogo de los documentos relativos a las Islas Filipinas existentes en el Archivo de Indias*. 8 vols. Barcelona, 1918–33.

Truyol Serra, Antonio. *Los principios del derecho público en Francisco de Vitoria*. Madrid, 1946.

Unamuno, Miguel de. *Del sentimiento trágico de la vida*. Tercera edición. Madrid, n.d.

Vanderpol, Alfred. *La doctrine scolastique de droit de guerre*. Paris, 1919.

———. *Le droit de guerre d'après les théologiens et les canonistes du moyen-age*. Paris, 1911.

Vázquez Menchaca, Fernando. *Controversiarum illustrium.* Ed. by Fidal Rodríguez Alcalde. 2 vols. Valladolid, 1931.

Wilson, Woodrow. *The Public Papers of Woodrow Wilson.* Ed. by Ray Stannard Baker and William E. Dodd. 6 vols. New York, 1925–27.

Winsor, Justin, ed. *Narrative and Critical History of America.* 8 vols. Boston, 1884–89.

Zavala, Silvio A. "Cristiandad e infieles según algunos autores medievales y renacentistas," *Estudios históricos* (Guadalajara, México, 1944), No. 3, pp. 7–24.

————. *De encomienda y propiedad territorial en algunas regiones de la América Española.* México, 1940.

————. *Ensayos sobre la colonización española en América.* Buenos Aires, 1944.

————. *Ideario de Vasco de Quiroga,* México, 1941.

————. *La encomienda indiana.* Madrid, 1935.

————. *La filosofía política en la conquista de América.* México, 1947.

————. "La propiedad territorial en las encomiendas de los indios," *Universidad,* IV (México, 1937), No. 20, pp. 34–37.

————. *La "Utopía" de Tomás Moro en la Nueva España.* México, 1937.

————. "Las Casas ante la doctrina de la servidumbre natural," *Revista de la universidad de Buenos Aires,* Año II (Buenos Aires, 1944), 45–58.

————. "¿Las Casas, esclavista?" *Cuadernos americanos,* Año 3 (México, 1944), No. 2, pp. 149–54.

————. "Las conquistas de Canarias y América," *Tierra Firme,* I (Madrid, 1935), 81–112; II: 89–115.

————. "Las encomiendas de Nueva España y el gobierno de don Antonio de Mendoza," *Revista de historia de América* (México, 1938), No. 1, pp. 59–75.

————. *Las instituciones jurídicas en la conquista de América.* Madrid, 1935.

————. "Las tendencias señoriales y regalistas en los comienzos de la colonización de América," *Boletín de la Academia Nacional de Historia,* XVIII (Buenos Aires, 1945).

————. *Los intereses particulares en la conquista de la Nueva España.* Madrid, 1933.

————. "Los trabajadores antillanos en el siglo XVI," *Revista de historia de América* (1938), No. 2: 31–67; No. 3: 60–88; No. 4: 211–16.

————. *New Viewpoints on the Spanish Colonization of America.* Philadelphia, 1943.

————. "Relaciones históricas entre indios y negros en Iberoamérica," *Revista de las Indias,* XXVIII (Bogotá, 1946), No. 88.

————. *Servidumbre natural y libertad cristiana, según los tratadistas españoles de los siglos XVI y XVII.* Buenos Aires, 1944. (Instituto de Investigaciones Históricas.)

————. "The American Utopia of the Sixteenth Century," *The Huntington Library Quarterly,* X (San Marino, 1947), 337–47.

————, and María Castelo, eds. *Fuentes para la historia del trabajo en Nueva España.* 8 vols. México, 1939–46.

Zurkalowski, Erich. "El establecimiento de las encomiendas en el Perú y sus antecedentes," *Revista histórica*, VI (Lima, 1919), 254–69.

6. LIST OF ABBREVIATIONS USED

Documentos inéditos de América. Colección de documentos inéditos relativos al descubrimiento, conquista y colonización de las posesiones españolas en América y Oceanía, sacados de los archivos del reino, y muy especialmente del de Indias. Ed. by Joaquín F. Pacheco, Francisco de Cárdenas, and Luis Torres de Mendoza. 42 vols. Madrid, 1864–84.

Documentos inéditos de España. Colección de documentos inéditos para la historia de España. Ed. by Martín Fernández de Navarrete. 112 vols. Madrid, 1842–95.

Documentos inéditos de México. Colección de documentos para la historia de México. Ed. by Joaquín García Icazbalceta. 2 vols. Mexico, 1858–66.

Documentos inéditos de Ultramar. Colección de documentos inéditos relativos al descubrimiento, conquista y organización de las antiguas posesiones de ultramar. Segunda serie. 21 vols. Madrid, 1885–1928.

INDEX

Ácoma, 134
Acosta, José de, 136, 167, 173
Adrian, Cardinal, 60, 65
Agüero, Jerónimo de, 43
Aguilar, Marcos de, 43
Aguilar, Pedro de, 93
Aguirre, Lope de, 6
Alberdi, Juan Bautista, 71
Alemán, Diego, 93
Alexander VI, Pope, 2, 25, 33, 171; interpretation of his bulls of donation, 26
Almagro, Diego de, 31, 92, 94
Altamira, Rafael, 122
Alva, Duke of, 98
Alvarado, Diego de, 44
Alvarado, Pedro de, 80
Álvarez Osorio, Diego, 134
Amaru, Inca Tupac, 136, 162
Ampiés, Juan de, 43
Andrada, Rodrigo de, 78, 94
Angulo, Pedro de, 78, 79, 93
Aquinas, Thomas, 23, 28, 120, 134, 188
Archive of the Indies, 8
Arcos, Miguel de, 149
Ardón, Marcos, 40
Arévalo, Bernardino de, 117, 119
Arévalo Martínez, Rafael, 176
Aristotle, 23, 28, 63, 114, 122, 124-27, 134, 176
Arriaga, Luis de, 55
Augustine, 74, 134, 188
Augustinus of Anchona, 23
Ávila, Pedro Arias de. See Pedrarias
Ayora, Juan de, 34

Barrionuevo, Francisco de, 47
Bayle, Constantino, 35
Bazán, Armando, 196
Beltrán de Heredia, Vicente, 27-28, 120, 151
Benalcázar, Sebastián de, 31, 89-90
Benavides, Miguel de, 140, 152, 158
Berlanga, 62
Bernal, Juan, 99
Berrio, Luis de, 61-62

Bertrand, Louis, 35
Betanzos, Domingo de, 68, 98, 103, 122; attitude toward Indians, 12
Beteta, Gregorio de, 159
"Black legend," 4, 88-91; bibliographical notes on, 195-96
Blakey, Robert, 40
Bodin, Jean, 126
Bolívar, Simón, 127
Box, Pelham, 91
Burgos, Laws of, 23-25, 147; Clarification of Laws of, 25

Cabezas, Alonso, 52
Cáceres, Alonso de, 44
Calderón, Melchor, 138
Calderón, Rodrigo, 93
Cáncer, Luis, 78, 79
Cano, Melchor, 114, 117, 129, 152
Capac, Maita, 166
Capac, Manco, 166
Casas, Bartolomé de Las, 3, 5, 8, 9, 11, 17, 29, 35, 45
    Life: appointed "Protector of the Indians," 42; attitudes toward, 177-78; colonization attempts, 54-70; consecrated Bishop of Chiapa, 95; conversion to defense of Indians, 21-22; early life of, 20-21; enters Dominican Order, 68; "General Representative of the Indians," 59; political theories, 153-55; purpose of conquest according to, 7; views on just war, peaceful preaching, 187-89
    Writings: Advice and Regulations for Confessors, 154; *Argumentum apologiae,* 118; *Apologetic History,* 69, 123-26; *Confesionario,* 130; *History of the Indies,* 22, 59, 61-63, 65, 66, 69, 73, 86; *Eighth Remedy,* 87-91; *Only Method of Attracting All People to the True Faith,* 72, 125; *Remedies for the Existing Evils, with Twenty Reasons Therefor,* 88; *Solution to the Twelve Doubts,* 163; *Thirty Very Juridical Propo-*

Casas, Bartolomé de Las (*continued*) sitions, 154; *Treatise Concerning the Imperial Sovereignty and Universal Pre-Eminence Which the Kings of Castile and Leon Enjoy over the Indies*, 153-55; *Very Brief Account of the Destruction of the Indies*, 73, 87-91, 170
Castañeda, Francisco de, 89
Castellanos, Miguel de, 68
Castro, Alfonso de, 138
Caupolicán, 6
Cayetano, Cardinal, 27
Centeno, Diego, 113
Cervantes de Salazar, Francisco, 157
Chacón y Calvo, José María, 177
Chamberlain, Robert S., 85
Charles V, Holy Roman Emperor (Charles I, King of Spain), 8, 10, 63, 83, 88, 90, 91, 93, 96, 100, 111, 124, 136, 147, 150, 177
Chávez, Pedro de, 142
Cholula, 6
Chrysostom, John, 75, 77-78, 121
Cieza de León, Pedro, 89
Cisneros, Cardinal, Jiménez de, 30, 42, 45
Clement V, Pope, 145
Cobán, 80
Colonization, early attempts at, 55-56, 58
Columbus, Christopher, 20, 25, 44, 55
Columbus, Diego, 18, 26, 103
Columbus, Pedro, 44
Conchillos, Lope, 31
Contreras, Rodrigo de, 134, 135
Copernicus, Nicolaus, 95
Córdoba, Pedro de, 18, 20, 24-25, 58, 59
Cortés, Hernán, 6, 71, 86, 94, 122, 133; attempts to erect statue to, 195
Covarrubias, Diego de, 138, 152
Cruz, Domingo de la, 98
Cuéllar, Juan de, 144
Cumaná, 58, 68

Dávalos, Melchor, 145
Dávila, Pedrarias. *See* Pedrarias
De Bry, 90
Díaz de Gibraleón, Juan, 96
Díaz del Castillo, Bernal, 6, 31, 133; purpose of conquest according to, 7
Diego, chieftain, 50
Don Quixote, 173

Drake, Sir Francis, 5
Dubois, William Burghardt, 176

Encomienda, bibliographical note on, 83-86, 182-83, 189; controversy in Philippines, 160; early history of, 19-20; history of (1512–42), 86-87; in Peru, 169; theory of, 19
Enriquillo, 69
Eraso, Francisco, 70
Ercilla, Alonso de, 6
Espinal, Alonso del, 23, 30

Falcón, Francisco, 171
Ferdinand II, King of Aragon, 8, 9, 18, 25, 26, 27, 29, 34, 55
Fernández, Diego, *Historia del Perú*, 168, 169
Fernández de Enciso, Martín, 111, 149; views on just war, 31-32
Fernández de Oviedo y Valdés, Gonzalo, 11, 31, 33, 34, 35, 47, 63; attitude toward Indians, 48
Fernández de Velasco, Don Iñigo, 62
Figueroa, Francisco de, 47
Figueroa, Rodrigo de, Indian experiments of, 45-47
Flemish courtiers, 66, 88
Flores, Diego, 171
Francis I, King of France, 148
Free speech, 8-10

Gama, Antonio de la, 46
Garcés, Julián, 69
García, Alonso, 103
García de Palacio, Diego, 134
García Icazbalceta, Joaquín, 72
Gasca, Pedro de la, 113
Gattinara, Don Mercurino Arborio de, 64
Gay Calbó, Enrique, 177
Getino, Luis, 151
Ginés de Sepúlveda, Juan, 3, 177, 196; biographical information on, 113-15; *Democrates alter, sive de justis belli causis apud Indos*, 114
González, Gil, 137, 138
González, Juan, 98
Gregorio, Licentiate, 23
Gregory XIV, Pope, 143
Grotius, Hugo, *On the Freedom of the Seas*, 25
Guarcai, Doña María Cusi, 170
Guerrero, Francisco, 50

Gutiérrez, Pedro, 164
Gutiérrez de Santa Clara, Pedro, 66

Henríquez Ureña, Pedro, 17
Henry of Susa (Ostiensis), 28, 134, 145, 155
Herrera, Antonio de, 148
Herrera, Diego de, 141
Herrera, Juan de, 137
Hojeda, Alonso de, 67
Hurtado de Mendoza, García, 137
Hurtado de Mendoza, Juan, 27

Incas, eulogy of their rule, 172
Indian experiment, to determine nature of Spaniards, 52
Indians, cannibalistic, 67; capacity of, 122-23; conversion in Guatemala, 78-81; disputes over baptism of, 40; hospital service for, 58; nature of, 10-13; theories concerning, 40-41
Infidels, 76
Inga, Topa, 164
Inquisition, 41, 145
Isabella, Queen of Castile, 8, 20, 26

Jeronymite friars, enquiry on Indian capacity, 42-45
Jesus Christ, 76, 78, 131, 136, 141, 153, 158
Jews, 60
Jiménez de Quesada, Gonzalo, 148, 150
Johnson, Samuel, 39, 148
Juárez, Hernán, 24
Juárez de Carvajal, Benito, 96
Julius II, Pope, 2

Keller, Albert G., 140
Knights of the Golden Spur, 63-64, 66

Land of True Peace, 81
Landa, Diego de, 41
Las Casas. See Casas, Bartolomé de Las
Lavezaris, Guido de, 142
Lebrón, Judge, 47
Legaspi, Miguel López de, 140
León, Nicolás, 72
León Pinelo, Antonio de, 90; Tratado de confirmaciones reales (1630), 85
Levillier, Robert, 104, 128, 152, 165, 171
Lizárraga, Reginaldo de, 136, 139
Loaysa, Alonso de, 18
Loaysa, García Jofré de, 88, 94, 100, 111, 114

Loaysa, Licenciado, 93
López, Gonzalo, 96
López, Gregorio, 93, 99, 118.
López de Gómara, Francisco, 64, 129
López de Velasco, Juan, 168
Luna, Tristán de, 159

Machuca de Zuazo, Diego, 134
Madariaga, Salvador de, 4
Major, John, his political theories, 183-84
Maldonado, Alonso de, 78-79, 117
Maldonado, Cristóbal, 137
Manzanedo, Bernardino de, 60
Mariana, Juan de, 148
Markham, Clements, 165, 171
Martín, Roque, 90
Martínez, Alonso, 134
Martyr, Peter, 49
Matienzo, Juan de, 136; Gobierno del Perú, 167
Means, Philip A., 165, 171
Mendoza, Antonio de, 89, 101, 133; attitude toward Indians, 12
Menéndez Pidal, Ramón, 177, 196
Mesa, Bernardo de, 23
Mexía, Pedro, 48
Mimbreño, Martín, 135
Minaya, Bernardino de, 135
Miranda, Bartolome dé, 117
Mirandola, Andrés de, 141
Missas, Francisco de las, 144
Moguer, Andrés de, 98
Montalbán, Francisco Javier, 140
Montejo, Francisco de, 31
Montesinos, Antonio de, 22, 23, 28, 173; revolutionary sermons of, 17-18
Montezuma, 75, 123
Moors, 60, 138
Morales, Luis de, 93
More, Sir Thomas, 56
Moslems, 154, 164
Mosquera, Juan, 43, 45
Motolinía, Toribio de, 9, 89
Muñoz, Honorio, 151
Münster, Sebastian, 90

Negroes, 57, 60, 125, 127, 176; in Hispaniola, 43
New Laws, 91-95; bibliographical note on, 190
Notaries, 34, 50; indispensable to Spaniards, 6

Núñez de Prado, Juan, 113
Núñez Vela, Blasco, 96, 165

Ocampo, Gonzalo de, 43, 67-68
O'Gorman, Edmundo, 124, 125, 192, 195, 196; criticism of his interpretation, 187-89; *Fundamentos de la historia de América*, 188
Oñate, Juan de, 134
Oñez de Loyola, Martín García, 138
Ortega, Francisco de, 142
Ortiz, Bartolomé, 103
Ostiensis. *See* Henry of Susa
Ovando, Nicolás de, 20, 26, 44
Oviedo, Hernando de, 98

Palacios Rubios, Juan López de, 32, 35, 57, 147; political theories, 29-30; *Of the Ocean Isles* (1512), 29-30
Paraguay "Reductions," 70
Pasamonte, Miguel de, 43
Paul III, Pope, 76, 135; bull on Indian capacity, 72-73
Paz, Matías de, 57, 147; political theories, 27-28
Pearl Coast, 59
Pedrarias, 30, 31, 33, 55
Peñalosa, Ronquillo de, 142
Pérez Dasmariñas, Gómez, 143, 144, 161
Pérez de Cabrera, Juan, 112
Pérez de la Fuente, Hernán, 118
Petrie, Sir Charles, 35
Philip II, King of Spain, 5, 8, 84, 100, 112, 130, 138, 144, 145, 159
Philip III, King of Spain, 139, 143
Pizarro, Francisco, 6, 92, 135, 166, 170
Pizarro, Hernando, 94
Polo de Ondegardo, Juan, 136, 164, 168
Ponce de León, Pedro, 119
Porras Barrenechea, Raúl, 195
"Protector of the Indians," 42
Puerto Rico, 67
Purchas, Samuel, 5

Quetzalcoatl, 176
Quevedo, Juan de, 63
Quinto, 46
Quiroga, Rodrigo de, 138
Quiroga, Vasco de, 56, 70, 176

Rada, Martín de, 140, 142, 158
Ramírez, Miguel, 48
Ramírez de Fuenleal, Sebastián, 87, 94, 100, 176

Ramírez de Haro, Antonio, 114
Ranke, Leopold von, 94
Repartimientos, 19
Requirement, 140, 149; composition, 31-32; contents of, 33; divergent interpretation of, 35; practice of, 33-35
"Revisionists," 4
Ribadeneyra, Pedro, 50
Ribera, Alonso de, 139
Ríos, Fernando de los, 5
Riva-Agüero, José de la, 165
Robertson, William, 3
Rodríguez de Fonseca, Juan, 19, 45, 64
Rojas, Manuel, 51
Roldán, Francisco, 25
Romero, Pedro, 43
Rousseau, Jean Jacques, 126

Salamanca, Miguel de, 86
Salamanca, University of, 11
Salazar, Domingo de, 8, 140, 142, 143, 152; life of, 158-59; *Treatise Concerning the Tributes to Be Levied on the Infidels of the Philippine Islands*, 160-61
Salcedo, Juan de, 142
Salmerón, Licenciado, 99
San Pablo monastery (Valladolid, Spain), 12
San Román, Juan de, 98, 100
Sánchez, Alonso, 143, 158
Santa María, Domingo de, 189
Santibáñez, Ignacio, 144
Santillán, Licentiate, 168
Santo Domingo, Bernaldo de, 44
Sarmiento de Gamboa, Pedro, 163, 164, 171; *Indian History*, 168, 170; life and works, 169-72
Schaefer, Ernest, 93
Scholes, France V., 84, 189
Scott, James Brown, 151
Scotus, Duns, 23
Sepúlveda. *See* Ginés de Sepúlveda, Juan
Serra, Mancio, 172
Serrano, Cristóbal, 43
Solórzano de Pereira, Juan, 90
Soto, Domingo de, 117-19, 123, 129, 134, 152
Soto, Hernando de, 31
Spaniards, character of, in America, 19; their legal formalism, 6; their pas-

sion for extremes, 6; their theological bent, religiosity, 5-6
Stevens, Henry, 91
Suárez de Peralta, Juan, 152

Tannenbaum, Frank, 175
Tello de Sandoval, Francisco, 96, 97, 118
Testera, Jacobo de, 93, 95, 135
Tierra de Guerra, 78
Tierra Firme, colonization in, 54-70
Tlaxcalans, 151
Toledo, Francisco de, 165-72; expedition against Chiriguanaes, 135-37
Torquemada, Cardinal, 28
Torres, Juan de, 93
Tuzutlán, 78

Urdañeta, Andrés de, 142
Urteaga, Horacio, 165

Vadillo, 51
Valdivia, Luis de, 138
Valdivia, Pedro de, 113
Vargas Machuca, Bernardo, 152
Vascones, Juan de, 139
Vázquez de Ayllón, Lucas, 44
Vázquez de Menchaca, Fernando, Illustrious Controversies, 127-28

Veblen, Thorstein, 4
Velasco, López de, 104
Velázquez, Diego, 133
Velázquez, Gutierre, 99, 118
Velázquez de Salazar, Juan, 157
Vera Cruz, Alonso de la, 152
Vico, Domingo de, 81
Villanueva, Alonso de, 96
Villasante, Antonio de, 44
Vitoria, Francisco de, 3, 11, 28, 74, 88, 94, 118, 130, 137, 138, 141, 145, 149, 158, 159, 164, 170, 171, 174, 177; comparison with Las Casas, 155; De Indis, 150, 152; De Jure Belli, 150
Vives, Luis, 188

Waltz, Otto, 126
Williams, Roger, 172
Wilson, Woodrow, 175

Yupanqui, Tupac, 165

Zambales, 144, 158
Zárate, Juan de, 98
Zavala, Silvio A., 3, 29, 103
Zuazo, Alonso, 60
Zumárraga, Juan de, 69, 93, 98, 112, 175
Zurita, Alonso de, 89, 152, 159

THE DEVELOPMENT OF LATIN AMERICAN HISTORY IN THE UNITED STATES, 1923–1988: REMINISCENCES, REFLECTIONS, AND RECOMMENDATIONS

THE problem of how historians present themselves to their colleagues cannot be easily solved. Some write autobiographies, many point to their publications, but my purpose will be to provide a memoir with an emphasis on the variety of historical topics that have attracted me over the years. There will also be considerable information on teaching problems and prospects, as well as proposals for new projects and ruminations on the role historians play in the contemporary world.

I was born in an Oregon village so small that births were not recorded, and when the State Department issued my first passport years later it was on the basis of an affidavit by my mother. But even in my birthplace in 1905 the centennial commemoration of the exploration of Oregon by President Thomas Jefferson's emissaries Meriwether Lewis and William Clark was noticed, and therefore on baptism my given names were Lewis Ulysses. My father always waxed indignant when my first name was spelled in the more usual French manner, and he explained that it had nothing to do with those decadent kings in Paris.

My middle name also had historical connotations, for my father was the son of an immigrant, a member of the Wendish minority in Germany, who had arrived in the United States during the presidency of Grant. Like many immigrants he became a patriotic American so that when his first son, my father, was born in Massachusetts he gave him as a middle name Ulysses. My father became a textile manufacturer but he always displayed special interest in the Civil War, and his favorite family vacation was a visit to its battlefields.

My mother's family, the Stevensons, were Scottish immigrants who first came to Connecticut in the late eighteenth century, probably from Northern Ireland for my mother had strongly Protestant inclinations all her life. Her grandfathers had pushed on to California in the middle of the nineteenth century, one by the perilous overland route with his wife and children. Her other grandfather had gone west alone during the Gold Rush days, and his family followed in due course via Panama, where one of the children died of fever.

None of these immigrants or their descendants apparently thought much about education, though my father was sent to Germany for a year or so for technical work in textiles, but he made a point of returning to Massachusetts before he became twenty-one to avoid being hustled into the emperor's army. One of my mother's grandfathers became well-to-do in California in the construction business, but his gift to each of his children was a well-built home— not higher education.

My own family, therefore, must have been very surprised when as a high school senior in a small Ohio town, I manifested a desire to attend Yale. Inasmuch as my father was a faithful Republican, he was not alarmed by this idea, for he knew that William Howard Taft had been a professor there. However, I failed the mathematics entrance exam and went instead to Northwestern University, which had the virtue in my mother's eyes of being a Methodist institution, but its attraction for me was that it then had a winning football team. At Northwestern there was one of the few American professors of Latin American history, a pioneer named Isaac Joslin Cox, and in 1924 at the age of nineteen I became the first descendant of those Scottish and German immigrants to receive a university degree. Inasmuch as by this time I had met a student named Kate Gilbert in an English composition class conducted by a young charismatic instructor named Bernard DeVoto, I decided to stay around for a master of arts degree and prepared a thesis at the ripe age of twenty on the Venezuelan Libertador Simón Bolívar. These university years also saw the beginning of my professional relations for, as a senior, I attended the annual meeting of the American Historical Association in 1923 in Columbus, Ohio, and there met Herbert Eugene Bolton, noted for his development of Latin American history in Berkeley.

AHA meetings were then modest affairs, and even undergraduate students could mix and mingle with the outstanding professors present. Charles E. Chapman was in Columbus, too, a younger scholar from California who had been instrumental in the establishment of the *Hispanic American Historical Review* a few years before. He had prevailed upon John Franklin Jameson, the famed editor of the *American Historical Review,* to persuade President Woodrow Wilson to send a special letter for publication in the first issue of *HAHR* when it appeared in 1918. Wilson expressed the hope, which must have seemed a quaint idea to some, that such a historical review would lead to better relations between the United States and our neighbors to the south.

During the summer of 1925, I was in Washington working on material relating to Bolívar in the State Department archives, long before the National Archives was built. During this hot experience, for there was no air conditioning and researchers were given makeshift quarters in which to work in the old State Department building, Cox took me to call on Jameson and invited me to lunch with James Alexander Robertson, then managing editor of *HAHR* in its early critical years. Keeping the review afloat was so difficult a task that the review had to cease operations for a time. Robertson, an accomplished scholar who had produced a large body of papers on the Philippines, kindly asked me whether I had a paper to submit for the review. I was too astonished to reply, but Cox wisely remarked for me that in time this might be possible.

The 1925 annual meeting of the AHA at the University of Michigan was even more significant, in my view. For now I had completed a master's degree at Northwestern and, due to a lucky fluke, was permitted, by the program chairman, William E. Dodd of the University of Chicago, to deliver a paper in Ann Arbor on "The Congress of Panama in 1826." Perhaps I should add that since 1925 I have never delivered a formal paper at the AHA until my presidential *discurso* in 1974. Fortunately for my reputation this feeble effort at Ann Arbor has never been published, but it did make possible a job interview for a position at the University of California at Los Angeles. All this occurred just a week before my twenty-first birthday. The interviewer from California, Waldemar Westergard, seemed to be interested perhaps because I had *not* studied at Berkeley. But on learning that I had only a master's degree he explained that the instructor they were to appoint had to have completed the doctorate, as Berkeley was skeptical of the newly founded branch and would be sure to object to anything less. Inasmuch as Berkeley then produced almost all the doctorates in Latin American history, the UCLA choice was limited. Today, dozens of well-trained young Latin Americanists prepared at a dozen or more centers would be happy to compete for a position at UCLA whose history department has flourished mightily since 1925.

After the interview, I had just enough money to spend the winter quarter of 1926 at the University of Chicago. Then after a few months in the Deep South as a publicity agent for Redpath Chautauqua, I was lucky enough to get a summer appointment at the University of Chicago, where someone was needed to teach Latin American history for the summer session which began in a few days. Dodd called me in and inquired whether I could substitute for Charles W. Hackett of the University of Texas who had suddenly and unexpectedly resigned. Dodd remarked that it was too late to find a suitable replacement, and Chicago felt it important to have the course offered because their Harris Lectures that summer were on Mexico, a country the United States was then having difficulties with. Being young and brash, I accepted Dodd's offer and spent a hectic but exhilarating period hastily assembling notes for the course during the next few weeks.

Only many years later did I learn, during a leisurely dinner at the Cosmos Club in Washington with Dana Munro of Princeton, the truth about the background for this episode. Hackett had abruptly resigned because the State Department had invited him to be a member of the United States delegation to attend the centennial commemoration of the 1826 Congress of Panama. The other two appointees were the current United States minister to Panama and the previous minister. Those were the days when American imperialism was being denounced throughout Latin America, and Argentina was playing its usual anti–United States role, but behind the scenes. The commemorative meetings were held in the ornate Panama Opera House, and the balcony was filled with politically active students. When Honduras, egged on by Argentina, proposed to the dignitaries on the stage that the Pan American Union be moved out of imperialist Washington, D.C., to Panama, there was enormous jubilation. Professor Hackett and the two United States ministers knew so little Spanish that they did not understand the motion and decided to join in the applause. Munro, as first secretary of the American Legation, sat in the front row of the audience and desperately tried by sign language to warn our representatives. Then another Central American representative stepped forth to propose a resolution condemning Yankee imperialism in the Caribbean. This time there was real pandemonium, and the United States representatives again applauded as vigorously as the others.

The next morning Munro hurried over to the foreign minister of Panama to explain that no resolutions of political substance could be acted on because the commemorative session was purely ceremonial. The foreign minister was adamant: the resolutions had been formally presented, and they would have to be voted on. Munro then insisted that the usual alphabetical voting procedure must be followed. Thus when Argentina was called upon to vote first, its representative, who had stirred up the resolutions, voted *no* as he had no instructions on the subjects in the resolutions, and the hapless Central Americans had to vote *no* as well since they lacked instructions too.

The Hawaii appointment was just as unexpected as the summer job. In the spring of 1926 at Chicago I came to know J. Fred Rippy, a Berkeley Ph.D. under Bolton. Another Bolton graduate, a professor at Hawaii, needed an inexpensive substitute for a year and the old-boy network prevailed. On the strength of this appointment, Kate Gilbert and I were married in August and sailed for Honolulu. Now that such arrangements are sometimes somewhat differently accomplished, let me say that we are still married and in a few months will have our sixty-second wedding anniversary.

So much for personal news. Let me now turn to the main focus of my remarks: how do graduate students decide what to write about? I shall concentrate on trying to explain how one Latin Americanist selected themes and topics for investigation. These in my case proved to be the life and times of Bartolomé de Las Casas, the colonial silver mining center in Potosí, and Spanish viceroys in America up to 1700.

DURING the last quarter century there has occurred a remarkable explosion of interest in the life and achievements of Las Casas, that sixteenth-century Spanish Dominican who devoted most of his long life (1484–1566) to a determined effort to protect the lives, the culture, and the independence of the American Indians. Ceremonies and conferences were held to mark the four hundredth anniversary of his death, and there were even more widespread commemorations to celebrate the five hundredth anniversary of his birth.

I had discovered as a graduate student in 1930 at Harvard that Las Casas had been in the forefront of those Spaniards who attempted to have their conquest of the New World carried on by just methods. After completing course work for the doctorate in 1932, I went to Spain with my family to search for documentation that would make possible a dissertation and had hoped particularly to locate the mass of books and manuscripts that surrounded Las Casas during the last years of his life in San Gregorio monastery in Valladolid. At the time he died the material he had collected and received from numerous correspondents in many parts of America was so great, we are told, that it was difficult to get in or out of his double cell. I still remember the sharp sense of defeat I felt in 1932 when I could not find this material in Spanish archives or libraries.

After some months of doubts and desperation, and after consultations with such outstanding scholars as Rafael Altamira and Fernando de los Ríos in Madrid and Emilio Ravignani in Buenos Aires, I stumbled on the truth that the contributions by Las Casas could be largely portrayed from his own copious writings. Great visions come to young students when they first begin to work in Spanish archives, particularly the Archivo General de Indias in Seville. As I examined bundle after bundle of manuscripts there, it gradually dawned on me that Spain had been the only European power that carried on its conquests amidst public doubts and disagreements of her people concerning the justice of the conquest. Las Casas was only one of the noble and erudite band of political thinkers and doers who distinguished sixteenth-century Spain.

But was this a suitable topic for research in Latin American history? Earl Hamilton of Duke University was then ransacking European collections for his fundamental investigations on the rise of prices in Europe caused by the Spanish conquest, and he saw no virtue whatsoever in my topic. He urged me to drop Las Casas and turn to some more important subject. However, soon I was so overwhelmed by the richness of the material in Seville that I could not stop, and after eighteen months in Spain returned to Harvard with enough documentation to write the kind of history I had in mind. In 1936 the dissertation, with the bland title "Theoretical Aspects of the Spanish Conquest of America," was accepted. Fortunately I did not attempt to publish this academic exercise, though I did draw off some of the more significant parts and was able to get them into print in order to indicate the trends of my research. *The First Social Experiments in America* (1935) came out in a series sponsored by the Harvard history department and "Pope Paul III and the American Indians" (1937) in the *Harvard Theological Review*.[1]

But despite the doctorate and some publications no teaching job was available during the five-year period after I returned from Spain in 1934. A part-time tutorship at Harvard and research assistance from the Carnegie Institution of Washington helped to keep the family alive. For eighteen months in 1937–1938 a post-doctoral fellowship from the Social Science Research Council enabled me to broaden my horizons by studying cultural anthropology with Robert Redfield and human geography with Preston James. It was a generous and imaginative fellowship which also permitted me to travel widely in Mexico, Central America, and Brazil. Thereafter the interdisciplinary approach to Latin American history seemed to me natural, even obvious. These were the years, too, that I began to edit the *Handbook of Latin American Studies* which flourishes these days and has become a fundamental research tool.[2] The SSRC grant also made possible discussions with Silvio Zavala in Mexico during which the

Revista de Historia de América was born; a period of several weeks in Agua Escondida in Guatemala observing Redfield as he studied this village; a trip up the Amazon and a stay at the rubber plantation established there by Ford; an exciting encounter with many Brazilian intellectuals, particularly Gilberto Freyre; and journeys across the great expanses of western Brazil in the company of James, who then settled down in Corumbá on the Bolivian border to pursue his researches in urbanization while we discussed human geography.

At the end of this fruitful period, a job finally appeared when Herbert Putnam decided to establish a new division in the Library of Congress, and on July 1, 1939, I became the first director of the Hispanic Foundation. For twelve years I labored there under the direction of the new librarian Archibald MacLeish and his successor Luther H. Evans, both of whom had a personal interest in Latin America and supported vigorously my efforts. The *Handbook of Latin American Studies* moved its editorial offices to the library, where they remain today and produce an annotated bibliography of the important books and articles on publications concerning the humanities and social sciences in Latin America, plus succinct interpretations of developments in the various disciplines by an impressive and dedicated band of scholars. The economic historian Miron Burgin edited the *Handbook* when it first moved to Washington, and he set a high standard that has been followed through the years. This is not the place to tell the story of other projects during the years 1939–1951, but strong leadership by MacLeish and Evans made possible such developments as the Assembly of Librarians of the Americas, the first Colloquium on Luso-Brazilian Studies, and the first meeting between Mexican and United States historians.[3]

Duties connected with these and other activities of the Hispanic Foundation kept me busy, particularly during World War II days, but I found it impossible to forget about Las Casas and his struggle for justice in the sixteenth century. While on shipboard en route to Brazil in 1941 I completed the introduction for the first publication of one of his principal treatises, on the need to preach the Christian faith by peaceful means alone. In 1943 the Carnegie Endowment for International Peace helped to make possible the publication in Mexico of a volume of manuscript treatises by other sixteenth-century Spaniards on the same topics that had occupied Las Casas—the just title of Spain to newly discovered America and justice for the Indians—which demonstrated how deeply Spaniards were concerned and how much controversy existed.

After World War II I was able to clarify and refine my views on these controversial issues by conversations with historians in Europe and America, and eventually prepared a large text on "The Struggle for Justice in the Spanish Conquest of America." Flushed with enthusiasm, I submitted it for a generous prize offered by Scribners for interpretive works. It failed to win the prize, but one of the judges, Dumas Malone, wrote me a greatly appreciated letter. Then a friend at the University of Chicago Press recommended that I try there. In due course an assistant editor wrote one of those bittersweet letters authors sometimes receive. It was an excellent manuscript, he said, and predicted that it would be published—but not by the University of Chicago Press, because an important member of their faculty had been so critical of the work the press could not accept it. This reader saw no usefulness in a work on the struggle for justice in the sixteenth-century Spanish America.

Still hopeful, I then sent the manuscript to the American Historical Association in competition for the Albert J. Beveridge Award, and it won the prize in 1947. The committee insisted that my manuscript be reduced in size, but by this time I was happy to comply especially since the original and much larger version had been accepted for publication in Spanish by the Editorial Sudamericana in Buenos Aires. Both editions appeared in 1949. French, Japanese, and Spanish translations of the Beveridge Award version have been published, and in 1988 the Sudamericana edition will come out in Spain with some additions to help commemorate the five hundredth anniversary of the discovery of America.

Much of 1949 was spent in Mexico on behalf of the Library of Congress, a period that enabled me to complete a study on "Las Casas: Historian" that served as introduction for the edition of Las Casas's *Historia de las Indias* (1951), a monograph which was soon published in English by the University of Florida Press (1952). Those months in Mexico, largely free of daily library duties and with the stimulus of various Mexican scholars, made possible more research and writing on Las Casas, and prepared the way for my later lectures in Havana, the University of Virginia, and the University of Pennsylvania. I remember the Havana experience well because at the end of my last lecture there, an angry and deeply offended Spanish priest rose up to challenge me to a public disputation on Las Casas, which he felt should take several days.

The Rosenbach Lectures in Philadelphia, published in 1952, were launched with poems, in the fashion so popular in seventeenth-century Spain, by the Pulitzer Prize–winning poet Leonard Bacon, by my wife Kate, and by our son Peter. The year before I had moved from the Library of Congress to the faculty of the University of Texas and found myself very busy with students and adjusting to the realities of academic life. There was no opportunity for further research, so I considered my life as a *lascasista* ended, and I even announced in the introduction to the Rosenbach Lectures on *Bartolomé de Las Casas: Bookman, Scholar, and Propagandist* that their preparation had "stimulated me to set down my final thoughts on Bartolomé de Las Casas, for these lectures terminate my researches and reflections on his great and controversial life." After so many years focused on this magnetic figure of the past, I decided the time had arrived for me to study other aspects of Latin American history. My wife and I knew that our friend Wilmarth Lewis of Yale had worked on eighteenth-century Horace Walpole so long and so exclusively that at one time he thought he was Horace Walpole, and we wanted to escape a similar fate for me with Las Casas.

Thirty-three years after bidding this definitive farewell to Las Casas I attended a conference on "Las Casas Lives Today" in Berkeley. And in all these years, it has been impossible to ignore him. This may be explained in part by the polemical nature of his writings and because few *lascasistas* have been able to avoid controversy. Sometime I may write on this diversified body of scholars in many countries whom I came to know since 1930, scholars noted for their erudition, for their individualism, and for their convictions. Not one of them appears to be fully in agreement with their colleagues devoted to Friar Bartolomé. Many of them appear to select from his writings what most appeals to them, a fact emphasized by the young Finnish historian Juha Pekka Helminen in his contribution to the 1985 meeting in Madrid,[4] where I spoke on "My Life with Bartolomé de Las Casas, 1930–1985" (1986).

The late Manuel Giménez Fernández of the University of Seville, who in many ways resembled Las Casas, characterized him as "the most remarkable of all the sons of Seville, without whose sublime qualities—disinterestedness, tenacity, energy, and above all courage to tell the truth, contrasted with his defects, his harangues, irritability, and unbridled enthusiasm—our colonization in the Indies would not have differed from the Dutch exploitation in Malaya or that by the Germans in South Africa."[5] For me the one treatise by Las Casas that holds a special meaning for us today is a manuscript that lay hidden in the National Library in Paris for centuries. Entitled "Defense Against the Persecutors and the Slanderers of the People of the New World Discovered Across the Seas," it is an attack Las Casas prepared against the Spanish Renaissance scholar Juan Ginés de Sepúlveda, who maintained that the Indians were inferior beings who could be conquered justly by the superior Spaniards. This treatise was first known to the world through an English translation by

Stafford Poole of the Latin original published by Northern Illinois University Press, and accompanied by my study entitled *All Mankind Is One* (1974).

This fundamental work of Las Casas has made him a more universal figure than ever before and should help the world to understand him, particularly in the light of the drastic changes that have occurred in the period since my discovery of Las Casas in 1930. The United States was then in the midst of an economic depression that was also felt throughout the world. Then came World War II that shook up the people of many parts of the world in many ways, when the problems of economic justice and political liberty afflicted millions in many countries. This was followed by the Vietnam War, the decolonizing movement in Africa and elsewhere, and the Civil Rights movement in the United States. More people than ever before in history became acutely conscious of the inequalities and the injustices in the world and the need for change.

Today, as we look back on the total encounter of Spaniards and Indians, we see that the doctrines Las Casas advanced in the sixteenth century have a decidedly contemporary ring about them. Two developments hold a special interest for us living as we do in a world society whose multiplicity and variety of cultures daily becomes more evident. For the first time in history, one nation—Spain—paid serious attention to the nature of the peoples it met; and, perhaps most striking of all, the controversies that proliferated in sixteenth-century Spain over the just method of treating the Indians led to a fundamental consideration of the nature of man.

The relevance of Las Casas to the problems of the twentieth-century world is being recognized ever more widely. No longer is his influence limited to those who argue over the justice of the Spanish conquest of America. For example, the Polish-born novelist Joseph Conrad wrote this on December 26, 1903, about Roger Casement, who had so long campaigned against Negro slavery in the Congo: "He is a limpid personality. . . I have always thought that some particle of Las Casas's soul had found refuge in his indefatigable body."[6]

Over thirty years ago, during a visit to Brazil, I was surprised to learn that General Cândido Rondon (1865–1958) knew about Las Casas's views on peaceful preaching to the Indians. Rondon put these ideas into practical effect during his exploration of the vast region of Matto Grosso. His injunction to his soldiers, "Die if you must, but never kill," became the motto of the Brazilian Indian Protective Service created under his direction in 1910. In the interview I had with him shortly before he died, he spoke of the impact

Las Casas had on his work and of the even more powerful influence of Positivist philosophy.[7]

Another example of how far Las Casas's doctrines have spread may be seen from the publications by Hidefuji Someda of Kyoto and from the article of Ishihara Yasunori entitled "Las Casas on the Conception of World History" selected as one of the best Japanese publications in 1980.[8]

The most dramatic example of the continuing vitality of Las Casas's views came a few years ago when the Canadian jurist Thomas R. Berger invited me to participate in a discussion of the rights of Alaskan natives. The Inuit Circumpolar Conference, an international organization of Eskimos from Alaska, Canada, and Greenland, had commissioned him in 1983 to review the Alaska Native Claims Settlement Act of 1971. For two years, Judge Berger traveled far and wide to obtain the opinions of Alaska's natives—Eskimos, Indians, and Aleuts. He took down thousands of pages of evidence in a large number of villages. Judge Berger has a wide-ranging mind, and he already had been familiar enough with the Las Casas–Sepúlveda argumentation at Valladolid in 1550 to publish a summary of it.

This explains how I came to browse in fields hitherto unknown to me, which resulted in a paper delivered in Anchorage, Alaska, in 1985 entitled "The Delicate Balance: A Consideration of some of the forces and circumstances that should be reckoned with today in a discussion of 'The Place of Native Peoples in the Western World,'" published in Chile in 1986.[9] There is no space now to summarize my argument, but Judge Berger has stated succinctly the fundamental proposition in his absorbing volume *Village Journey: The Report of the Alaska Native Review Commission.* "Las Casas called upon the Spanish to consider by what right one race could impose its own laws and institutions on another race. We are struggling still with the implications of that question, though it does not arise in precisely the same terms as it did" in the sixteenth century.[10] To help the world understand the implications of that struggle, there exists now an ever enlarging flood of publications. In New Orleans in March, 1988, at the Latin American Studies Association XIV International Congress there were two sessions on Las Casas bringing new material on his life and works and new insights on his theology by Helen Rand Parish of Berkeley and by Gustavo Gutiérrez of Peru.[11]

AFTER I said good-bye to Las Casas in 1952, gradually my attention turned to the history of the greatest single mining center in the Spanish empire, discovered at Potosí in 1545. Very little has been published on this great mountain of silver in colonial Peru and even today it would not require a large room to hold those who have made serious studies of its colorful and violent history. Therefore it was an exciting day when, during a search in Spain in 1932–1933 for material to prepare a dissertation on Las Casas, I happened to find in the royal library in Madrid an extensive two-volume manuscript history of Potosí.

The newly established Spanish Republic had opened this rich and then largely unknown collection to researchers, and the late France V. Scholes of the Carnegie Institution of Washington and I were privileged to be among the first historians permitted in the palace library. Though it was the depth of the depression, though my principal concern was Las Casas, and though my wife, two small sons and I were all trying to exist in Spain on a fellowship designed to keep one thin graduate student alive, I managed to buy a microfilm copy of the manuscript.

A few years later, on the way to Sucre, Bolivia, in 1935 to study some Las Casas manuscripts in a monastery there, I visited Potosí, went down in the mine, and began to realize how little the world knew about its history. While working on the struggle for justice in Spanish America I could not forget that many battles on this subject had been waged in Potosí. After bidding farewell to Las Casas in 1952, I began to think about the Villa Imperial de Potosí in comparison with Las Casas. In 1954 I published in Sucre a brief volume in Spanish which came out in English in the Netherlands on *The Imperial City of Potosí: An Unwritten Chapter in the History of Spanish America* (1956).

In this preliminary essay I concluded that the truly unique aspects of Potosí were its size and dramatic history. Other mining centers existed in the empire and developed somewhat similar societies and sets of institutions. But Potosí came to exhibit those common characteristics of all mining societies in such a theatrical way that it became symbolic of the process that was going on everywhere. Perhaps herein lies the real justification for assigning to Potosí a long and significant chapter in the history of Spain in America. Just as the vociferous and learned Dominican Bartolomé de Las Casas, although not the only defender of the Indians, most persistently captured the imagination of his contemporaries and later generations, so Potosí exemplified, in the gaudiest and most memorable colors, the passion for wealth that drew many Spaniards to the New World. Bernal Díaz del Castillo, the famous and articulate foot-soldier of Cortez, exhibited the remarkable combination of "Gott Und Gewinn" which characterized the Spanish conquest of America when he exclaimed: "We came here to serve God, and also to get rich." As the mountain of Potosí towers above the surrounding peaks, so will this mine, once its story is adequately told, stand as the towering symbol for the spirit of all Spaniards who came to the New World to get rich.

Convinced of the historical significance of Potosí, I began to search for relevant manuscripts. There turned up in the apparently inexhaustible archive in Seville a report by a Spaniard named Luis Capoche. It was not a formal history, but rather a description of the discovery of Potosí in 1545 and its enormous immediate development, as well as an account of its economic and social life up to 1589. After publishing this report in 1959 in Spain, I began an unsuccessful but pleasant search in Portuguese archives for a history supposedly written in the sixteenth century by a Portuguese miner Antonio de Acosta. This investigation resulted in my article on "The Portuguese in Spanish America with Special Reference to the Villa Imperial de Potosí" (1961).

These studies naturally led me to look again at the manuscript obtained years before in Madrid which had been written in Potosí in the early eighteenth century by Bartolomé Arzáns de Orsúa y Vela grandiloquently entitled "The Imperial City of Potosí: The Incomparable Wealth of Its Famous Mountain, the Greatness of Its Generous Citizens, Its Civil Wars and Other Memorable Events." This history was finally published in its entirety, thanks to the support of the Bicentennial Committee of Brown University and to the cooperation of my friend and colleague Gunnar Mendoza, Director of the National Library and National Archives of Sucre, Bolivia. We labored together for almost five years in complete harmony on the task of editing it.

There is not time here to describe and analyze the work in detail, but the large three volumes that appeared in 1965 provide much information on the author as well as on his history and a complete text of the work. Few visitors go to Potosí these days—because of the cost, the inconvenience, and the cold—but those who do see there the great hill that contained the silver ore, rising some 2,000 feet above a plain and seemingly sterile land, itself 13,000 feet above sea level. Below the mountain there still may be seen impressive churches, the enormous mint, and many other signs of departed glory. But there are still no printed collections of the many basic sources available on the history of Potosí, many of them in the excellent National Archives in nearby Sucre meticulously organized and administered by Mendoza. Some scholars have recently produced monographs on Potosí, but much remains to be done before the world will more fully understand the true significance of this great

mining center—one of the most important urban concentrations in
the history of the Americas—as may be seen from the list of research
projects awaiting historians set forth in my article on "What Needs to
Be Done on the History of Potosí" (1972).

Bolívar spent seven weeks in Potosí in 1825 and announced there
the end of his long struggle for independence from Spain. There
were gay receptions, a three-day fiesta and other rejoicings, and on
October 25 he ascended the mountain itself accompanied by various
generals and "all the persons of distinction in Potosí." The ascent was
made at the end of the winter season while raw winds still whipped
around the top of the mountain, but the ceremony was carried out
with pomp and, of course, oratory. With the flags of newly liberated
Argentina, Bolivia, Colombia, Chile, and Peru flying in the breeze,
Bolívar ended his peroration with these words: "I consider the
opulence [of Potosí] to be of no importance when compared with
the glory of having borne the standard of liberty victoriously from the
tropical shores of the Orinoco to plant it here on the peak of this
mountain which is the admiration and envy of the world."[12] Thus the
Liberator reached a very Spanish kind of climax. For at the moment
when he celebrated the final act of political independence from the
mother country, the Liberator was also proclaiming one of the fundamental ideas deeply embedded in Spanish character—that men
ought to seek virtue, not wealth. What could more dramatically illustrate the power of Spain to mold her people than the words of this
successful revolutionary general, standing among his brilliantly
uniformed officers at the summit of the desolate mountain high in
the Andes that had been for centuries one of the principal produc-
ers of wealth in all the territory ruled by Spain?

Let me record, too, that Potosí has helped to mold the character
of those who study its history. During the years of preparing Arzáns's
History, Mendoza and I had dreamed of the possibility of an international conference on the history of Potosí, but nothing came of this
project. When the three-volume work was finally published in 1965,
however, the citizens of Potosí were appropriately grateful. Mendoza
and I were made Honorary Citizens of Potosí and there was a ceremonial meeting at which lofty speeches were made. A local choir
sang the Bolivian national anthem in the Indian language Quechua,
and the band played the Star Spangled Banner—probably for the
first, and last, time in Bolivia. A formal dinner was organized by the
municipality of Potosí, at which we all wore our overcoats because of
the intense cold. There was, however, a lively and heated discussion
of the English historian Arnold Toynbee, because he had written

something that offended the Potosinos, who are still as proud of their city as Arzáns was in the eighteenth century.

THE history of Potosí must of course be studied as a part of the Spanish Empire, which means the viceregal system established by Spain to govern its vast holdings in America. The sixteenth-century viceroy Francisco de Toledo in Peru interested me early on because of his strong desire to make certain that Spain's title to the New World was just and legal. Years later, after the Arzáns history of Potosí was published, the University of St. Thomas in Houston invited me to deliver the Benjamin Kopper Smith Lecture there (1972), and this turned my attention toward a more systematic study of viceregal history.

The viceregal documentation available in Seville and elsewhere must be seen to be believed. Bundle after bundle of minutely detailed letters on all aspects of colonial administration have been available for centuries, often accompanied by extensive reports on matters referred to in the letters—Indian tributes, silver production, reports on foreign corsairs in the empire, Negro uprisings, lists of persons who should be considered for appointment, and friction with ecclesiastics. Few of these letters or reports have been published. When something did appear, such as the remarkably detailed report on the Indian population of Lima prepared in 1613 for Viceroy Marqués de Montesclaros, the information was hailed at once as information of fundamental importance for understanding the economic and social history of the empire. The judges who carried on the formal investigations of each viceroy at the end of his rule collected information of great value to historians. One such *visitador* Alonso Fernández de Bonilla spent the years 1590–1600 examining the record of Viceroy Conde del Villar in Peru and required 43,601 sheets of paper for his report. This officer was such a supreme procrastinator that I published in 1975 an analysis of his unique career and the formidable documentation he produced.

Here too I discovered controversy over the role of Spain. Some historians considered viceroys unimportant, and that they left little behind them except paintings of themselves in elegant robes. The revolutionary wars that began in 1810 and ended in 1825 with Bolívar in Potosí stirred up much anti-Spanish spirit, and historians since have shown little interest in viceroys and their administrations. Despite meetings in Texas and at Columbia University I had been unable to arouse any enthusiasm for the study of viceroys, partly because there was so much to be done and because of a generally unfavorable attitude toward Spain and her colonial administration.

Toward the end of my teaching career and the beginning of a blessed retirement period I decided to work on the project again, and was fortunate enough to obtain financial support as well as the cooperation of an active and competent associate editor, Celso Rodríguez. We focused on the Hapsburg period, 1535–1700. With the sponsorship of the Biblioteca de Autores Españoles assured through its director, Ciriaco Pérez Bustamante, twelve volumes of documents and bibliographical information gradually appeared in this series (1976–1980) during my retirement years at the University of Massachusetts, Amherst. A detailed three-volume description of additional viceregal sources in Spain came out in Germany (1977), and a final volume was devoted to viceregal sources in Spanish America (1980). This last volume contains a notable description and analysis of material in the National Archive in Sucre, Bolivia, by Mendoza.

There is neither time nor need here to provide more information on the contents of these sixteen volumes. Suffice to say that they should be useful to students of the key Hapsburg period of the Spanish Empire in America. This mass of material, largely awaiting the scrutiny of scholars, demonstrates that while Spaniards argued over the justice of their empire in America, a remarkable quantity and quality of sources exist for a fuller understanding of its nature.

My story thus far on Las Casas, Potosí, and viceregal documentation indicates that a historian's life may include much more than publications, though these will usually be an indispensable element. Another fundamental activity for most of us is teaching—how to present Latin American history to our students. Teaching was a subject no one mentioned in my graduate courses at Northwestern and Harvard. In that first unexpected summer job at the University of Chicago in 1926 and the following year at the University of Hawaii my pressing task was to bring together enough information to last during the lecture period, not how to teach effectively.

The same situation prevailed in my years (1927–1930) at the American University of Beirut, in Syria [Lebanon was at the time generally considered a part of a "greater" Syria], though I do remember corresponding with Carl Becker of Cornell on possible approaches to teaching and methodology. During twelve years at the Library of Congress (1939–1951) there was no focus on teaching. At the University of Texas from 1951 to 1961 I cannot remember any discussion with my colleagues on how to teach. But this experience did convince me that anyone attempting to teach Latin American history was hampered by the lack of adequate teaching materials. Students had almost no knowledge of Latin America, and many of them lacked a reading knowledge of Portuguese or Spanish.

Not until I arrived at Columbia University in 1961 did questions on teaching and teaching materials enter my life, but that imaginative publisher and friend of historians, the late Alfred A. Knopf, thought it would be a good idea to start a new series, the Borzoi Books on Latin America, to help teachers by providing carefully edited collections of documents and interpretations on significant topics. It proved to be a valuable learning experience for me to select the authors and then ride herd on them until the thirty volumes of the series were in press.[13] Whenever possible, I scheduled before publication a meeting of my seminar with the authors, which usually led to frank discussions and probing questions by the graduate students, who were happy to have an opportunity to exercise their critical faculties.

Shortly before I moved from Texas to Columbia, Louis Snyder induced me to prepare a couple of paperback volumes for general consumption on *Modern Latin America* (1959), and shortly before I left Columbia for Irvine, California, Little Brown Co. published my two-volume collection designed for university students, *History of Latin American Civilization: Sources and Interpretations* (1967). The second edition of this textbook has been recently described by the Venezuelan historian José Antonio Carbonell: "no hay ningún estudio sobre Venezuela, sus aportes en la Economía, Arte, Arquitectura Colonial; sus hombres, no figuran en ella aparte de ligeras citas sobre Simón Bolívar y Andrés Bello y mas para criticarnos, reflejo creo de algunos historiadores venezolanos; Simón Rodríguez, Páez, Guzmán Blanco, sus artistas, historiadores, escritores, no son tomados en cuenta por el Hispanista Hanke."[14] Then follows the most detailed description I have seen of the contents of this textbook. This is not the place to comment on this review, except to remark upon the difficulty historians of Latin America encounter when they publish large general works.

A particularly valuable event for me was the special summer session for about thirty high school teachers at the end of my Columbia period. These lively teachers from many parts of the country had an unusual opportunity to study Latin American history under the aegis of a *veterano*, Charles Nowell, and a younger scholar, E. Bradford Burns. A collection of several hundred paperbacks was assembled as a kind of private library, and at the end of the session the students took home the volumes of interest to them. Richard Morse and the art historian Pál Kelemen were among the outside scholars who presented stimulating lectures. It was a wonderful summer for all of us, and I was encouraged to think more about suitable materials for teaching. One result was that Van Nostrand Co. brought out a two-volume selection of articles from the *Hispanic American Historical Review* (1966), since our students were becoming sophisticated enough to profit from such solid material, as well as a volume of text and documents entitled *Contemporary Latin America* (1968). Inasmuch as practically all of my research had concentrated on the colonial period, all these experiences inevitably broadened and deepened my own views on the nature of Latin American history, and how to teach.[15]

Opportunities continued to present themselves causing me to refine and reconsider my opinions on Latin America and how to teach its history. Norman F. Cantor and I spent a pleasant and profitable day discussing "Iberian Civilization in the Old and the New World," which became a part of his 1971 volume on *Perspectives on the European Past: Conversations with Historians.* Cantor forced me to realize the long-standing and permanent relationship of Latin America to Europe. The same may be said in general about my participation in *The Columbia History of the World* (1972). As the Spanish cruelty to the Indians theme never seems to die, in 1971 the *HAHR* published my polemical comments in "A Modest Proposal for a Moratorium: Some Thoughts on the Black Legend." Indeed, in glancing back, I find it easy to see that some of the basic positions in my 1949 volume on *The Spanish Struggle for Justice in the Conquest of America* are often to be found, in various guises, in my later writings.

During my final years of teaching at the University of Massachusetts at Amherst (1969–1975), my colleague Jane Meyer Loy and I regularly discussed problems of teaching, and she prepared an innovative report on music and films.[16] About this time the American Historical Association received funds for using feature films for teaching purposes, which enabled me to produce an edited version of Paul Muni's film depicting the life of Mexico's leader Juárez as well as a booklet entitled *Benito Juárez and the French Intervention in Mexico* (1971) with a section on "An Informal Critical Judgment on Historical Films."

While organizing the Borzoi series, some Columbia students invited me to contribute an essay on "How a Historian Works" to a volume they were planning to publish, which appeared in 1964. About this time I devoted almost a whole summer to analyzing the methods and what seemed to me the prejudices of one of Spain's most venerable and outstanding scholars, Ramón Menéndez Pidal, in his biography of Las Casas. Thus my earlier determination to leave Fray Bartolomé was abandoned, and there resulted a long article entitled "More Heat and Some Light on the Spanish Struggle for Justice in Conquest of America" (1964).

This polemical writing and many discussions with students and with editors of the volumes in the Borzoi series made me aware as never before of the influence of parochialism and patriotism in the writing of history. In reading the revealing letters by John Franklin Jameson on the development of history in the United States, I learned that he had been so shocked by the ignorance of British historians of American history that he worked hard to bring over half a dozen scholars from Britain to participate in the 1926 annual meeting of the AHA and then to lecture at various universities. Charles Homer Haskins devoted his 1922 AHA presidential address to recounting American contributions to European history, as if to make certain that historians across the Atlantic understood how much had been accomplished here. This famous medievalist also made several statements that have stuck in my mind over the years and which may well be considered by United States Latin Americanists today: "Many historians find it easy to be historically minded respecting everything save only history," and "the temptation to write much and frequently on topics of current interests—'hot stuff on live subjects'—must be withstood if the historian hopes to accomplish a considerable and finely matured work."

It should not surprise us, therefore, to find that some of our own historians have displayed what has been called a certain "condescension toward Latin America." I first encountered this attitude in Texas. Though long before I arrived there in 1951 the University of Texas had recognized the importance of Latin America, this was not always so. In the early years of this century, Bolton had begun his career there after completing a dissertation at the University of Pennsylvania on "The Free Negro in Pennsylvania before the Civil War." In Austin he studied Spanish and traveled into Mexico. When he proposed that he be allowed to give a course at the University of Texas on Mexico, the long-time chairman George P. Garrison is supposed to have replied: "Young man, there never has been, and never will be, such a course at this university as long as I am chairman of the history department."

So Bolton went on to Stanford, and shortly thereafter to the University of California at Berkeley, where he soon had more than a thousand students in the course that he offered for many years on the "History of the Americas." In addition, Bolton attracted so many graduate students that two *festschrifts* were published for him over the years, probably a world record. His success alienated some of the Berkeley faculty; I was told on good authority in 1925 in Berkeley that one member was so infuriated that he conspired to have one of Bolton's graduate students voted down at the oral examination. This background helps to explain why on reaching the University of Texas I had a thoughtful graduate student named Charles Eastlack prepare a master's essay on Bolton, and why later on I brought out a volume on *Do the Americas Have a Common History? A Critique of the Bolton Theory* (1964). During my ten years in Texas I took a peculiar pleasure in going to my office in Garrison Hall, named in honor of the chairman who vowed never to have a course on Latin America in his department.

Later on other events occurred to convince me that the AHA, or some members of it, were still somewhat parochial. Once as a member of the committee to nominate the next president I knew enough not to propose Arthur P. Whitaker to lead the AHA as he was a Latin Americanist, but I did put forward the name of John King Fairbank because of his distinguished work in Chinese history. Our chairman, a Europeanist, politely listened to this and other suggestions and then concluded by remarking that inasmuch as a historian of the United States was the last president, the next one should be in European history (or vice versa). And so it was done.

In 1974, as AHA president, I had the temerity to propose that there should be a wider range of historians honored by prizes, even though no funds were available and the awards would have to be symbolic. The council had heard of Alexis de Tocqueville, my first proposal, so there was no opposition there. The next proposal, for the recognition of the significance of teaching by honoring James Harvey Robinson, was approved in principle, though questions were raised on how best to select the recipients. It was the first and, so far as I know, the only AHA award for teaching. The next proposals on behalf of John Franklin Jameson and Waldo Gifford Leland, to my great astonishment, were received by the council in silence. I was stunned to learn how little the council knew of the past of the AHA. Evidently no one had heard of Leland, despite his powerful efforts in establishing the National Archives and in many other historical projects from 1903 onward, and there was only slight knowledge of Jameson's long service as editor of the *American Historical Review* and for many years as one of the principal pillars of the AHA.

The council hesitated to turn me down flatly; they appointed a committee to consider the suitability of Leland and Jameson for awards. The chairman of this committee, a Europeanist, reported favorably in due course explaining that he had tried out both names on various candidates for positions in American history in his university. He was surprised that all but one candidate knew about Jameson's many contributions. Leland was not so well known, but when it was discovered that he had served as secretary of the AHA for over ten years and had prepared some basic guides for the Carnegie Institution in Washington, he scraped by too. So it came to pass that today the AHA offers the Tocqueville Award for historians abroad who write on American history, the Robinson Award to recognize contributions to teaching history, the Jameson Award for outstanding documentary collections, and the Leland Award for reference works of significance to historians. Let me hasten to conclude by emphasizing that the presidency of the AHA has been open for a decade or more to a broader representation of the total range of historical scholarship in the United States, and that fresh winds are blowing in many directions in the AHA itself.

I believe that there has also occurred a revolution in both teaching and research in Latin American history since my first appearance at the AHA in 1923. The Conference on Latin American History has become one of the largest and certainly one of the most active groups in the AHA. The basic printed and manuscript materials for the study of Latin American history in the United States have enormously increased in size and in quality, so much so that the problem of recording them has proved to be formidable. The *HAHR* has likewise steadily improved in quality as well as in coverage, not a mean achievement. I can personally testify to these developments on the basis of my watch as managing editor of the review during the years from 1954 to 1960. An editor matures very rapidly while confronting the circumstances large and small that make up the daily experiences with members of the Advisory Board, book reviewers, would-be authors, and staff members. If my own experience is any guide, editing our flagship review provides a unique overview of the field and may lead to a kind of mild hubris.

The annual meetings of CLAH have become increasingly comprehensive and provide an opportunity for our members to participate in professional discussions of a wide variety of historical topics. It has also sponsored a number of solid publications, from Howard F. Cline's two-volume collection on *Latin American History: Essays on Its Study and Teaching* (1976) to the volume edited by Kenneth J. Grieb and others entitled *Research Guide to Central America and the Caribbean* (1985). The other items in this series, such as Russell H. Bartley's *Soviet Historians on Latin America: Recent Scholarly Contributions,* are also noteworthy reference works that every library seriously concerned with Latin America should possess. But improvements can still be made. Relatively little has appeared in the *HAHR* on art history, the history of literature, or on religious topics. We do have a kind of new theology in the recent emphasis on dependency theory and quantitative methods, though nothing on liberation theology despite its sixteenth-century origins. Nor is there yet a critical review of that massive and imaginative research program carried on by the Carnegie Institution in Washington, probably the most important single project ever achieved in Latin America.

Thus we should not be complacent, for there are still frontiers to be crossed. Two specific needs seem to me particularly important: (1) professional scrutiny of textbooks and teaching materials, and (2) an annual report on developments outside the United States in teaching and research.

Evaluations of teaching materials in historical reviews are long overdue. James Axtell of the College of William and Mary has recently broken new ground by publishing in the *American Historical Review* some penetrating comments on "Europeans, Indians, and the Age of Discovery in American History Textbooks," which stimulated lively comments by readers and a response by the author. Axtell produced another valuable statement on "Forked Tongues: Moral Judgments in Indian History" for the section of Teaching Innovations in *AHA Perspectives*.[17]

The *HAHR* has not adopted a policy of reviewing regularly textbooks and teaching materials in Latin American history. It did once notice a textbook that devoted more space to Honduras than to Colombia, but this was an exception. Has not the time arrived for the *HAHR* or the CLAH *Newsletter* to review such materials regularly? If so, it would be well to consider enlisting the advice of students who are the consumers. Robert F. Berkhofer, Jr., of the University of Michigan reported that his experiment of having students write reviews of assigned books produced evaluations "better than most of the reviews that appear in professional journals."[18] And Harold D. Woodman of Purdue University, West Lafayette, has found that students also become expert in interpreting new documentary material if given an opportunity.[19] Both Berkhofer and Woodman described their teaching experiences in the section on Teaching Innovations in *AHA Perspectives*. We certainly should not abdicate the responsibility of evaluating these developments and teaching materials to interested publishers who are always ready to advertise their wares with complimentary blurbs. I am happy to see that the CLAH Committee on Teaching and Teaching Materials is gradually becoming more and more active.

The second need seems to me equally pressing. Much more could be done to acquaint our colleagues with activities outside the United States. Latin American history is now cultivated in Australia, China, Japan, and the Soviet Union, to mention only some of the larger countries. Much goes on in both eastern and western Europe that we hear little about. Even in Latin America the same may be said. The preparation and publication of a carefully designed report on current developments outside the United States of interest to historians concerned with Latin America would be a unique contribution which CLAH is in an excellent position to make.

These international connections would surely involve political considerations. I first became aware of this at the end of my period as managing editor, when I arranged to have translated a Soviet analysis and criticism of the *HAHR* in the November 1960 issue. By the time protests were made by some of our readers there was a new editor, Donald Worcester, and he wisely decided not to encourage a flurry of passionate letters protesting the Soviet bias.

The political problem continues, as I found out in my first visit to Moscow and Leningrad in 1971. Following this, several of the Soviet Latin Americanists were invited to visit our Latin American centers by the International Exchanges and Research Board in New York, but none was able to accept. The splendid volume by Bartley provides a valuable report on Soviet writings on Latin American history, but much remains to be done to make historians concerned with Latin America aware of the contributions to this field outside the United States.

The same may be said for historical source material on Latin American history scattered in many countries. This is particularly true for sources produced after 1900, and I am encouraged to learn that Celso Rodríguez of the Organization of American States is hoping to remedy this lack. Many teachers and many researchers today concentrate their attention on this period, and probably will continue to do so. Yet many of the basic sources for an understanding of Latin American history since 1900 remain locked up in archives unavailable for study and in many cases unorganized whether in Latin America or elsewhere.

To end this section on teaching, let me pose a question that is difficult if not impossible to answer: what effect do students have on teachers? My long and continuing concern to ensure a balanced treatment of Brazilian history was due to experiences during the SSRC fellowship, and in this instance I like to believe that I may have influenced some students to agree, though this is speculation. But none followed my research interests, nor did I encourage them to do so. My motto was that of Walter Bagehot: a teacher has the right to be consulted and the right to warn students. Otherwise they are on their own. Of course they learned from each other and from the ideas swirling about among historians after World War II, currents which were strong at both Texas and Columbia. It thus seemed to me particularly appropriate that two of my students conspired with others to bring out a volume of essays of new approaches to Latin American history, which included fresh treatments of old problems and even concerned such subjects as prosopography and psycho-analysis.[20]

Anyone making a list of the titles of the masters' theses and doctoral dissertations prepared under my general guidance would discover a wide range of topics and approaches, and my conclusion is that discussions over years with students and with the editors of the Borzoi Books on Latin America naturally broadened and deepened my own views.

In looking back at developments since I first attended a meeting of the AHA sixty-five years ago, it is clear that the study of Latin American history has been solidly established in the United States. Today even the history of Brazil, that immense and fascinating country, steadily receives more attention in our teaching and research after a long period of relative neglect. Is it not a sign of our maturity that we recognize that our sources can never be wholly complete, our linguistic capabilities too narrow, our literary styles too inadequate, and our prejudices and other limitations too evident, for any of us to be satisfied?

But Latin Americanists in the United States are particularly fortunate because it is customary for us to associate professionally with historians in Latin America, Spain, and elsewhere. Since 1949 there have been regular meetings with Mexican historians.[21] The forty-seven volumes of the *Handbook of Latin American Studies,* largely developed by historians, have been a spectacular demonstration of the interdisciplinary approach and how impossible it is to study Latin America without taking into account sources and interpretations written in many languages.

Indeed, this is the message which will certainly be heard during the forthcoming activities and publications stimulated by the Columbus Quincentennial. About a decade ago I argued in a lecture in Japan (1979) that the discovery of America was the true beginning of the modern world, because for the first time in history serious attention was paid to the people of other languages, other religions, other colors, and other cultures so well exemplified by the magnificent anthropological contributions of the sixteenth-century Spanish Franciscan Bernardino de Sahagún in Mexico. Thus was born, in my opinion, the world we call modern.

This conviction was expressed in a somewhat different way in my remarks published in 1986 on "The Importance of Learning about the Rest of the World: What Would Emerson Say Today?" There I quoted John Brademas, a former congressman and university president, that "there is a special responsibility on the part of the colleges and the universities of the United States to help educate the American people about the other peoples of the world—who, after all, populate most of it."

One of the best ways historians can learn about other peoples is to know how they interpret their own history. The Conference on Latin American History not only therefore has an opportunity to improve the teaching of Latin American history in the United States, but also to report on the way it is taught and studied elsewhere. And we may take satisfaction in the steady development since 1918 of *The Hispanic American Historical Review.* There exists a healthy variety of opinions among us. Many topics await serious study, and many sources need to be made better known. What more can any historian in any field ask for?

Lewis Hanke
ca. 1988

NOTES

This article has greatly benefited from the literary skill
and judgment of my wife Kate.

[1] For detailed bibliographical information on my publications referred to in this article, see "The Writings of Lewis Hanke," *Inter-American Review of Bibliography* 36:4 (1986), 427–451. Additional biographical and bibliographical information is in Cynthia D. Bertelson's master's thesis on "Lewis Hanke: Historian and Propagandist" (University of Wisconsin, River Falls, 1975).

For information on the early years and marriage to Kate Ogden Gilbert on August 12, 1926, see the fifty-six-page unpublished memoir "Recollections and Suppositions of Lewis Hanke" dated in Warsaw, Poland, March 25, 1980, in Tulane University Latin American Library.

[2] Volume 3 of the *Handbook of Latin American Studies* appeared in 1939, and reflected my discovery during the SSRC (should this be defined?) fellowship of the richness and variety of Brazilian history, for it included many special articles in commemoration of the centennial of the Instituto Historiografico y Geografico Brasileiro. The *Revista Hispanica Moderna* at Columbia University published in the same year my "Gilberto Freyre: vida y obra. Bibliografia-antologia," and a new review established by Harvard graduate students, the *Quarterly Review of Inter-American Relations,* included a shorter version in English. These were among the first descriptions of the ideas of this influential Brazilian historian. During my years at Texas Donald Cooper, Richard Graham, and David Hall Stauffer began to work on Brazilian topics. While at Columbia 1961–1967 Stanley Stein, as an occasional visiting professor, helped to stimulate an interest in this field as the work of E. Bradford Burns, Robert Conrad, Ralph Della Cava, Joseph L. Love, Stuart B. Schwartz, and others testifies. Michael M. Hall and the late Peter Eisenberg decided to teach at a Brazilian university, and continued their research there.

With the strong support and leadership of Francis M. Rogers of Harvard, we were able to organize the first Colloquium on Luso-Brazilian Studies at the Library of Congress in 1950. The six meetings of this unique gathering of scholars concerned with Brazil and Portugal provided an opportunity for Luso-Brazilianists, many of whom were historians, to meet and exchange ideas. Scholars from Brazil, Portugal, the United States, and several other countries—such as Charles R. Boxer, the English historian—made these meetings memorable events.

Ernesto Da Cal discussed with me my experiences in the Luso-Brazilian world in a program aired by the United States Information Service c.1966. The records are available in the Latin American Library in Tulane University.

For my publications in Brazil see *Writings,* 1938, 1939, 1948, 1958, 1961, 1968, 1983.

[3] For more information on the years in Washington, see my interview with Mary Ellis Kahler on experiences in the Library of Congress and elsewhere. Recorded in Washington on March 30, 1979, and available in the Library of Congress Phonoduplication Division. The related administrative developments are in the library's archives.

[4] Juha Pekka Helminen, "Bartolomé de Las Casas en la historia. Un ejemplo de como las personas historicas pueden ser aprovechadas para diferentes finalidades," *En el quinto centenario de Bartolomé de Las Casas* (Madrid, 1986), 61–72.

244

⁵ Manuel Giménez Fernandez, *Nuevas consideraciones sobre la historia, sentido y valor de las bulas alejandrinas de 1493 referentes a las Indias* (Seville, 1944), 149.

⁶ Zdzislaw Najder, *Joseph Conrad: A Chronicle* (New Brunswick, 1973), 295.

⁷ One of my students at Texas prepared a monograph on Rondon's contributions, which are not yet fully recognized. See David Hall Stauffer, "Origem e fundação de Serviço de Proteção aos Índios," *Revista de Historia*, 10:37 (Sao Paulo, 1959), 73–96. For other chapters of this dissertation see the same review, 10:37 (1959), 73–95; 11:42 (1960), 435–453; 11:43 (1960), 165–183; 11:44 (1960), 427–450; 12:46 (1961), 413–433. I have found no adequate biography of Rondon, but John Hemming's *Red Gold: The Conquest of the Brazilian Indians* (Cambridge, 1978) provides a recent and devastating account of what actually happened.

⁸ *The Japan Foundation Newsletter*, 8:8 (Tokyo, February–March, 1981), 13.

⁹ *Historia*, 21 (1986), 379–401.

¹⁰ Thomas R. Berger, *Village Journey: The Report of the Alaska Native Review Commission* (New York, 1985). 174.

¹¹ My remarks were entitled "New Discoveries about the Life and Writings of Bartolomé de Las Casas."

¹² Lewis Hanke, *Bartolomé Arzáns de Orsúa y Vela's History of Potosí* (Providence, 1965), 42–43.

¹³ For a list of the Borzoi volumes, see *Writings*, 1964.

¹⁴ The review appeared in the *Boletín de la Academia Nacional de la Historia*, 69:273 (Caracas, January–March, 1986), 231–245. The quotation is on p.231–232.

¹⁵ In selecting material for a volume of my writings (1979), I was not surprised to find that there had to be a section on Teaching and Teachers. Since Columbia days, these questions have been a regular part of my life, as shown by these articles: "Studying Latin America: The Views of an Old Christian" (1967); "The Care and Feeding of Latin Americanists: Some Remarks on the Most Important Instrument in Teaching—the Teacher" (1975); "Sobre cómo enseñar historia latino-americana en los Estados Unidos" (1968); "The Quiet Revolution" (1969); "Typologies of Academic Pollution in the Good Neighborhood" (1972).

¹⁶ Jane Meyer Loy, *Latin America: Sights and Sounds. A Guide to Motion Pictures and Music for College Courses* (Gainesville, 1973).

¹⁷ *American Historical Review*, 92 (June, 1987), 621–632. For the subsequent discussion of the issues raised, see *ibid.*, 93 (February, 1988), 283–286. The second Axtell article is in *AHA Perspectives*, 25:2 (February, 1987), 10–13.

¹⁸ "Demystifying Historical Authority: Critical Analysis in the Classroom," *AHA Perspectives*, 26:2 (February, 1988), 13–14, 16. The quotation appears on p.16.

¹⁹ Harold D. Woodman, "Do Facts Speak for Themselves? Writing the Historical Essay," *AHA Perspectives*, 25:4 (April, 1987), 18–20.

²⁰ *New Approaches to Latin American History*, edited by Richard Graham and Peter H. Smith (Austin, 1974). The variety, vigor, and independence of my students have always impressed me. At Hawaii there was a young man from Tokyo who undertook to show me the Japanese side of life in Honolulu—the Buddhist temple where an English priest officiated, the language schools where children studied Japanese after regular school hours at the cost of their parents, and the night schools where the ancient martial arts were learned. In my second and final semester I was allowed to offer a course on Latin American history in which the wife of the professor of physics enrolled, to my surprise and pleasure. When I inquired how she came to be interested in the subject, she explained that my course fit her baby's bathing schedule. Never again did I raise such a question with a student!

At Beirut the American University had recently admitted women, and there were always a few of them in my classes. The men were exceptional. One from Damascus went on to receive a doctorate from Princeton and in time became an outstanding educator; another, from Baghdad, after a doctorate at Chicago became a leading scholar in Islamic studies at the School of International Studies of Johns Hopkins University; and another student from Baghdad entered his country's diplomatic service.

As previously mentioned, some of my students at Texas began to specialize in Brazilian history, but there were also a retired Chilean air officer, a couple of Jesuits, two Protestants who were concerned with missions in Latin America, and an unusual youngster with a Harvard undergraduate double major of mathematics and Spanish who prepared a master's thesis on Bolton and then went on to a career in computers. One has devoted his time to college teaching after completing a dissertation on a colonial topic.

At Columbia there was a flood of able students who are now out in the world performing in different ways. Many are teaching in institutions large and small, one is a United Press International editor in South America, one is editor of the United States Naval History Publications, and another is the Roman Catholic chaplain connected with the American Embassy in Moscow. Outstanding women students began to appear in my classes, and they have participated actively in the development of women's history, as well as in other aspects of Latin American history. One edited the basic *Encyclopedia of Latin America*. Another completed a dissertation on colonial Peru and later became an activist in Roman Catholic circles. Both women and men have found administrative positions in United States government cultural organizations. Two neither teach nor administer, but continue to publish. Some have chosen to teach abroad, in Brazil, Israel, and the Netherlands.

Foreign students were a regular part of the Columbia scene. A Spanish Jesuit came from Japan, and a Panamanian young woman who agreed under pressure to write a master's thesis on a non-Panamanian topic. I was even able to persuade a Mexican to prepare a master's thesis on a topic in Brazilian intellectual history, after which he entered the Mexican diplomatic service. An English student came across the Atlantic and produced an unusual master's thesis on transportation in colonial Argentina. One student with an excellent topic—Mormons in Mexico—somehow or other never completed the work.

My Irvine experience was brief, and I taught only undergraduates. But one Swiss student later went on to graduate school and became the director of the Ethnographic Museum in Geneva. Another became an activist, and some years later I ran across him in Paraguay, where he was an undercover agent for Amnesty International.

During my last teaching period, at the University of Massachusetts, Amherst, my students were mostly undergraduates but there were some graduate students. One now teaches at the Universidad Central de Venezuela, and another is in the cultural section of the Organization of American States in Washington.

[21] Our students of United States history do not enjoy this advantage. Notable contributions have been made to our history by foreign scholars, as may be easily seen in the five-volume *Guide to Studies on United States History outside the U.S., 1945–1980* (White Plains, 1985). But much remains to be done before our historians make adequate use of these contributions, many of which are published in languages they do not know.